CADOGAN CHESS BOOKS

Attack with Mikhail Tal

CADOGAN CHESS BOOKS

Chief Advisor: Garry Kasparov
Editor: Andrew Kinsman
Russian Series Editor: Ken Neat

Other titles in this series include:

ALEKHINE, A.
On the Road to the World Championship 1923-1927

AVERBAKH, Y.
Comprehensive Chess Endings
   Vols. 1-5

GELLER, Y.
The Application of Chess Theory

KARPOV, A.
Chess at the Top 1979-1984

KASPAROV, G. et al.
Kasparov - The Ultimate Grandmaster

LIVSHITZ, A.
Test Your Chess IQ Books 1-3

NEISHTADT, I.
Queen Sacrifice

POLUGAYEVSKY, L.
The Sicilian Labyrinth Vols. 1 & 2

POLUGAYEVSKY,L. & DAMSKY, I.
The Art of Defence in Chess

SHEKHTMAN, E. (Compiler)
The Games of Tigran Petrosian
   Vols. 1 & 2

SHERESHEVSKY, M.
Endgame Strategy

SHERESHEVSKY,M. & SLUTSKY, L.
Mastering the Endgame Vols. 1 & 2

SMYSLOV, V.
Smyslov's 125 Selected Games

SUETIN, A.
Three Steps to Chess Mastery

TAL, M., CHEPIZHNY, V. &
   ROSHAL, A.
Montreal 1979

VAINSTEIN, B.
David Bronstein: Chess Improviser

For a complete catalogue of CADOGAN CHESS books (which includes the
former Pergamon Chess and Maxwell Macmillan Chess list) please write to:

Cadogan Books, London House, Parkgate Road, London SW11 4NQ
Tel: (071) 738 1961
Fax: (071) 924 5491

Attack with Mikhail Tal

by

Mikhail Tal & Iakov Damsky

Translated and Edited by Ken Neat

CADOGAN CHESS
LONDON, NEW YORK

CADOGAN BOOKS DISTRIBUTION

UK/EUROPE/AUSTRALASIA/AFRICA
Distribution: Grantham Book Services Ltd, Isaac Newton Way,
Alma Park Industrial Estate, Grantham, Lincs NG31 9SD
Tel: 0476 67421; Fax: 0476 590223

USA/CANADA/LATIN AMERICA/JAPAN
Distribution: Paramount Distribution Center, Front and Brown Streets,
Riverside, New Jersey 08075, USA
Tel: (609) 461 6500; Fax: (609) 764 9122

English Translation Copyright © 1994 Ken Neat

First published 1994 by Cadogan Books plc, London House, Parkgate Road,
London SW11 4NQ

British Library Cataloguing in Publication Data
A CIP catalogue record for this book is available from the British Library

ISBN 1 85744 043 9

Cover design by Mark Levitt

Typeset by Ken Neat, Durham

Printed in Great Britain by BPC Wheatons Ltd, Exeter

Contents

Mikhail Tal: A Personal Tribute

YOUNG PLAYERS of today may find it difficult to appreciate what the name of Mikhail Tal means to chess devotees of my generation. In the late 1950s I became passionately interested in the game and began subscribing to *Chess* Magazine, where I first read about Tal. In particular I remember his exploits in the 1958 USSR Championship, where he was striving to retain the title he had sensationally won the year before. Going into the last round level with Tigran Petrosian, Tal had Black against Boris Spassky, who himself needed to win at all costs, in order to progress to the next stage of the World Championship cycle. Petrosian prudently agreed an early draw, but after five hours' play Spassky and Tal were still locked in battle, and their game was adjourned in a position that looked grim for Tal. I can still recall the words of Salo Flohr, as they appeared in *Chess*: "Tal and all Riga slept badly that night". As it happens, the reader can follow this game in Chapter 8, and see how Tal defended heroically, before finally breaking out with a decisive counterattack to win his second USSR Championship gold medal.

The next year, 1959, saw the thrilling Candidates Tournament in Yugoslavia, in which Tal and Keres fought out a ding-dong battle, Tal in particular taking huge risks in striving to win in virtually every game. Even the legendary Botvinnik was unable to resist his fiery play, but, not long after wresting the World Championship in 1960, Tal suffered the first bout of ill-health that was to dog him for the rest of his life. And after losing the Return Match the following year, he was never again to contest the title, although he reached the Candidates stage on several occasions.

With the passing years his playing style inevitably mellowed and became more solid, although in almost every event he could be relied on to provide at least one combinational flash recalling the Tal of old.

I vividly recall one occasion in 1970 at the Moscow University Chess Club, when Tal came to give a talk about the recent "Match of the Century" in Belgrade. He spoke modestly and wittily to the packed audience, and a wonderful evening was rounded off by a 12-player lightning tournament, into which the grandmaster threw himself wholeheartedly. As one of the leading foreign players at the University Club, I was invited to take part, but in my game with Tal was too over-awed, and after losing dismally in under 20 moves I felt too ashamed to engage the great man in conversation...

The pleasure I have gained from translating this book, and which I hope will be shared by its readers, is tinged by the regret, felt throughout the chess world, that the incomparable Mikhail Tal is no longer with us.

Ken Neat   July 1994

Introduction

ON THE ONE HAND, this is not a textbook. Because in chess, in the opinion of the authors, this name can be given only to an explanation of the rules — the bishop moves diagonally, the rook vertically or horizontally in any direction — and also, perhaps, to the principles of checkmating the lone king with pieces of different values. These are indisputable — they are axioms.

Everything else in chess consists of theorems, and they need to be demonstrated. Sometimes they drag on for many years, and sometimes stretch far into the distant future. Indeed: does the truth lie in a strong pawn centre, or the attack on it? Who will give a definitive answer? And when?

On the other hand, this is nevertheless a textbook. Similar to those that set out the basics of versification, the metres and peculiarities, say, of Alexandrine verse. It is true that, after studying all this, you will not necessarily become an Alexander Pushkin, a William Shakespeare, or a Johann Goethe — geniuses themselves make paths in the endless world in the name of creativity, but... Neither Pushkin, nor Shakespeare, nor Goethe would have become who they were, had their knowledge of poetry (feelings and thoughts we introduce into this conversation in brackets; they are primary and lay at the very foundation) remained at the level of prehistoric, primitive people, who made single-line drawings on their cave walls of the desired objects of their hunting, but nothing more...

And so, dear readers, what you have before you is a guide. Since it is fully admitted that this is a field in which there are many more exceptions than rules, this book has the aim merely of suggesting: where and on which paths in the dense forest of variations are concealed those very indicators — imperceptible or altogether invisible — that will allow you to replace quiet forward movement with a much more rapid tempo, or to switch from a positional struggle to an attack. It is not always explosive, sacrificial — on the queenside things very often do not come to this. But if the target of the pursuit becomes the king, the sacrifice becomes both a basic weapon, and the main "performer" of that army which is mounting the offensive. This is why reference points and prompts are so important, in deciding whether or not it is the right time for a sacrifice.

The theory of sacrifices has already been studied — true, not especially often, and not very recently — by chess researchers, including grandmasters Rudolf Spielman in the mid-thirties, and Leonid Shamkovich in the late sixties. The classification of sacrifices compiled by them was correct, although also not altogether complete: life in chess does not stand still. But the aim of this book is different: it is to demonstrate the practical application of these sacrifices, to give typical attacking procedures, and — most important — to point out those very "symptoms" of a position, which indicate the existence, at its heart, of a combinational, sacrificial solution to the problem. However — and the reader can see this for himself — the correctness of an attack on the kingside may sometimes depend on whether the white a-pawn is at a2, a3 or a4...

So then, let's be off. The authors have endeavoured to differentiate the sections as far as possible, although, of course, in practice attacks only on h6 or exclusively on the light squares do not occur. But the main idea may be suggested by one particular feature of the position — and it is this that gives the name to this or that chapter. Each chapter is accompanied by illustrative games: at the demand of one author (**I.D.**) they are taken from the "personal collection" of the other (**M.T.**). The basis for this selection was the record number of special prizes, the vast majority for "brilliance in attack", which overcame the feeble resistance of one author against the other, and Attack was victorious.

May the readers of this book also be victorious.

1 The Main Indicator - King in the Centre

"IT IS A PROFOUND MISTAKE to imagine that the art of combination depends only on natural talent, and that it cannot be learned. Every experienced player knows that all (or almost all) combinations arise from a recollection of familiar elements."

I.D. This thought of Richard Réti (with certain doubts regarding the numerical grounds of "all or almost all combinations") can be considered indisputable. And the king in the centre is a stable "familiar element" of possible combinational attacks.

M.T. At any event I can admit: as long as my opponent has not yet castled, on each move I seek a pretext for an offensive. Even when I realise that the king is not in danger.

I.D. Is such an expenditure of time and effort justified?

M.T. Well... It is more likely that doubts are unjustified, as shown by the following instructive episode. It occurred in the 4th game of my Candidates Semi-Final Match with **Bent Larsen** in 1965. After **1 e4 ♘f6 2 e5 ♘d5 3 d4 d6 4 ♘f3 dxe5** (to some extent a Larsen patent) **5 ♘xe5** there suddenly followed **5...♘d7**.

Had this been a simultaneous display, I would have decided that my opponent had simply overlooked 6 ♘xf7 ♔xf7 7 ♕h5+, when, against his will, the black king is forced to "go for a walk".

But Larsen could not have overlooked this, and I began examining possible variations. My intuition insistently kept telling me that the sacrifice had to be correct, but I decided to calculate everything "as far as mate", spent some 50 minutes, but then in one of the innumerable variations I found something resembling a defence, and... rejected the sacrifice. This was a betrayal of myself, I saved the game only by a miracle after the adjournment, and in general I barely, in a "war of nerves", won the match.

Of course, I should have begun the attack without thinking, and only after the forced 7...♔e6 8 c4 ♘5f6 9 d5+ ♔d6 10 ♕f7 ♘e5 11 ♗f4 studied the position. This is no place to give variations: in certain of them the black king is mated not even on the central files, but at b2 or a1! And so that this should not sound totally unreal, here, cleared of a whole network of branches, is a continuation which, though not of course obligatory, is very pretty — 11...c5 12 ♘c3 a6 13 ♖d1!! g6 14 ♗xe5+ ♔xe5 15 d6 g5 (defending against 16 f4) 16 ♖d2 ♗f5 17 ♖e2+ ♔d4 18 ♖e4+!! ♗xe4 19 ♕e6!!, with the threat of 20 ♘e2+ ♔d3 21 ♕h3+ ♔c2 22 ♕b3+ ♔b1 23 ♘c3+ ♔a1 24 ♗d3 ♗xd3 25 ♔d2+ ♗b1 26 ♖xb1 mate.

And so, the attack on the king. It includes many components. If there is a lead in development, if the king's pawn shelter is weakened or files and diagonals have been opened, if a secure piece outpost or a striking force has been created — all these are sufficient grounds for an offensive, and a discussion of them will follow. But for the moment — the assault on the king that is still in the centre.

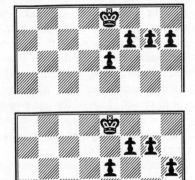

These are the most natural kingside pawn formations, arising almost invariably in many semi-open and closed openings. They can be broken up only by a direct blow — by a sacrifice at e6 or f7. The offensive then proceeds either along the opened central files, or else along either the h5-e8 diagonal (if it has been weakened beforehand, this often serves as a "prompt" for the attack) or the a2-g8 diagonal.

However, usually the attack is mounted down both central files.

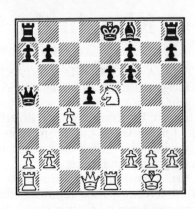

Nezhmetdinov-Kamyshov
Russian Federation Championship
Yaroslavl 1951

This can be considered a classic example: a preceding pawn sacrifice for the initiative, an energetic exploitation of a lead in development, and — an attack with limited forces!

17 ♘xf7!! ♔xf7

17...♖g8 18 ♕h5 ♖g6 19 ♘h8! is also bad.

18 ♕h5+ ♔e7 19 cxd5 e5 20 f4 ♕xd5 21 fxe5 f5 22 e6 ♔f6 23 h4!

Preparing mate at f7 or g5.

23...♗c5+ 24 ♔h1 ♕xe6 25 ♕h6+ Black resigns.

Rudolf Spielmann called such a sacrifice "preventive" — after it the king does indeed lose the opportunity of ending up in its customary and therefore safest place, and is "invited" to face the full force of the attack. Most often this draught threatens not just a cold, but terminal pneumonia...

Kupreichik-Grigorian
Leningrad 1974

By a temporary pawn sacrifice Black appears to have gained good counterplay on the g-file, and is intending, at the least, after 17 ♘f3 ♘xh4 18 ♕xh4 b5 (there is no point in hurrying to restore material equality; the threat of ...b4 forces White to waste a tempo) 19 a3 ♗b7 to complete his development, and, more important, to create the preconditions for a counterattack, in particular on e4.

All this would be right, were it not for the fact that the black king is still in the centre, and that White has the possibility of "inviting" it to face the storm.

17 ♘xf7! ♔xf7

The interposition of 17...♘xh4 18 ♕xh4 ♔xf7 changes little: after 19 ♕h7+ ♖g7 20 ♗h5+ ♔f8 21 ♕h8+ ♖g8 22 ♖xf6+ Black loses immediately, while 19...♔f8 is insufficient, if only because of 20 ♘d5!, renewing the threat of ♗h5.

18 ♗xf6 ♗xf6 19 ♖d5!

Preventing the black queen from switching to the centre or the kingside, where it could have taken on the role of central defender.

19...b5

Not through choice: if 19...♕d8 White has both 20 ♖g5 with the irresistible threat of ♗h5, and 20 ♖xd6 ♕e7 21 ♘d5 exd5 22 ♖dxf6+ ♕xf6 23 ♖xf6+ ♔xf6 24 ♕d6+, which is also good enough to win. And 19...exd5 20 ♘xd5 ♕d8 21 ♖xf6+ is similar to this second variation.

20 e5

20 ♖g5, as given above, would have been more quickly decisive, but on the other hand White now attacks "with checks".

20...dxe5 21 ♖xf6+ ♔xf6 22 ♘e4+ ♔f7 23 ♕f2+ ♔g7 24 ♕f6+ ♔h7 25 ♘g5+ ♔h6 26 ♖d3 ♕e1+ 27 ♗d1 ♕h4 28 ♖h3 ♕xh3 29 ♘f7+ ♔h7 30 gxh3 ♗d7 31 h4 ♖g7 32 h5 ♘f4 33 ♗f3 ♘d5 34 ♕h6+ ♔g8 35 ♕h8+ ♔xf7 36 ♕xa8, and White soon realised his material advantage.

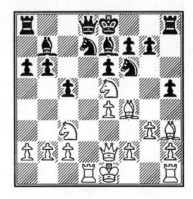

Tal-Sveshnikov
41st USSR Ch., Moscow 1973

Objectively speaking, White does not need to hurry, since he has achieved all that he could dream of: he has brought his central attacker, the knight at e5, into a striking position, he has his sights set on e6, and his queen's rook and queen are both active. In addition, the advanced h-pawn hinders Black's castling, and therefore 12 0-0 was perfectly possible, in order to begin the assault a move later. But what chess player will defer his enjoyment without extreme necessity?

12 ♘xf7! ♔xf7 13 ♗xe6+ ♔f8

The bishop is taboo - 13...♔xe6 14 ♕c4+ (a "left hook"), winning immediately.

14 0-0

14 e5 ♗xh1 15 exf6 is also sufficient, when both 15...gxf6 16 ♖xd7 and 15...♘xf6 16 ♖xd8+ ♖xd8 17 f3 give White a great advantage.

14...♕c8 15 ♖xd7 ♘xd7 16 ♖d1 ♗c6 17 ♘d5 ♕b7 18 e5 ♔e8, and now White had a straightforward win by 19 ♗xd7+ ♕xd7 20 e6 ♕xd5 (otherwise 21 ♘c7+) 21 ♖xd5 ♗xd5 22 ♕e5 ♗c6 23 ♕c7 (but not 23 ♕xg7? ♖f8 24 ♗c7 ♗f6) 23...♗b5 24 c4 ♗xc4 25 ♗d6, or the more prosaic 25 ♕c6+, with mate in three moves.

Today the episode, known in its time as the "Argentine tragedy", has been largely forgotten. It occurred in the 14th round of the Göteborg Interzonal Tournament, 1955, when by the will of the draw an unusual USSR v. Argentina match took place: **Geller** had White against **Panno**, **Keres** against **Najdorf**, and **Spassky** against **Pilnik**. Specially for that day, the Argentine grandmasters prepared an innovation

in a well known variation of the Sicilian Defence.

Here Black struck the flank blow **9...g5**, and after **10 fxg5** he continued **10...♘fd7**, planning to regain the pawn and obtain the "eternal" e5 square for his knight. After this his f7 pawn would be securely defended, and time would be gained for the development of his queenside forces.

Black's plan could have been fully justified, had not for an instant the h5-e8 diagonal been weakened and his e6 insufficiently defended.

The first to notice this was Yefim Geller.

11 ♘xe6(!) fxe6 12 ♕h5+ ♔f8 13 ♗b5!

Aimed indirectly against the black outpost at e5; to support it with the other knight from c6 will not now be possible.

13...♘e5

This continuation, prepared in advance, loses, as does 13...♔g7, played by the other Argentine grandmasters. The strongest defence was found much later, after a debate in virtually all the world's chess magazines. It consists in 13...罝h7!, covering f7 in a different way, when after 14 0-0+ 含g8 15 g6 罝g7 16 罝f7 奥xh4 17 豐xh6 罝xf7 18 gxf7+ 含xf7 19 豐h7+ 含e8 White either gives perpetual check, or continues the attack with 20 豐h5+ 含f8 21 罝f1+ 奥f6 22 e5, although here too Black nevertheless has a draw.

14 奥g3!

Essential accuracy. After the move order 14 0-0+ 含g8! 15 奥g3 the offensive could have been parried by 15...hxg5! But now it is all over!

14...奥xg5

Alas, here 14...含g8 is met by 15 奥xe5 dxe5 16 豐g6+, while 14...含g7 loses to 15 奥xe5+ dxe5 16 0-0 豐g8 17 奥e8!

15 0-0+ 含e7 16 奥xe5 豐b6+

Nothing is changed by 16...奥e3+ 17 含h1 dxe5 18 豐xe5 奥d4 19 ②d5+ 豐xd5 20 豐c7+.

17 含h1 dxe5 18 豐f7+ 含d6 19 罝ad1+ 豐d4

If 19...含c5 White wins most quickly by 20 豐f2+, mating.

20 罝xd4+ exd4 21 e5+ 含c5

A rare, pure mate in the centre of the board results after 21...含xe5 22 豐c7.

22 豐c7+ ②c6 23 奥xc6

Black resigns: 23...bxc6 24 豐a5+ 含c4 25 b3 mate.

The other two games concluded in similar fashion.

Of course, in the next diagram White has the possibility of further activating his forces - his king's rook, but in this time Black will endeavour to simplify the position, in particular by ...罝d8. Bringing up the knight by 17

②e4 is parried by the natural and strong centralisation of the queen — 17...豐e5!, and so White resorts to a typical solution:

Nezhmetdinov-Suetin
Russian Federation Ch., 1947

17 奥xe6! fxe6 18 豐xe6+ 奥e7

After the alternative defence 18...豐e7 White has a choice between 19 豐b3 奥g7 20 罝g1 (but not 20 罝e1 奥e5 21 罝xe5 豐xe5 22 豐xb7 0-0, when the advantage passes to Black) 20...罝f8 21 罝g4, and the more convincing 19 豐f5! 奥c8 20 豐f3! Black still cannot castle, 20...罝a7 is met by 21 ②e4, and after 20...豐c7 all the white forces unite with 21 罝e1+ 奥e7 22 罝g1 罝f8 23 豐h5+ 含d8 24 罝g7 罝e8 25 ②d5! 豐a5 26 ②xe7! (or 26 豐xe8+) 26...豐xh5 27 ②xc6 mate!

19 ②e4 奥c8 20 ②f6+ 含f8 21 罝d7!

Another typical decision: Black's central defender — his light-square bishop, is removed from the game. We shall be studying this procedure in detail in a later chapter.

21...♗xd7 22 ♘xd7+ ♔e8 23 ♘f6+ ♔d8

Or 23...♔f8 24 ♖g1!, and by the threat of mate at g8 White wins both black rooks. But what is he to do now, since Black has prepared 24...♕b6 ?

24 ♔e2!!

This decides the game.

24...♕d6 25 ♖d1 ♕xd1+ 26 ♔xd1 ♗xf6 27 ♕xf6+ ♔c7 28 ♕e7+ ♔b6 29 c4, and a few moves later **Black resigned**.

Sometimes it is not so easy to approach e6, but any "customs duties" will be recovered on the way. There are many examples, of which one of the most striking is a game from more than half a century ago.

Ravinsky-Panov
Moscow 1943

The player with a lead in development is obliged to attack. But there is simply no other target, other than e6, and it appears to be quite securely covered by the black knights. Securely?

20 ♖xd7!! ♘xd7 21 ♘xe6 fxe6 22 ♕xe6+

The result is the same, the only difference being that White has had to pay a higher price.

22...♗e7

The king cannot escape from the centre: 22...♔d8 23 ♗g5+ ♔c7 24 ♕c6+ ♔b8 25 ♗f4+ ♖c7 26 ♗xc7 ♕xc7 27 ♕a8 mate.

23 ♖e1 ♕c5

In this way Black coordinates his forces and takes control of the important g5 square, since it is clear that White cannot manage without including his reserves in the attack.

The other defence against the immediate mate, 23...♘b6, is weaker on account of the overloading of the black queen. White quickly wins by 24 ♗g5 (24 ♗e3 allows Black to defend by giving up his knight — 24... ♕d7; this is where the price, paid by White for the sacrifice on e6, tells) 24...♖c7 25 ♗c6+ ♔f8 26 ♖e3, and Black has no adequate defence against 27 ♖f3+.

24 b4!

Destroying Black's coordination. With 24...♕xb4 he loses control over g5, and after 25 ♗g5 he does not have the defence 25...♘f6. Nevertheless, according to analysis by grandmaster Reuben Fine, it was in this line that Black should have sought salvation: 25...♕xe1+! (once again reminding White that in his attack he has not sacrificed, as usual, a minor piece, but a whole rook!) 26 ♕xe1 ♘f6 27 ♕e6 ♖xc2 28 ♗c6+ ♔f8 29 ♕c8+ ♔f7 30 ♕xh8 ♖xc6 31 ♗xf6 ♗xf6 32 ♕xh7, and there is still a lot of play to come. After the move in the game Black's king remains for ever under fire.

24...♘f8 25 ♕g4 ♕c3 26 ♖xe7+!

Leaving the king totally exposed.

26...♔xe7 27 ♗g5+ ♔d6

The alternative was 27...♔e8 28 ♕e2+! ♔f7 (28...♔d7 29 ♕e7 mate) 29 ♗d5+ ♔g6 30 ♕e4+ ♔xg5 31 ♕f4+ ♔h5 32 ♗f7+ g6 33 ♕h4 mate.

28 ♕d1+! ♔c7 29 ♗f4+ ♔b6 30 ♕d6+ ♔a7 31 ♕e7+ ♖c7 32 ♗xc7 ♕a1+ 33 ♗f1 ♘g6 34 ♕c5+ ♔b7 35 ♗a5, and Black did not in fact succeed in avoiding mate.

I.D. Misha, the whole world knows of that unusual ease with which you "squander" material in an attack. I realise that this ease is purely superficial, yet is there a limit to your generosity, is there an inner censor, which sometimes places a veto on tempting attacking ideas?

M.T. I hope that we are talking not about those attacks, that are calculated to the end, but about those, in the correctness of which one is persuaded by experience, knowledge and intuition? I once discussed this with grandmaster Yefim Geller, and we generally agreed that in intuitive attacks there is a limit to the amount of material that can be sacrificed.

I.D. That is what the Tal of the early 1990s thinks. But what did, say, the Tal of 1960, the World Champion, think?

M.T. Mmmm... If you were to give me that Tal now, I would show him what's what. No, Geller is right: if for an attack on the king you have to give up a piece for one or two pawns, and there is the prospect, even in the absence of a mate, of winning two pieces for a rook, then there is nothing to think about. If you sacrifice a rook for a pawn, it would be good at least to be sure of perpetual check. Of course, this is the most abstract viewpoint, and in concrete terms you could have, for example, two minor pieces and positional compensation for a queen.

I.D. In short, if the beauty of a combination does not depend, as one of the old writers said, on the "thickness" of the sacrificed piece...

M.T. ... then in an attack one still has to make one's demands commensurate with one's possibilities. And don't look at me like that: I have been an ex-World Champion for 30 years!

The e6 square may also provide the altar for a "free" offering: a piece intrudes in here with the same idea - of enticing the black pawn away from f7, thereby opening the h5-e8 diagonal.

Tal-Bilek
Amsterdam Interzonal 1964

The rejoinder **15 ♘e6** is logical and quite correct: after 15...fxe6 16 ♕h5+ ♔d7 17 ♕g4 the black king's path to a7 is blocked, and White has numerous threats, including 18 ♕xg7 and 19 d6, or 18 d6 immediately.

15...♕d6 16 ♘xg7+ ♔f8 17 ♘e6+ ♔e8

Here in the event of 17...fxe6 the black king is completely defenceless.

18 ♖hf1 ♗g5+ 19 ♔b1 b5 20 ♕h5 ♗f4 21 ♗b3 a5 22 ♘c7+!

The quickest, although 22 a4 or even 22 g3 is quite sufficient.

22...♕xc7 23 d6, and **Black resigned**, since on 23...♕d7 there would have followed the obvious 24 ♖xf4 exf4 25 ♕e5+.

An alternative to the direct blow against a king in the centre is the attack on it from the flank. In practice this most often reduces to the attacking pieces breaking through to g7 (usually the queen) or on the a4-e8 diagonal (again, usually the queen).

M.T. Of course, we are formulating things somewhat abstractly, rather in the style of Mikhail Moiseyevich (Botvinnik - **I.D.**), but, strangely enough, a great variety of attacks reduce to this...

I.D. In your games too!

Tal-Vooremaa
Tallinn 1971

14 ♕g3

The only possibility of maintaining the initiative, even if at the cost of a piece: after 14 fxe5 ♗xe5 15 c3 d6 Black has nothing to fear.

14...exd4 15 ♕xg7 ♖f8 16 e5 ♗e7 17 f5 f6

Otherwise White himself would advance his pawn to this square.

18 ♘f4 ♖f7 19 exf6! ♘e5

The queen is clearly immune — after 19...♖xg7 20 fxg7 ♔f7 21 f6 the threats of 22 ♗c4+ and 22 ♗h7 are irresistible, and also after 21...♗xf6 22 ♘xh5.

20 ♗c4!!

Diverting the knight both from the e-file, and away from g6 square beside the king, from where in certain variations the queen will continue the attack.

20...♘xc4 21 ♕g8+ ♗f8

Or 21...♖f8 22 ♕g6+ ♖f7 23 ♘d5 ♕d6 24 fxe7 ♕xd5 25 f6.

22 ♘xh5

Again threatening a blow from the flank.

22...♘d6 23 ♖ae1+ ♔d8 24 ♖e7!

This essentially concludes the game.

24...♕b5 25 ♖fe1 ♕d5 26 ♘f4 ♕xa2 27 ♘e6+ ♕xe6

After 27...dxe6 28 ♖xf7 ♘xf7 29 ♕xf8+ ♔c7 30 ♕xf7+ ♔b6 31 fxe6 in the near future White will obtain as many queens as he wants.

28 fxe6 ♖xf6 29 ♖f7 Black resigns.

In the next diagram Black is intending to complete his queenside development with gain of tempi, after which he will have at least equal chances. The hopes for White, who up till now has been conducting an attack through the centre, involve a flank continuation of it.

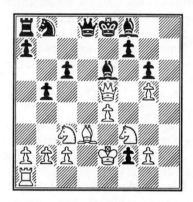

Tal-Gufeld
Gori 1968

20 ♘xb5! cxb5 21 ♗xb5+ ♘d7 22 ♖d1 ♕e7

The best defence was 22...♗e7, after which White appears to have nothing better than to go into an equal endgame: 23 ♕h8+ ♗f8 24 ♘e5 ♕xg5 25 ♗xd7+ ♗xd7 26 ♘xd7 ♕g4+ 27 ♔xf2 ♕xd1 28 ♕xf8+ ♔xd7 29 ♕xa8. But now the black king is drawn out into the firing line.

23 ♖xd7! ♗xd7 24 ♗xd7+ ♔xd7 25 ♕d5+ ♔c7 26 ♕xa8 ♕c5 27 c3, and White's pawn preponderance decided the outcome.

The same idea is embodied in the illustrative game Tal-Larsen (p.24), but for the moment here is another typical flank operation by White. There is a second theme - the intrusion of the heavy pieces onto the 7th rank, but it is only extremely rarely that any procedures occur in pure form.

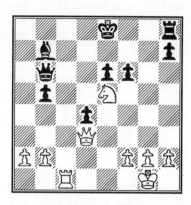

Botvinnik-Euwe
The Hague/Moscow 1948

The position is very sharp. The white rook has occupied the open file, and for the moment — but not for ever — the black king is stuck in the centre. On the other hand, Black has an excellent bishop and a phalanx of central pawns. In short, after the retreat of the knight each side will have his chances.

But, as it turns out, the retreat is not obligatory, since White has a different way of proceeding.

22 ♕g3! fxe5 23 ♕g7 ♖f8 24 ♖c7

The invasion has taken place, mates at d7 and e7 are threatened, and the bishop is "hanging" — things are bad for Black. He fails to save the game by 24...♕d6 25 ♖xb7 d3 26 ♖a7 ♕d8 27 ♕xh7, with unavoidable mating threats. Therefore he gave up his queen — **24...♕xc7**, but was soon forced to resign.

In all these cases the path for the attacking queen to land a "right hook" was already open. The same goal may be achieved, if first the way has to be cleared by an advance of the pawns. The subsequent invasion of the pieces can then usually be supported by the far-advanced infantry.

Nezhmetdinov-Paoli
Bucharest 1953

This position also illustrates to an equal degree the next theme of our discussion: how incautious it is to voluntarily leave the king in the centre. True, kingside castling is not possible here — White is well prepared for an attack on this area of the board, but the "normal" 12...♞e5 (essential now or on the following move to neutralise the queen's X-ray pressure on f7) 13 ♕e2 0-0-0 would have given the game a "normal" course. But Black, hoping for a counterattack, leaves his king in the centre, and White lands an energetic knock-out blow from the flank.

12...♖c8? 13 g5 hxg5 14 hxg5 ♞e5 15 ♕g2! ♞g8 (15...♞fg4 16 ♗f4) **16 f4 ♞c4 17 ♗xc4 ♕xc4 18 f5 b5 19 ♔b1 b4 20 g6! e5**

After 20...bxc3 21 gxf7+ ♔xf7 White wins most simply by the direct

22 ♕xg7+ ♔e8 23 ♕xh8, although he also has the more elegant 22 b3! ♕c7 23 ♕g6+ ♔f8 24 fxe6, mating. But now f7 is defended by the queen, and the white knights are attacked...

21 b3!

Now, in contrast to 21 ♞d5, Black does not have time to block the position by 21...f6.

21...♕xc3 22 gxf7+ ♔d8 23 ♕xg7 exd4 24 ♗xd4!

The quickest, most accurate (weaving a mating net) and prettiest solution.

24...♕xc2+ 25 ♔a1 ♖h2 26 ♗b6+ ♖c7 27 ♕xg8+

Black resigns, since he is mated in two moves. White's play was rewarded by the first brilliancy prize.

Larsen-Spassky
"Match of the Century"
Belgrade 1970

Black has the initiative, but at first sight it appears difficult to approach the white king. Of course, it can be forced to remain for ever in the centre, but the price for this (11...♖xd2 12 ♞xd2 ♞xe3 13 ♕c3 ♖d8) is perhaps too great. And so Black begins an attack from the flank.

11...h5 12 h3

Practically forced. Firstly, because the knight, which has been "launched into the penalty area" (we will be talking about this attacking procedure later, in Chapter 3) cannot be tolerated for long, and secondly, because the concrete 12 ♘c3 is refuted by the equally concrete 12...♖xd2!!, when after 13 ♕xd2 ♗xe3 14 ♕c2 ♗f2+ White has to part with his queen.

12...h4! 13 hxg4

The interposition of 13 ♗xg4 ♗xg4 and now 14 hxg4 would have led to variations, similar to those that occurred in the game: 14...hxg3 15 ♖g1 ♖h1!! 16 ♖xh1 g2 17 ♖g1 ♕h4+ 18 ♔e2 ♕xg4+ 19 ♔e1 ♕g3+ 20 ♔e2 (or 20 ♔d1 ♕f2 21 ♕xe4 ♕xg1+ 22 ♔c2 ♕f2, winning) 20...♕f3+ 21 ♔e1 ♗e7, when the outcome is decided.

13...hxg3 14 ♖g1 ♖h1!! 15 ♖xh1 g2 16 ♖f1

There is no choice: if 16 ♖g1 Black has the decisive 16...♕h4+ 17 ♔d1 ♕h1 18 ♕c3 ♕xg1+ 19 ♔c2 ♕f2.

16...♕h4+ 17 ♔d1 gxf1=♕+

White resigns. After 18 ♗xf1 ♗xg4+ mate is inevitable.

I.D. This confirms what you said in an interview, given after the "Match of the Century" in Belgrade: "Spassky... won a game, that will undoubtedly find its way into the books"...

M.T. In my opinion, only Nostradamus has made faultless forecasts, decades and centuries beforehand. Besides, the attack from the flank was carried out brilliantly by Boris, but there was no sacrifice on f2, the theme of this section...

I.D. Well, what of it? All the same, examples cannot be clinically pure, procedures and themes are interwoven and, incidentally, we should now make a slight digression and jump ahead.

The sacrifice on f7, drawing out the king, can also be made after it has moved away from the centre into its shelter. The double defence of this point makes it less vulnerable, of course, but even so the pawn linkage "e6 + f7" continues to draw the attention of the attacking side, and nearly always requires additional defence by other pieces. Otherwise disaster can strike here.

This eternal truth is sometimes forgotten by even the most experienced grandmasters.

Smirin-Smyslov
55th USSR Ch., Moscow 1988

Of course, Black stands worse, and the powerful piece outpost at e5 simply obliges him to keep an eye not only on his queenside pawn weaknesses, but also on the "e6 + f7" link of his pawn chain. Therefore 21...♗d7 was essential, and if 22 ♘g5 ♘fd5, at least blocking the dangerous diagonal.

21...♗a6?

This activity leads to disaster.

22 ♘xf7! ♖xf7 23 ♗xe6 ♘ed5 24 ♘e5 ♖aa7 25 ♖xc6

25 ♘xc6 ♕b6 26 ♘xa7 ♕xa7 27 g5 would also have won.

25...♘f4 26 ♖xa6! ♖xa6 27 ♗xf7+ ♔h8 28 ♕f3 Black resigns (28... ♕xd4 29 ♘c6).

Kaplan-Radulescu
Hungary 1980

Black is cramped over the entire front. Especially unpleasant is the rook at c7, preventing him from completing his queenside development. It would be good to send it home by 18...♘d5, but then for an instant the black king remains completely undefended, and 19 ♕h5 leads to a quick mate. Hence his natural desire to first drive away White's "central striker", also removing his h7 pawn from attack.

18...h6 19 ♘xf7!

It turns out that now this is possible.

After **19...♔xf7 20 ♗xf6 ♕xc7** (20... gxf6 or 20...♔xf6 allows a quick mate) **21 ♕h5+ ♔f8 22 ♗xg7+! ♔xg7 23 ♕g6+ ♔f8 24 ♕xh6+ ♔f7 25 ♗g6+ ♔f6** from the several possible mates White chose **26 ♗h5+ ♔f5 27 ♕g6+ ♔f4 28 ♕g4** mate.

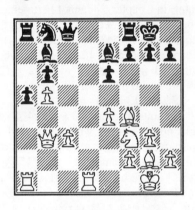

Adorjan-Tarjan
Riga Interzonal 1979

Not one of White's pieces is "looking" at the kingside. But for the moment Black's main forces too are blocked in on the left corner of the board, and so White can calmly prepare an attack on the classic point f7.

17 ♘e5!

An essential prelude, planned long beforehand, otherwise the black knight leaps via d7 to c5.

17...♖a7 18 ♗h3 ♗a8 19 ♘xf7! ♔xf7

Alas, forced: 19...♖xf7 20 ♗xe6 ♕f8 21 ♗xb8.

20 ♗xb8 ♕xb8 21 ♕xe6+ ♔e8 22 ♖d7 ♖xd7 23 ♕xd7+ ♔f7 24 ♕e6+

White contents himself with perpetual check. The alternative was 24

♗e6+ ♔f6 25 ♗d5 (threatening mate in one move) 25...♕c8 26 e5+ ♔g6 27 ♕xe7 ♗xd5 28 ♕d6+ ♗e6 29 ♕xb6 h6 30 ♖xa5 ♔h7 when, although in the endgame (31 ♕c6) Black has nothing to fear, and with the queens on the white king might come under a counterattack, even so White's chances look preferable.

24...♔e8 25 ♕d7+ Draw agreed.

And, finally, another motif may suggest the preparation of this typical combination: the deployment on the a2-g8 diagonal of the black rook and king, or in the following instance, of even the queen and king.

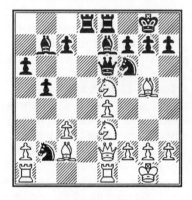

Keres-Geller
Budapest 1952

18 ♘xf7! ♕xf7

Capturing with the king would have allowed White the same possibilities, plus one more: the inclusion in the attack at the required moment of the queen from h5.

19 ♗b3 ♘c4 20 ♘xc4 bxc4 21 ♗xc4 ♘d5 22 ♗xe7 ♕xe7 (or 22... ♖xe7 23 ♕d2) **23 exd5 ♕xe2 24**

♖xe2 ♖xe2 25 ♗xe2 ♗xd5 26 a4, and in the endgame White was a pawn up.

Botvinnik-Vidmar
Nottingham 1936

In this example the same motif dominates, the only difference being that the black pawn has already gone from e6, and White has acquired an additional factor: along the h3-c8 diagonal his queen has its "sights" set on the rook.

20 ♘xf7! ♖xf7

Things are very simple after 20... ♔xf7 21 ♗xd5+.

21 ♗xf6 ♗xf6 (or 21...♘xf6 22 ♖xf6 and 23 ♕xc8) **22 ♖xd5 ♕c6 23 ♖d6!**

Avoiding a little trap: 23 ♖c5 ♗xd4+, when White has to agree to a draw.

23...♕e8 24 ♖d7

Whereas now **Black resigned**.

But let us return to the main theme of this chapter - the attack on the king, caught in the centre. In all primers, even those for beginners, this factor is mentioned as a sure indicator of a possible attack. There is probably no sense in once again listing all those difficulties that a king, remaining on its initial square, causes its troops. They are well known. But also known is this paradoxical fact: for centuries, in one tournament after another, their participants forget to concern themselves about their king, and in such instances the response of the opponent can and should be appropriate. In short, it must be said again and again: the king in the centre is the signal for an attack. Because a delay in evacuating the king can cost a player very dearly.

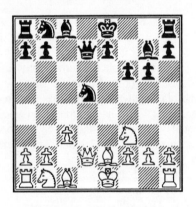

Nezhmetdinov-A.Zaitsev
Kazan 1964

Here, for the first time, Black should have castled, maintaining equality: 11...0-0 12 ♗c4 ♖d8 13 0-0 ♔h8, or 12 c4 ♘c7, when White's light-square bishop is not too well placed. But Black was tempted by something different.

11...e5 12 0-0 ♘e7 13 ♗c4

Now, even after the exchange of queens, it becomes uncomfortable in the centre for the king: 13...♕xd2 14 ♘bxd2, with the threat of ♘e4-d6+.

13...b5 14 ♗b3 ♘a6 15 ♕e2 ♘c5 16 ♖d1 ♕c6 17 ♗c2 ♗e6

Castling would now be bad: 17... 0-0? 18 b4 ♘b7 19 ♗e4 ♕e8 20 a4 bxa4 21 ♕c4+ ♖f7 (21...♕f7 loses a piece after 22 ♕c7) 22 ♘a3, and there is literally nothing that Black can move.

18 ♘bd2 ♖d8?

This second voluntary rejection of castling, for the sake of simplification, leaves Black on the verge of disaster.

19 ♘b3 ♖xd1+ 20 ♕xd1 ♘b7?

This third rejection of castling leads to a crushing defeat, although for his previous errors Black would have had to suffer mounting difficulties in the variation 20...0-0 21 ♘xc5 ♕xc5 22 ♗e3 ♕c7 23 ♗b3.

21 a4 a6 22 axb5 axb5

Black is not afraid of the check at a8: there would appear to be no way of approaching his king at f7. But...

23 ♘bd4! exd4 24 ♘xd4 ♕d7 25 ♘xe6 ♕xe6 26 ♖a8+ ♘c8

Alas, the f7 square has become "mined" on account of the weakening of the a2-g8 diagonal.

27 ♗b3 ♕d7 28 ♕e2+ ♔d8 29 ♗e6 ♖e8

Is everything in order?

30 ♖xc8+! ♕xc8 31 ♕d1+ ♔e7 32 ♗xc8 ♖xc8 33 ♕e2+ Black resigns.

(see diagram next page)

After playing the opening without any particular pretensions, White should have concerned himself about his king - 10 ♗e2 and 11 0-0.

Gromek-Veresov
Poland v. Belorussia 1954

But the premature sortie **10 ♘d5** placed him on the verge of disaster, especially after **10...♖c8 11 ♗e2**.

Now came a piece sacrifice.

11...♘xd5! 12 exd5 ♘b4 13 dxe6

The game would have lasted longer after 13 c4 ♗f5 14 ♘d4 ♗xd4 15 ♗xd4 ♘c2+, but with the same result.

13...♘xc2+ 14 ♔f2 ♘xe3 15 ♔xe3 ♕b6+ 16 ♘d4

Or 16 ♔d3 ♗h6 17 exf7+ ♖xf7 18 ♘d4 ♕a6+ 19 ♔e4 d5+! 20 ♔xd5 ♕d6+ 21 ♔e4 ♖f4+.

16...fxe6 17 ♕d3 ♖c2!

Not the only continuation, but the most efficient. Now 18...♗xd4+ is threatened, and if 19 ♕xd4 ♖xe2+.

18 ♖hd1 ♖xb2 19 f4 e5 20 fxe5 dxe5 21 ♕c4+ ♔h8 22 ♗f3 ♖b4 23 ♕d5 ♖xd4 24 ♕xb7 ♖e4+! White resigns.

But, as a rule, a king does not remain in the centre voluntarily: it has to be forced to do so, and not "for free". The price may vary: from sacrifices to positional concessions, which may be very diverse.

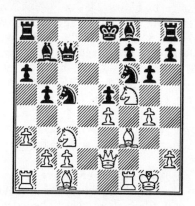

Nezhmetdinov-Tal
29th USSR Championship, Baku 1961

Here such a concession was **15 ♘h6**, which seems to place the white knight into an offside position. This was the reaction of one of the authors, who decided at this point to "punish" the opponent for his anti-positional decision.

In principle this would have been right, had not the audacious knight covered all these drawbacks with one trump: it blocks the king's path to a secure shelter.

15...♘e6 16 ♗g2 ♗g7 17 ♖xf6!

To the positional "sacrifice" is added a normal one, but now the invasion at d5 becomes possible.

17...♗xf6 18 ♘d5 ♕d8 19 ♕f2 ♘f4?

White would have encountered greater difficulties had Black first played 19...♗xd5 (now or on the next move), when there appears to be no clear-cut win. For example: 20 exd5

♘f4 21 ♗xf4 exf4 22 ♕xf4 ♕b6+ 23 ♔h1 0-0-0 24 c3!! (the direct exchange of blows 24 ♘xf7 ♗xb2 25 ♖f1 ♖hf8 26 ♕b4 ♗g7 27 ♘xd8 ♖xf1+ 28 ♗xf1 ♕f2 29 ♗h3 leaves Black with the advantage after 29... ♕f3+ 30 ♔g1 ♕xd5, but not 29... ♗d4? 30 g5+ ♔xd8 31 ♕d6+ etc., when White wins) 24...♖hf8 25 g5 ♗e7 26 ♗h3+ ♔b7 27 ♘xf7 ♔a7! 28 ♗e6, and although White has a serious advantage, there is still a struggle in prospect.

20 ♗xf4 exf4 21 e5! ♗xe5

Alas, Black is obliged to open the central files, along which he comes under attack.

21...♗h4 is very strongly met by 22 ♕d4!, with the threat of e5-e6, and after 22...♖f8 23 ♖d1 ♗xd5 24 ♗xd5 ♖c8 25 ♕a7 ♕c7 26 ♕xa6 White must win, since 26...♕xc2 is bad on account of 27 ♗xf7+ ♖xf7 28 ♕e6+ ♖e7 29 ♕g8+.

If 21...♗g5 White has time for 22 ♘f6+ ♔f8 23 ♗xb7 ♖b8 24 ♗f3 ♗xh6 25 ♖d1 ♕e7 26 ♕h4 ♗g7 27 ♘d7+ ♔e8 28 ♕f2 ♖c8 29 ♕d4, when Black cannot parry the numerous threats, the chief of which is 30 ♗b7 ♖c7 31 ♗xa6.

And after 21...♗xd5 all the same the e-file is opened, and White wins the queen: 22 exf6! ♗xg2 23 ♖e1+.

22 ♖e1 f6 23 ♘xf6+! ♕xf6 24 ♕d4! ♔f8 25 ♖xe5 ♕d8

Or 25...♖d8 26 ♖e8+! ♔g7 27 ♖e7+.

26 ♖f5+ gxf5 27 ♕xh8+ ♔e7 28 ♕g7+ ♔e6 29 gxf5+ Black resigns.

This ability — to prevent the opponent from removing his king to safety — was also possessed by the top players in the earlier era of romantic chess.

P.Morphy-E.Morphy
USA 1850

12 e5! dxe5 13 ♖fe1 ♗d7 14 ♖ab1

The black king has not been allowed across to the kingside, but on the queenside too it will evidently be uncomfortable. But there is no alternative.

14...0-0-0 15 ♗a6! ♘a5 16 ♖ec1 ♗c6 17 ♕xa5 bxa6 18 ♕xa6+ ♔d7 19 ♖xc6 and White won (19...♕xc6 20 ♖d1+).

I.D. However, let us leave in peace the shadows of our great predecessors. Their opponents played rather naive chess, and on the whole they defended weakly (here, for example, more tenacious was 15...bxa6 16 ♕b3 ♗g4 17 ♕b7+ ♔d7 18 ♖bd1+ ♕e8 19 ♖xd8+ ♔xd8! 20 ♕a8+ ♗c8 21 ♖d1+ ♘d4, although White still retains an attack - 22 ♕d5+). More instructive, in my opinion, are modern games even at the level of masters, to say nothing of grandmasters, candidates and champions.

M.T. Alas, I am forced to agree. In my youth I gained enormous pleasure from examining the games of the old masters, but when the so-called "Tal School" opened in Riga, at the very first meeting I said to my young friends: "For pleasure you can read the games collections of Anderssen and Chigorin, but for benefit you should study Tarrasch, Keres and Bronstein."

In modern chess the art of defence has grown greatly, and it is becoming increasingly difficult to win a won position. But the basic principles of attack are eternal. Moreover, the assault need not necessarily resemble a meteorite, be instantaneous and be calculated from beginning to end: the king in the centre can be the target of a lengthy, multi-stage offensive, with one phase logically developing into another.

An example — and a brilliant one! — is provided by the following game.

Chiburdanidze-Dvoiris
Tallinn 1980

White is fully mobilised, and essentially cannot even strengthen the placing of her pieces: they are extremely actively placed. Black, by contrast, has made several "superfluous" pawn moves, his queen has gone to b6 in two moves, and as a result not all his forces are in play. And yet he needs only one tempo for queenside castling... The player with the advantage is obliged to attack!

12 ♘d5!! exd5

The other knight is taboo: 12... ♕xd4? 13 ♗xf6 gxf6 14 ♗xb5 and 15 ♘xf6+.

13 ♘c6!!

Before opening the c-file, White cuts off the black king's escape to the saving shelter at c7.

13...♗xc6

The attacking file cannot be kept closed: 13...d4 14 e5!

14 exd5+ ♗e7 (14...♔d8 15 dxc6 ♘c5 16 c7+) **15 dxc6 ♘c5 16 ♗xf6 gxf6 17 ♗f5!**

And once again the black king has nowhere to go.

17...♕c7

Forced, since Black has to defend both his bishop, and his d6 pawn, and also the advanced white pawn has to be blocked.

18 b4 ♘e6 19 ♕h5 ♘g7 20 ♗d7+

Erecting a barrier in front of Black's queen, which is obliged to look after his bishop.

20...♔f8 21 ♕h6 d5

The main point is to bring the queen out to d6, but in passing Black sets a little trap.

22 ♖xe7! ♔xe7 23 ♖e1+!

The trap — 23 ♕xg7? ♕xf4+ 24 ♔b1 ♖ag8, when Black wins — fails to operate.

23...♔f8 24 ♕xf6 ♔g8 25 ♖e7 ♖f8 26 ♗e6!

It's all over!

26...♕xe7 27 ♕xe7 fxe6

Or 27...♘xe6 28 f5 ♘g7 29 c7.

28 c7 h5 29 ♕xf8+ Black resigns.

This theme received a quite amazing interpretation in the following world-famous game.

M.T. I am happy to admit that I watched this game with envy, and would have readily exchanged my silver medal of that championship for the right to sign the scoresheet — the white half, of course.

I.D. And when White's next move was announced in the press centre, we decided that the impregnable Ratmir Kholmov, the "central defender" as he was then called, had for a moment taken leave of his senses.

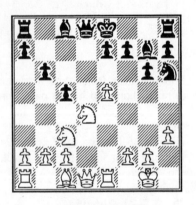

Kholmov-Keres
26th USSR Championship
Tbilisi 1959

12 ♘c6(!!)

The following variation is not too complicated: 12...♕xd1? 13 ♖xd1

♗b7 (or 13...♗d7) 14 ♘d5, when 14...♗xc6 is bad in view of 15 ♘c7+ ♔f8 16 ♘xa8 ♗xa8 17 ♖d8 mate, and otherwise after 14...0-0 White simply picks up the e7 pawn with check. But Black has another possibility.

12...♕d7(!)

This is what was played, and how can White now save his piece?

13 ♘xe7!!

Once again two exclamation marks, although this is merely a continuation of White's brilliant conception. White forces the black king to remain in the centre, since in the event of 13...♕xe7 14 ♘d5 ♕d8 15 ♘f6+ ♗xf6 (or 15...♔e7 16 ♕f3 ♗e6 17 ♗g5, and Black loses material) 16 exf6+ ♗e6 17 ♗xh6 ♕xf6 18 ♕g4! without sacrificing anything White has a powerful initiative, which is merely strengthened by the opposite-colour bishops. And totally bad is 13...♕xd1 14 ♖xd1 ♔xe7 15 ♗g5+ ♔e6 16 ♖d6+ ♔f5 (16...♔xe5 17 ♖d5+, mating) 17 f4, with various mating threats.

13...♔xe7 14 ♗xh6!

Again a paradoxical decision. The bishop, which was predestined for an attack along the weakened dark squares, is exchanged for the "off-side" knight.

M.T. But on the other hand, a major attacking principle is maintained — "a tempo". The time that we don't have is more precious than the piece that we do have.

14...♗xh6 15 ♕f3 ♗g7!

The best defence. Now after 16 ♕xa8 ♗b7 17 ♕xa7 ♕c6 18 f3 ♖a8 19 ♘d5+ ♕xd5 20 ♕xb6 the outcome is unclear.

16 ♘d5+ ♔d8

Forced, since Black loses quickly after both 16...♔e8 17 ♘f6+ ♗xf6 18 exf6+ and 19 ♕xa8, and 16...♔f8 17 e6 ♕b7 18 e7+ ♔e8 19 ♕f6!

17 ♖ad1 ♗b7

To find the strongest continuation 17...♕b7 at the board would be practically impossible, in view of its paradoxical nature. True, even in this case after 18 e6! White has a very strong attack, e.g. 18...fxe6 19 ♘b4+ ♔c7 20 ♕g3+ e5 21 ♖xe5! cxb4 22 ♖c5+, mating.

18 ♕b3 ♗c6 19 ♘xb6 axb6 20 ♕xf7 ♗xe5 21 ♖xd7+ ♗xd7 22 ♖xe5, and White won.

More complicated are instances when both sides appear to have the right to play actively, and when it is more difficult to decide: should one continue attacking or now switch to defence? Here the deciding role is played by an accurate appraisal of all the factors "for" and "against".

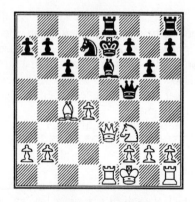

Karpov-Yusupov
55th USSR Championship
Moscow 1988

Both kings have lost the right to castle, and, in addition, the positions of each side have their pluses and minuses. White, for example, is for the moment playing without his king's rook, and at least three tempi are required to bring it into the game. Black, for his part, is clearly weak on the dark squares, but he only needs to bring his king to f6, when he could think of seizing the initiative. This could have happened, for example, after 16 ♕a3+ ♔f6 17 ♗d3 ♕d5 18 ♕xa7 ♗g4!, or 16 ♗xe6 fxe6 17 ♕a3+ ♔f6 18 ♕xa7?? ♕b5+ 19 ♔g1 ♖a8 winning, or 16 ♘g5 ♔d8! (here 16...♔f6 is weaker in view of the concrete 17 ♗xe6 fxe6 18 ♘e4+, when White wins the exchange) 17 ♘xe6+ fxe6 18 ♗xe6 ♕b5+ 19 ♔g1 ♖e7! with counterplay; in this last variation 17 ♗xe6 fxe6 18 ♘xe6+ ♔c8 19 ♕b3 ♖e7! also favours Black.

The correct evaluation of the position is only established by the typical attacking device carried out by the ex-World Champion.

16 d5!!

At the cost of the isolated pawn the black queen's path to b5 is cut, and more important — the weak dark squares become glaringly weak! After all, now White can also attack along the long dark-square diagonal from c3. And another achievement for White becomes apparent on his next move.

16...cxd5 17 ♗b5!

Revealing another target — the knight at d7, which is insufficiently protected, as best illustrated in the variation 17... ♔f8 18 ♕c3 ♖g8 19 ♘d4, 20 ♘xe6+ and 21 ♗xd7.

17...a6 18 ♕a3+ ♔d8

Alas, forced: 18...♔f6 19 ♗xd7 ♗xd7 20 ♕c3+.

19 ♕a5+ ♔e7

On the queenside the king would have had altogether no defenders, and no chance of surviving: 19...♔c8 20 ♖c1+ ♔b8 21 ♕c7+ ♔a8 22 ♘d4 ♕e4 23 ♗xa6! ♖b8 24 ♕a5! ♕xd4 25 ♗xb7+ ♔xb7 26 ♖c7 mate. And although this variation is not forced (for example, 22...♕f6 is possible), all the same the sacrifice on a6 destroys the king's shelter and wins.

20 ♕b4+ ♔f6

Exploiting a tactical nuance, Black tries to save his king (21 ♗xd7 ♕d3+), but the a1-h8 diagonal is on the point of collapse.

21 ♕d4+ ♔e7 22 ♗d3 ♕h5

22...♕f6 23 ♕b4+ is even worse, but now in this variation the black king can try to slip away to g7 via f6.

23 h4

With the terrible threat of 24 g4.

23...♔d8 24 ♘g5

Renewing the same threat of 25 g4, strengthened by the possibility of 25...♕h6 26 ♖xe6 fxe6 27 ♘f7+.

24...♖hf8 25 ♗e2! ♕h6 26 ♗f3

White is effectively a queen up!

26...♖e7 27 ♕b4 ♘f6 28 ♕d6+ ♖d7 29 ♕f4 ♘g8 (29...♕g7 30 ♖xe6) **30 ♗g4 ♔c8** (30...♗xg4 31 ♕b8 mate) **31 ♗xe6 fxe6 32 ♖c1+ ♔d8 33 ♘xe6+ ♔e7 34 ♕xf8+ ♕xf8 35 ♘xf8**, and White had a winning material advantage.

The basic solution to this position was provided by a breakthrough in the centre, about which we will have more to say later. But the theme itself —

"the attack on the king in the centre" — is practically inexhaustible, and all of the above examples are merely milestones on the way.

However, sooner or later we have to draw the line, and we do this with the following position, which as though encapsulates the entire chapter.

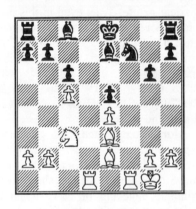

Ivkov-Kagan
Rio Interzonal 1979

The queens are no longer on the board, neither is there any pawn tension, and all the white pieces are based on their own territory, on the first three ranks.

Yet with a clear conscience Black can resign.

He did this, a little later, after **17 ♘b5! cxb5 18 ♗xb5+ ♔f8 19 ♗h6+**, forcing mate or crushing gain of material.

Here there was everything about which we talked earlier: a lead in development, open files and diagonals, but most important — the opponent's king, caught in the centre.

Tal-Portisch
Candidates Quarter-Final, Bled 1965
Caro-Kann Defence

1 e4 c6

Strangely enough, an unexpected reply, since the Hungarian champion adopts this defence very rarely, and we (or more precisely, I) had somehow not thought up any plans against the Caro-Kann. When, during our pre-match preparations, my trainer asked me what I was intending to play against 1...c6, I simply replied that this defence would not occur.

It immediately became clear that the Hungarians had carefully studied the records of my matches with Botvinnik, and therefore, without any prepared "mines", it would have been inexpedient to employ the variations with h2-h4 (2 d4 d5 3 ♘c3 dxe4 4 ♘xe4 ♗f5 5 ♘g3 ♗g6 6 ♘1e2 ♘f6 7 h4, or 2 d4 d5 3 e5 ♗f5 4 h4).

After Portisch's first move I began frantically trying to recall which of the variations I had not hitherto employed in my tournament games. Perhaps, 2 ♘c3 d5 3 ♘f3? It was this plan that I decided to try, especially since the Hungarian grandmaster had never played against it.

2 ♘c3 d5
3 ♘f3 dxe4

This reply shows that White's choice was a happy one. 3...♗g4 has long been considered best here, not yielding White an inch in the centre. Who knows, perhaps Portisch did not like the variation 4 h3 ♗xf3 5 gxf3!?, as I played in the third game of my first match with Botvinnik? But now White

makes the advance d2-d4 unhindered, obtaining a slight but enduring advantage.

4 ♘xe4 ♗g4
5 h3 ♗xf3
6 ♕xf3 ♘d7
7 d4 ♘gf6
8 ♗d3 ♘xe4
9 ♕xe4 e6
10 0-0

10 c3 is perhaps more accurate, in order to retreat the queen to e2 after it is attacked. White, however, has something different in mind...

10 ... ♗e7
11 c3 ♘f6

The first critical position. Portisch's reasoning is clear: Black has a slightly passive position, but one that White will be hard-pushed to crack. He handles such positions with great precision.

Now the following natural plan suggests itself for White: ♕e2, then ♗d2 or ♗f4, when after the obligatory ...c5 and the exchange on c5 he obtains a queenside pawn majority plus the two bishops — Black faces a gruelling defence. And I, of course, realised that 12 ♕e2 was a natural and strong move.

But nevertheless I was attracted by another idea.

12 ♕h4

This provokes Black's reply:

12 ... ♘d5

In a number of variations Black strengthens his defences by the manoeuvre ...♘f6-d7-f8, but now from d5 it is difficult for the knight to reach f8. However, this is achieved at the cost of several tempi, and Black has time to stabilise the position.

13 ♕g4 ♗f6

Not, of course, 13...0-0 14 ♗h6 ♗f6 15 ♕e4, winning the exchange.

14 ♖e1

Initially I had been intending to complete the queen manoeuvre by 14 ♕e4, keeping the black king in the centre, but then I noticed that after 14...♘e7 followed by ...♘f5 White's initiative would quickly peter out.

Allowing Black to castle is by no means evidence of White's good nature — after 14...0-0 he succeeds in advantageously regrouping his pieces: 15 ♗h6 ♖e8 16 ♖ad1 ♕b6 17 ♗c1, when the bishop returns to what is perhaps its best position, and the rook is actively placed in the centre. So Portisch prevents the development of White's queenside:

14 ... ♕b6

The second critical position. Up till now Portisch had played quickly and confidently. White has clearly not achieved what he could have expected from the opening: the queen is pressing on the b2 pawn, pinning down the

bishop at c1. Therefore "correct" (one can also write it without the inverted commas) was the reserved 15 a3, with the hope, in a protracted struggle, of exploiting the illustrious bishop pair. All this is true. But for 14 moves the black king has remained with impunity in the centre of the board. Is there no way of exploiting this and at the same time abruptly changing the course of the game?

This was how the idea arose of the rook sacrifice at e6. An amusing variation flashed though my mind — one that was by no means forced, but highly camouflaged, which afforded a certain aesthetic pleasure. And I concluded that, even if the sacrifice might lead only to a draw, it was correct, and in addition the change in the character of the play was bound to be unpleasant for Portisch.

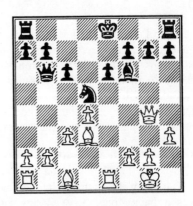

15 c4?! ♘b4

On 15...♘e7 I was intending to play 16 d5! cxd5 17 cxd5 ♘xd5 18 ♕a4+, at least preventing Black from castling.

16 ♖xe6+ fxe6

17 ♕xe6+

Here Black was faced with the problem of how to punish his opponent for his "recklessness". It is clear that this aim is least of all answered by 17...♔d8: White has 18 ♕d6+ ♔e8 19 ♕e6+ etc. I did not see anything better during the game, nor do I now.

My hopes were mainly associated with the "refutation" 17...♗e7, when White does indeed lose after 18 ♗g5 ♕c7 19 ♖e1 ♘xd3! 20 ♗xe7 ♕d7! He can, however, obtain a very attractive position by interposing 18 ♗g6+!, when Black cannot play 18...hxg6 19 ♗g5 ♕c7 20 ♖e1 with the threat of 21 ♕xg6+! Therefore he must reply 18... ♔d8 19 ♗f5 ♕xd4 (not 19...♕c7 20 ♗f4 ♕c8 21 ♕e4) 20 ♗f4. This position greatly appealed to me, and a continuation of the variation (not exactly forced, it is true) revealed a most attractive idea: 20...♖e8 21 ♖e1 g6? 22 ♗e3 ♕d6 23 ♗xa7! ♕xe6 24 ♗b6+ ♔c8 (not 24...♔d7 25 ♗xe6+ ♔d6 26 c5 mate) 25 ♗xe6+ and 26 ♗d7. However, in this variation too Black could have defended.

After the game Portisch admitted that he had seen the rook sacrifice, but had not considered it dangerous; and when it in fact took place, he became ill at ease. Only this nervousness can explain why he instantly, without thinking, replied

17 ... ♔f8

I was even upset: so much time and effort had been spent on the analysis of the most complex and attractive variations, and not one of them was to occur on the board...

18 ♗f4 ♖d8

The only good move. Insufficient is

18...♖e8 19 ♗d6+ ♗e7 20 ♖e1 ♕d8 21 ♖e3!, or 18...♕d8 19 ♖e1 g5! 20 ♗d6+ ♔g7 21 ♗xb4, when White has a very strong attack with level material. By parting with his queen, Black can face the future with confidence.

19 c5 ♘xd3!
20 cxb6

Still out for blood... My first intention here had been at last to force a draw by 20 ♗h6, to which Black's only good reply is 20...♕xb2! (less good is 20...♕c7 21 ♕xf6+ ♔g8 22 ♗xg7!). But not every c-pawn can reach a7! Therefore White decided on the again rather risky, but not losing capture of the queen.

20 ... ♘xf4
21 ♕g4 ♘d5
22 bxa7

The third critical position. Initially it appeared to me to favour White, but when, awaiting my opponent's reply, I began examining the plan with ...g6 and ...♔g7, I had to change my evaluation: chances were roughly equal. Of course, were Black to succeed in coordinating his forces, his

position would become clearly preferable. But there are two factors that hinder this: the audacious pawn at a7, which at the very least frightens Black, and, although only temporary, the difficulties in developing his king's rook. With his next move Portisch tries simultaneously to solve both of these problems, but the further course of the game shows that the plan chosen is incorrect.

22 ...   ♔e7

"Suicide?", was my first thought. But then I realised that Black's manoeuvre was not without its logic: the king heads for the a7 pawn, and any checks will only act as a "favourable wind", for example 23 ♖e1+ ♔d6 24 ♕g3+ ♔d7 25 ♕g4+ ♔c7.

But Portisch did not see my next move, which, incidentally, would have occurred to a player with an attacking style. Therefore it would have been stronger, without further ado, to play 22...g6. How the game would have developed in this case, I honestly do not know. But at the board it seemed to me that to a considerable extent the a7 pawn "insures" White against defeat. In a number of variations he is able, by giving it up with a8=♕, to pick up both of Black's queenside pawns in compensation.

23 b4!

Preparing a "warm reception" for the enemy king. It is bad to take the pawn because of 24 ♖b1, but after b4-b5 White either exchanges on c6, opening lines, or advances it further, when the lone a7 pawn is transformed into a pawn tandem a7/b6.

Here Black could have held the position by 23...♘c7, suggested by Aronin. But the picture had been so unexpectedly transformed, that Portisch succeeded in losing a defensible position in a matter of moves.

23 ...   ♖a8

If not 23...♘c7, then Black should at least have chosen 23...♔d6 24 b5 ♔c7, not abandoning, for the moment, the pursuit of the pawn. In any event, Black will not have time to take it.

24 ♖e1+   ♔d6
25 b5   ♖xa7

This loses instantly, but by now Black's defence was very difficult. White has at his disposal two threats: the attacking 26 bxc6 bxc6 27 ♕e6+ ♔c7 28 ♖c1, and the constricting 26 b6!, after which Black must either agree to the a7 pawn being a constant threat, or nevertheless go in for the extremely dangerous opening of the b-file (after 26...♘xb6 27 ♖b1).

26 ♖e6+   ♔c7
27 ♖xf6   Black resigns

Tal-Larsen
Candidates Semi-Final, Bled 1965
Alekhine's Defence

1	e4	♘f6
2	e5	♘d5
3	d4	d6
4	♘f3	dxe5
5	♘xe5	e6

So, once again this dubious (there is no other word for it) variation. Directly after the Larsen-Ivkov match the Yugoslav grandmaster showed me the final game of that encounter, and "scolded" himself for making the pseudo-active move 6 ♕h5. At the same time, he offered the following opinion: that 6 ♘d2 is the quietest reply, and 6 ♕f3, although committing, is the strongest, with which, after a cursory analysis, I agreed. Of course, in the existing match situation, the committing nature of White's move was by no means a hindrance.

6   ♕f3   ♕f6

6...♘f6 is perhaps stronger, agreeing to a slightly passive position. White would have replied 7 ♗e3, preparing queenside castling. After Larsen's move the black queen proves to be badly placed, and he has to waste precious time defending it.

7   ♕g3   h6

8 ♗g5 was threatened.

8   ♘c3

White must play energetically, in order to exploit the better placing of his pieces. Since exchanging on c3 would only strengthen White's centre, and his queen's knight is threatening to move with great effect to e4, Black continues manoeuvring with his knight, hoping to divert White from his intentions.

8   ...   ♘b4
9   ♗b5+   c6
10 ♗a4   ♘d7

The transference of the bishop to the rather inactive post at a4 does not signify that White has given up ideas of an attack. After ♘e4 and c2-c3 the bishop can be advantageously switched to the important b1-h7 diagonal.

Here White thought for quite a long time. The advantages of his position are perfectly clear: a lead in development, Black's difficulty in evacuating his king, but all this must be

effectively exploited. In such a position victory is doubly necessary: if I could not win from such a position, the psychological shock would be too great — it would mean that I had altogether forgotten how to win.

Here White has several very tempting ways to develop his initiative. The first that suggests itself is the tactical possibility of 11 a3 ♘d5 12 ♘xc6. Then 12...bxc6 loses quickly to 13 ♗xc6 ♘5b6 14 ♘b5! But the idea proves insufficient after 12...♘xc3 13 bxc3 (13 ♕xc3 ♘b6 14 ♘b8+ ♔d8) 13...♘b6 14 ♗b5 ♗d7 15 ♘xa7 ♕d8.

The positional 11 ♗f4 does not give anything decisive after 11...♘d5.

White gains good attacking chances by 11 ♘e4 ♕f5 12 f3, and objectively this was perhaps the strongest continuation, although after 12...♘xe5 13 dxe5 ♗d7 14 a3 ♘d5 15 c4 ♘b6 16 ♗c2 ♕h5 it is not so easy to continue the attack. I was intending to continue my analysis of this variation, when suddenly my attention was drawn to the possibility of the piece sacrifice that occurred in the game within a few moves. This idea seemed very tempting.

11 0-0   ♘xe5

This knight cannot be tolerated for long.

12 dxe5   ♕g6
13 ♕f3

White could have obtained the better ending by exchanging queens, but this would have been a small achievement.

13 ...   ♕f5

Not altogether successful. Black drives the queen to a more comfortable position. Stronger was 13...♗d7, defending c6, on which I was intending to play 14 ♕e2, with the idea of ♘e4 and c2-c3, bringing the light-square bishop into play.

Of course, 13...♘xc2 14 ♗xc6+ was out of the question.

14 ♕e2 ♗e7

Black appears not to have seen the intended sacrifice. White's intention was that if 14...♘d5 15 ♘b5!, an idea that it is still possible. However, if 14...♗d7 (which would have ruled out the knight sacrifice) the manoeuvre ♘e4, c2-c3 and ♗c2 would have gained in strength.

Now, however, 15 f4 would be met by 15...0-0 16 ♘e4 b5! 17 ♗b3 c5! and if 18 c3 c4, not allowing the bishop onto the b1-h7 diagonal.

15 a3

Had the following move not been available, this would have been a serious mistake, leading to the loss of the initiative.

15 ... ♘d5

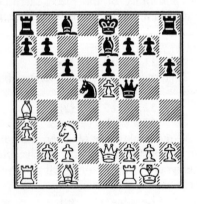

15...♘a6 can also be answered by 16 ♘b5, although with the slightly different idea of 16...cxb5? 17 ♗xb5+ and 18 ♗d3, winning the queen.

16 ♘b5!

A move which came as a surprise to my opponent. White is intending to play his knight to the ideal square d4. After, for example, 16...0-0 17 ♘d4 ♕h7 18 c4 ♘b6 19 ♗c2 Black's position is extremely difficult, and so the acceptance of the sacrifice is forced.

16 ... cxb5
17 ♕xb5+

But here 17 ♗xb5+ ♔f8 18 ♗d3 fails to 18...♘f4!

17 ... ♔d8
18 c4

The critical position. Where should the knight move to? Larsen follows the path of least resistance: he gives back the piece, but the position of his king in the centre allows White easily to mount a decisive attack without any significant material sacrifice.

White saw that after 18...♘b6 19 ♕a5 he would also regain his piece, since 19...♗d7 20 ♗e3 ♔c7 21 c5 is bad for Black. Stronger is the immediate 19...♔c7 20 c5 ♔b8 21 cxb6 axb6 22 ♕b5 ♖a5 23 ♕b3, although here too White has very good attacking chances.

The main variation of White's combination was 18...♘f4 19 ♖d1+ ♔c7 20 ♖d7+ ♗xd7 21 ♕xd7+ ♔b8 22 ♕xe7 ♕xe5 23 ♗e3 ♘g6 (24 ♖d1 was threatened) 24 ♕xf7 ♕f6 25 ♗e8! This is the point: 25...♕e7 (25...♘e5 26 ♗f4) 26 ♕xg6 ♖xe8 27 ♗c5! ♕d7 28 ♗d6+ ♔c8 29 c5, and the bishop at d6 is much stronger than a rook.

18 ... ♕xe5

19	cxd5	♗d6
20	g3	♕xd5
21	♕e2	

It becomes clear that for the pawn White has much more than sufficient compensation. The black king is a long way from any sort of peaceful refuge, and White only needs to develop his queen's bishop, for all his pieces to join in a decisive attack.

21	...	♔e7
22	♖d1	♕a5
23	♕g4	♕f5

This clever possibility does nothing at all to help Black. White considered here 23...e5, after which neither 24 ♕h4+ f6 nor 24 ♗g5+ hxg5 25 ♕xg5+ ♔f8 26 ♖xd6 ♗e6 27 ♖ad1 f6! is altogether convincing. But by continuing 24 ♕xg7 ♗e6 (or 24... ♕xa4) 25 ♗xh6 White gains an irresistible attack.

24	♕c4

24 ♕xg7?? ♗e5! would have been a terrible blunder.

The queen manoeuvre emphasises just how hopeless Black's position is, since after 24...♖d8 25 ♗e3 he has no good move.

24	...	♕c5
25	♕d3	♕d5
26	♕c3	

It is for this square that the white queen has been aiming. Now 26...♕e5 is not possible on account of 27 ♗f4. Black is forced to worsen still further the placing of his pieces.

26	...	♗e5
27	♕e1	

27 ♕e3 ♕a5 28 ♗d2 was also perfectly adequate, but there were already many ways to win.

27	...	♕c5
28	♗d2	♔f6
29	♖ac1	

Now everything is clear. The onslaught of the white pieces is quite impossible to withstand.

29	...	♕b6
30	♗e3	♕a6
31	♕b4	

Threatening, incidentally, 32 ♗b5.

31	...	b5
32	♗xb5	♕b7
33	f4	♗b8
34	♗c6	

Black resigns. Out of his 33 moves, 13 were made by his queen.

Tal-Hecht
Varna Olympiad 1962
Queen's Indian Defence

Although the cascade of sacrifices in this game was linked by the single general aim of attacking the king caught in the centre, at the same time it was, as it were, divided into stages. Thus, when he gave up a pawn, White was not counting on further sacrifices, but was prepared to content himself with the initiative. And since a "primary" sacrifice does not exist — there is only the first, the second, and so on, so as the attack developed the aim also changed.

1	d4	♘f6
2	c4	e6
3	♘f3	b6
4	♘c3	♗b4
5	♗g5	♗b7
6	e3	h6
7	♗h4	♗xc3+
8	bxc3	d6

9	♘d2	e5
10	f3	♕e7
11	e4	♘bd7
12	♗d3	♘f8

Black stubbornly avoids breaking the pin at the cost of any weakening. Earlier he could have chosen 7...g5 8 ♗g3 ♘e4, and now he could have followed Keres in his game with Botvinnik, 12th USSR Championship, Moscow 1940: 12...g5 13 ♗f2 ♘h5 14 g3 ♘g7 15 ♕e2 h5, gaining counterplay sufficient for equality.

Now, however, by getting his blow in first, White initiates unfathomable complications. However, the move played is not necessarily the strongest continuation in this position. He could have obtained a favourable position by the "Spanish" manoeuvre 13 ♘f1 followed by ♘e3 and ♘d5 (or ♘f5).

13 ♕a4+ was also good, and if 13...♕d7 14 ♕c2. And yet the move played is the one most in the spirit of the position: White is able to open up the game, for which he happily sacrifices a pawn.

13	c5	dxc5

On 13...bxc5 there could have followed 14 d5, when White gains control of c4 and b5, as well as the open b-file.

14	dxe5	♕xe5

Now White has a pawn majority in the centre, i.e. on the part of the board where he is intending to begin active play. But Black's defensive resources are, of course, quite adequate.

15	♕a4+	c6?

A mistake, after which White also gains the use of the d6 square for his attack.

15...♘6d7 was much stronger, although here too after 16 ♕c2 White's initiative would have been quite appreciable.

16	0-0	♘g6

After 16...♕xc3 both 17 ♗a6 and 17 ♘c4 b5 18 ♘d6+ ♔d7 19 ♘xb5 cxb5 20 ♗xb5+ are unpleasant for Black. But now White has to hurry, since a position has been reached where every tempo may be decisive. Black only needs to "hide" his king, and for the pawn White will have no compensation. If 17 ♗g3 the strongest is 17...♕e7, when 18 ♘c4 fails to 18...b5.

17	♘c4	♕e6

Not 17...b5 18 ♘xe5 bxa4 19 ♘xg6 fxg6 20 e5, when Black can resign.

18 e5!

As already mentioned, White's chief aim is to keep the king at e8. With his 18th move he begins a combination, in anticipation of... a favourable endgame. The position does not promise anything better.

18	...	b5

18...♘xh4 was interesting. After 19 ♘d6+ ♔f8 it is unfavourable for White to take any of the three pieces that are en prise: on 20 ♕xh4 or 20 ♘xb7 there follows 20...♕xe5. The e5 pawn is more valuable than any of the black minor pieces, and therefore White had decided to play the positional 20 ♖ae1, since with one move the threats to the three pieces cannot be eliminated.

(see diagram next page)

19 exf6!!

This move brings to mind the well known game Lilienthal-Capablanca, Hastings 1934/35, in which White, then a young master, quickly forced the ex-World Champion's capitulation.

Hecht made his reply without thinking... Of course, anyone with the black pieces would be very happy to play 19...0-0. Then three of White's pieces are en prise, and if he moves his queen, 20...♘xh4 leads to a position where Black is under no threat.

But against 19...0-0 White has the very strong rejoinder 20 ♖ae1! If 20...♕d5 there can follow 21 ♕c2 ♘xh4 22 ♘e5 with a powerful attack, while after 20...♕xe1 21 ♖xe1 bxa4 22 ♗xg6 fxg6 23 ♖e7 Black cannot play 23...♖f7 on account of 24 ♘d6.

At this point the effusive Miguel Najdorf, who was watching the game, came up and... kissed me (M.T.).

19	...	bxa4
20	fxg7	♖g8
21	♗f5!!	

The culmination of the combination! After 21...♕xc4 Black will be a whole queen up(!), but he loses: 22 ♖fe1+

♕e6 23 ♖xe6+ fxe6 24 ♗xg6+ ♔d7 25 ♖d1+ ♔c7 26 ♗g3+ ♔b6 27 ♖b1+ ♔a6 28 ♗d3+ ♔a5 29 ♗c7+ mate. Meanwhile, 21...♕xf5 leads to a hopeless ending: 22 ♘d6+ ♔d7 23 ♘xf5 ♖xh4 24 ♖ad1+ ♔c7 25 ♘xh4 ♖xg7 26 ♖fe1, and the variation 21...♘xh4 22 ♗xe6 fxe6 23 ♘d6+ demonstrates the "agility" of the white knight.

Black chooses the best defence, having in mind a counterblow on the next move.

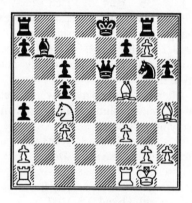

| 21 | ... | ♘xh4 |
| 22 | ♗xe6 | ♗a6 |

How is White to save his piece?

| 23 | ♘d6+ | ♔e7 |
| 24 | ♗c4! | |

This concludes the combination, which has brought White a marked advantage in the endgame.

| 24 | ... | ♖xg7 |
| 25 | g3 | ♔xd6 |

A mistake, since in positions of this type a bishop is stronger than a knight. Black would have retained some drawing chances after 25...♗xc4 26 ♘xc4 ♖d8.

26	♗xa6	♘f5
27	♖ab1	f6
28	♖fd1+	♔e7
29	♖e1+	♔d6
30	♔f2	c4

Creating a shelter for the king at c5. Nevertheless 30...h5 was more tenacious, for the moment maintaining the knight at its important post.

31	g4	♘e7
32	♖b7	♖ag8
33	♗xc4	♘d5
34	♗xd5	cxd5
35	♖b4	♖c8

Black should at least have exchanged a pair of kingside pawns by 35...h5 36 h3 hxg4 37 hxg4 f5, although even this would hardly have saved him.

After the move played, which leads to a "mutual elimination" of pawns, everything is clear.

36	♖xa4	♖xc3
37	♖a6+	♔c5
38	♖xf6	h5
39	h3	hxg4
40	hxg4	♖h7
41	g5	♖h5
42	♖f5	♖c2+
43	♔g3	♔c4
44	♖ee5	d4
45	g6	♖h1
46	♖c5+	♔d3
47	♖xc2	♔xc2
48	♔f4	♖g1
49	♖g5	

Black resigns: 49...♖xg5 50 ♔xg5 d3 51 g7 d2 52 g8=♕ d1=♕ 53 ♕b3+.

WHAT WOULD YOU HAVE PLAYED?

No.1

Black is attacking the knight that has crossed the demarcation line. To where should it retreat?

No.2

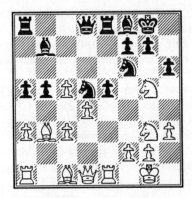

Here too the white knight has the right to choose...

No.3

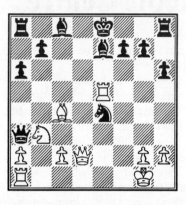

But here there would not appear to be any choice: the knight must be taken and the black king will finally castle...

No.5

White plans to get rid of the enemy outpost at d4, and then, according to circumstances, either queenside castling with chances of an attack (♗h6, h2-h4 etc.), or else the quieter kingside castling. But it is Black to move...

No.4

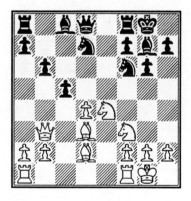

Black has just played 12...c5?, evidently expecting the theoretical 13 ♘xf6+...

No.6

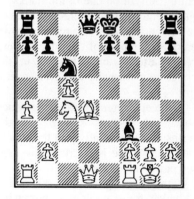

After 15 ♕xf3 ♕xd4 Black gains a tempo by attacking the white knight, castles, and then sets about realising his advantage. Correct?

2 Breakthrough in the Centre

A CERTAIN FRENCH GENERAL went down in history for the following dispatch to his commander: "My centre is broken, my flanks are retreating, I attack"...(**I.D.**)

M.T. Mmm... This might do — in a tournament for beginners.

But at our and your level of chess - hardly. True, a "retreating" or even absent queenside does not prevent a desperate assault on the kingside, but the domination of one player in the centre completely rules out activity by the other. Deviations from this rule are more likely to be found in studies, than in practical play.

On the other hand, an advantage in the centre almost always allows an attack to be obtained. Whether in the centre itself, or on one of the flanks — this depends on the concrete features of the position. With a mobile pawn centre the strength of the attack grows greatly after a breakthrough in the centre, which usually achieves several aims:

— the opening of lines, along which rooks and bishops situated on the queenside can instantly join the attack; often their scope is restricted by their own pawns in the centre;

— the vacating of a central square, via which, for example, a slow-moving queen's knight can join the attack, or which, like a spring-board, can be used by a rook for a subsequent switching along the rank;

— finally, the disruption, if only for a certain time, of the coordination of the enemy pieces.

In short, a breakthrough in the centre is always the start of an attack, which, however, is by no means bound to be swift and explosive, but can grow by degrees, like the seventh wave in the sea.

This is why voluntarily conceding the opponent a mobile pawn centre, or perhaps only a single pawn in the centre that is capable of advancing, is equivalent to voluntarily entering the lion's cage. This comparison is perhaps evoked by the following game, in which the player with White was a grandmaster by the name of Lev.

(A play on words: *lev* is the Russian word for *lion* - Translator's note).

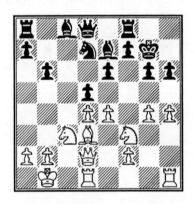

Polugayevsky-C.Hansen
European Team Ch., Plovdiv 1983

In the opening Black has clearly underestimated the possible pawn offensive by his opponent on the king-side, and stands worse. But never-theless, even with the two bishops, he should not have opened the centre and given White a dynamic pawn at d4. The correct 15...♗b7 (15...♘f6 16 g5, and the king's pawn shelter collapses) 16 exd5 exd5 would yet have given him hope of gradually neutralising the attack. But...

15...dxe4? 16 ♗xe4 (gaining a tempo) **16...♖b8 17 g5 h5 18 d5**

The central files and the long dark-square diagonal are opened (18...e5 fails to 19 d6) and White's lead in development quickly decides.

18...exd5 19 ♘xd5 ♘c5 20 ♕c3+ ♔h7 21 ♗c2 ♗e6

21...♗g4 is no better, being well met by the quiet 22 ♘e3.

22 ♘f4 ♕c8 23 ♘xh5, and without waiting for the completion of the attack after 23...♖g8 24 ♘f6+ ♗xf6 25 gxf6 followed by 26 ♘g5 and h4-h5, **Black resigned**.

Of course, such gifts of fate do not occur in every round. For a break-through in the centre one usually has to battle — and pay.

In the next diagram, the game has hardly passed out of the opening stage, but the pawn formation is already largely determined, and the two sides are considering their strategic plans. If the game were to take a quiet course, Black, after completing his develop-ment, could hope to use the strength of his dark-square bishop, which has no opponent.

But... White makes excellent use of the trumps of his position, including the advanced position of the black queen, to develop a powerful initiative by means of a central breakthrough.

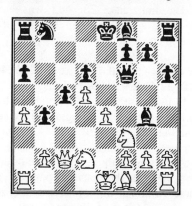

Chernin-Miles
Tunis Interzonal 1985

12 e5! dxe5 13 ♘e4 ♕f4 14 ♘fd2!

The white offensive is not "in a hurry", but now two of Black's pieces become targets for attack, and he is forced to lose time.

14...♗f5 15 ♗d3 ♗xe4 16 ♘xe4 ♘d7 17 g3 ♕g4 18 h3 ♕h5 19 d6

The development of Black's kingside is hindered, his queen has been driven to the edge of the board, and his king is still in the centre (as is White's, but Black's is under attack).

The pawn sacrificed is a miserly price for all this.

19...♕g6 20 ♖d1!

The outpost at d6 is supported, and now 21 ♘xc5 is a real threat. Black's tactical attempts to confuse matters are ignored by White.

20...b3 21 ♕e2

Not allowing the black rook to move off a light square with gain of tempo (21 ♕xb3 ♖b8).

21...f5 22 g4! c4 23 ♗b1 fxg4 24 ♕xc4 ♕f7 25 ♕c6 ♖d8 26 hxg4

The immediate 26 ♘c5 was also possible, since 26...♕f3 fails to the bishop check at g6.

26...g6 27 ♘c5 ♖g8 28 ♗e4 ♗g7 29 ♘xa6 ♕f4 30 ♘c7+ ♔f7 31 ♕c4+ ♔f6 32 ♘d5+ Black resigns.

In this case the breakthrough in the centre was merely strengthened by the fact that the stranded black king was pursued.

After a breakthrough, a piece offensive against the castled position is more common, as one of the authors experienced in the following game.

Polugayevsky-Tal
37th USSR Championship
Moscow 1969

This position had already occurred in previous games, and who could have known that, in the quiet of his study, White had worked out a variation giving him a decisive advantage, or... a forced win.

16 d5! exd5 17 e5!

By breaking through in the centre,

White has imparted a great deal of energy to his e-pawn, but more important — he has opened a way for his pieces to the kingside.

17...♘c4 18 ♕f4 ♘b2

After 18...h6 White would have won by 19 ♕f5 g6 20 ♕h3 ♗g7 21 e6 fxe6 22 ♘d4, while if 18...♖c6 he has 19 ♘g5 h6 20 ♗h7+ ♔h8 21 ♘xf7+ ♖xf7 (or 21...♔xh7 22 ♘xd8 ♖xf4 23 e6!) 22 ♕xf7 ♔xh7 23 ♕xb7.

19 ♗xh7+ ♔xh7 20 ♘g5+ ♔g6 21 h4!!

With the unequivocal intention of giving mate in the variation 22 h5+! ♔xh5 23 g4+ ♔g6 24 ♕f5+ ♔h6 25 ♘xf7+, and 21...f5 fails to save Black on account of 22 ♖d4! (with the same idea of h4-h5) 22...♕e7 23 h5+ ♔h6 24 ♘f7+ ♔h7 25 ♕xf5+ ♔g8 26 e6 ♖xf7 27 exf7+ ♕xf7 28 ♕xf7+ ♔xf7 29 ♖f4+ ♔g8 30 ♖e7.

21...♖c4 22 h5+ ♔h6 23 ♘xf7+ ♔h7 24 ♕f5+ ♔g8 25 e6 ♕f6 (there is no other defence against 26 h6) **26 ♕xf6 gxf6**

And now, after inaccuracies by both sides, White won easily: **27 ♖d2** (27 ♘d6 was more energetic) **27...♖c6 28 ♖xb2 ♖e8** (and here 28...♗c8 was more tenacious) **29 ♘h6+ ♔h7 30 ♘f5 ♖cxe6 31 ♖xe6 ♖xe6 32 ♖c2 ♖c6 33 ♖e2 ♗c8 34 ♖e7+ ♔h8 35 ♘h4 f5 36 ♘g6+ ♔g8 37 ♖xa7 Black resigns.**

In the next diagram White has achieved a strategically won position. There is nothing to support Black's counterplay on the queenside, whereas around his king there are many weaknesses, and his pieces (queen and knight) are far from ideally placed.

Nevertheless, it is only by a breakthrough that White can capitalise on all the advantages of his position.

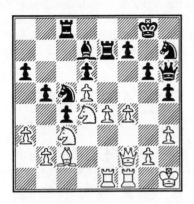

Ribli-Gheorghiu
Riga Interzonal 1979

27 e5! f5
Otherwise absolutely all the lines are opened.
28 ♘c6
Also good enough to win was 28 e6 ♗e8 29 ♗xf5 gxf5 30 ♘xf5 ♕f8, when 31 ♘xe7+ and 31 ♘xd6 are equally strong. But White prefers, firstly, to clear the e-file, and secondly, to include in the attack the only piece that is not participating — the knight at c3.
28...♗xc6 29 dxc6 ♕f8 30 ♘d5 ♖xc6
The exchange is lost in any case, and that is not all.
31 exd6 ♖xe1 32 ♖xe1 ♕xd6 33 ♘e7+ ♔f7 34 ♘xc6 ♕xc6 35 ♕e3 ♘f8 36 ♕e7+ ♔g8 37 ♖d1 ♘ce6 38 ♖d6 ♕c8 39 ♗d1
The bishop heads for d5, and Black can resign, which he did in fact do

after **39...c3 40 bxc3 ♕c4 41 ♗f3 h4 42 ♕xh4 ♕xc3 43 ♗d5 ♕e3 44 ♖xa6**.

Szabo-van Seters
Hilversum 1947

Although nominally Black has completed his development, his position gives serious cause for alarm. Ideally aimed against the black king is the bishop at a2, which together with the queen can also operate on the b1-h7 diagonal, and the e-file is open for the white rook. Nevertheless, a rapid success can be gained only by increasing the number of targets to attack, and this is ideally achieved by a breakthrough in the centre.
17 d5!! ♘xd5
The alternative capture 17...exd5 is refuted by the simple 18 ♗b1 g6 19 ♖xe7 (this demonstrates the superiority of the 17 d5 breakthrough over the immediate 17 ♗b1). After 17...♘a5 18 ♘e5 ♖dd8 19 ♗b1 g6 20 ♘b5 ♕b8 21 d6 Black loses material, while the attempt to exploit the pin on the audacious white pawn, 17...♖cd8, is

refuted by 18 ♗xf6! ♗xf6 19 ♕e2!, exploiting the weakness of the back rank to create an irresistible threat against e6.

18 ♗xd5! ♕d8

The same idea, but with 18...♖cd8, is refuted by the thematic 19 ♖xe6! But now the second white bishop is also attacked.

19 ♕e4!

Renewing the attack on e6 (19... ♗xg5 20 ♗xe6!).

19...exd5 20 ♘xd5 ♗xg5 21 ♘xg5!

Here we can sum up the outcome of the central breakthrough. The white pieces have closed in, and a weakening of the black king's position is inevitable. In addition its main defenders have been exchanged, and the final assault now commences.

21...g6 22 ♕h4 h5 23 ♘f6+ ♕xf6 24 ♖xd7 ♘d8 25 ♖e8+ ♔g7 26 ♖xf7+, and **Black**, who is losing his queen, **resigned** (26...♘xf7 27 ♘e6+).

I.D. Every player has a "game of his life", a victory in which he seemingly moves onto a higher chess plane. You first became champion of your country, and at the same time a grandmaster, by defeating the highly experienced Alexander Tolush in the final round of the 1957 USSR Championship.

M.T. Surprisingly, it was also the first time in my serious chess career that I made such an effective breakthrough in the centre (*see diagram next column*).

White has of course made more progress in the preceding complications, and for the pawn he has a strong attack. But for 30 ♗d2 followed by

g4-g5 he has neither the time, nor the right: firstly, Black will establish a piece at e5, and secondly, counterplay on the b-file is already imminent. Besides, White must include his reserves — his knight and light-square bishop.

All this is achieved with a single thematic move.

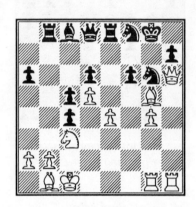

Tal-Tolush
24th USSR Championship
Moscow 1957

30 e5! ♖xe5

30...fxg5 also opens the f-file for White, and after 31 ♗xg6 hxg6 32 ♕h8+ ♔f7 33 ♖h7+! he gives mate in a few moves.

31 ♗xg6 ♖b7

For the moment both bishops are immune: the light-square one on account of the same variation, and the dark-square one in view of 31...♖xg5 32 ♗xh7+ ♔f7 33 ♘e4.

32 ♘e4!

Another gain from the breakthrough.

32...fxg5 33 ♖f1 ♖xe4

There is no other defence against 34 ♘f6+.

34 ♗xe4 ♖g7 35 ♖f6 ♗xg4 36 ♖hf1 ♘d7 37 ♖xd6 ♕e7 38 ♖xa6 ♔h8 39 ♗xh7! ♘b8 40 ♗f5+ ♔g8 41 ♗e6+ ♗xe6 42 ♖xe6 **Black resigns**.

Geller-Spassky
*25th USSR Championship
Riga 1958*

Here too White has gained a clear positional advantage, with the two bishops, the better pawn formation, and - the possibility at the necessary moment of a breakthrough in the centre.

23 ♖ce3! ♘e6 (23...♘fxe4 can be met by 24 ♗xe7 ♖xe7 25 ♘g5!) **24 e5!**

It is in this way, by ridding Black of his pawn weakness, that White imparts additional dynamic strength to his rooks, which dominate on the e-file, overloaded with black pieces.

24...♘g4

24...dxe5 25 ♖xe5 would also have led to the loss of a pawn.

25 hxg4 ♘xg5 26 exd6 ♘xf3+ 27 gxf3 ♗g5 28 a4

The ending with two extra pawns is

easily won after 28 ♗c4 ♕d7 29 ♖xe8 ♖xe8 30 ♖xe8+ ♕xe8 31 d7 and 32 ♗xa6. But for the moment White decides to stay in the middlegame.

28...♕d7 29 ♖xe8 ♖xe8 30 ♖xe8+ ♕xe8 31 d7 ♕f8

If 31...♕e7 White has the decisive 32 f4.

32 ♕e2

White is in no hurry to go into the pawn ending after 32 ♗xf7 ♕xf7 33 d8=♕+, but creates the simple threat of 33 ♕e8.

32...♕e7 33 ♕d3 h6 34 ♗c4!

Enticing the black a-pawn into an attack and effectively deciding the game.

34...a5 35 ♗xf7 ♗h4

Or 35...♕xf7 36 d8=♕+ ♗xd8 37 ♕xd8+ ♔h7 38 ♕xa5, and the f3 pawn is immune in view of the exchange of queens.

36 ♔g2 ♗f6 37 ♗c4 ♕d8 38 ♕d5 ♗g5 39 ♕f7 Black resigns.

Against the threat of 40 ♕e8+ ♔h7 41 ♗d3+ there is no defence.

Spassky-O'Kelly
San Juan 1969

This game can be considered a model example of this type of operation.

27 ♗xf5! gxf5

The h5 pawn has been weakened, and a path towards the king from g5 has been opened, but... Black's centre has been strengthened, he has gained control of e4, and there is the prospect of his knight reaching there.

28 d5!!

This breakthrough is the key to White's plan. At the cost of a pawn he occupies the centre with his pieces, and the next stage of the game commences.

28...♗xc3 29 ♕xc3 cxd5 30 ♘d4 ♕d7

The threat of 31 ♘xf5 forces Black first to concede the queenside.

31 c5! ♘h7 32 b4 a6 33 a4! ♖c8

Alas, 33...♕xa4 fails to 34 c6! bxc6 35 ♖a1, trapping the queen.

34 b5 axb5 35 axb5 ♖f8

The black knight has hopes of occupying e4, but at the point when this is achieved disaster is all ready to strike.

36 c6 bxc6 37 bxc6 ♕d8 38 ♖c1 ♘f6 39 c7 ♕d7 40 ♕e3!

White has tied down the black forces with his c7 pawn, and now, with his control of the centre, he switches his sights to the kingside, where his attacking queen is unopposed.

40...♘e4

The dream is realised, but a longer resistance could have been offered by 40...♘h7 41 ♖ec2 ♔g7 42 ♕e5+ ♔g8, although after 43 ♖c6 White has the irresistible threat of ♘d4-b5-a7(d6); he can also play for a mating attack with 44 f3 followed by g3-g4.

41 f3 e5 42 fxe4 f4 43 gxf4 exd4 44 ♖g2+

Black resigns: 44...♔h7 45 ♕f3 ♕d6 46 ♕xh5+ ♕h6, and now the simplest is 47 ♕xh6+ ♔xh6 48 exd5.

Spassky-Tal
Tallinn 1973
Nimzo-Indian Defence

1	d4	♘f6
2	c4	e6
3	♘c3	

I took this to be the first sign of Spassky's aggressive intentions. When in a more peaceable mood he plays 3 ♘f3, which usually leads to the relatively quiet Queen's Indian Defence.

| 3 | ... | ♗b4 |
| 4 | ♗g5 | |

Throwing down the gauntlet. This, the Leningrad Variation, which is quite often employed by Spassky, usually leads to a sharp and complicated battle.

4	...	h6
5	♗h4	c5
6	d5	b5

The challenge is accepted. This sharp continuation seems to me quite logical, although Black also has other, quieter moves, such as 6...d6, 6...e5 or 6...♗xc3+. The move 6...b5 is akin to the Volga (Benko) Gambit, which has recently been played quite frequently.

| 7 | dxe6 | |

Very complicated play results from 7 e4 g5 8 ♗g3 ♘xe4 9 ♗e5, which occurred in the game Levenfish-Estrin (USSR Championship Semi-Final, 1951). White also suffered a reverse in the game Korchnoi-Durasevic from the USSR-Yugoslavia Match (Belgrade 1956). It was then that grandmaster

Tolush suggested for White a different plan, involving the win of a pawn, and subsequently he successfully employed it. This is the course that Spassky chooses. True, to me it seems more correct to say not that White wins a pawn, but that Black sacrifices it.

7 ... fxe6
8 cxb5 d5

Now Black has an active pawn centre.

9 e3 0-0
10 ♘f3

Better, perhaps, was 10 ♗d3 d4 11 exd4 cxd4 12 a3, or the immediate 10 a3. It is on this possibility that the evaluation of the entire variation depends.

10 ... ♕a5
11 ♗xf6

This exchange is forced in view of the threatened 11...♘e4.

11 ... ♖xf6
12 ♕d2

12 ♕c1 is more accurate, so that after a subsequent a2-a3 the black bishop should be immediately attacked, since the rook at a1 is defended. True, Black can reply 12...c4.

12 ... a6!
13 bxa6

A risky move. 13 b6 or 13 ♗e2 axb5 14 0-0 was more circumspect.

13 ... ♘c6

Black, of course, does not take on a6, but intensifies the threat of ...d4.

14 ♗e2

Here too 14 ♕c1 came into consideration, in order to answer 14...d4 with 15 a3 ♗xc3+ 16 bxc3. In this case White would have been in no immediate danger.

14 ... d4!

15 exd4

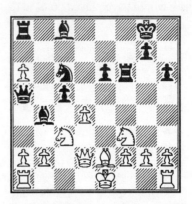

15 ... ♖xf3

This combination leads by force to an advantage for Black.

16 ♗xf3 cxd4
17 0-0

Interesting variations arise after 17 ♖c1. In this case I was intending to play 16...♗xa6 (17...dxc3 18 bxc3 is unpromising) 18 ♗xc6 ♖d8, when Black must win, e.g. 19 ♕c2 dxc3 20 bxc3 ♕e5+ 21 ♗e4. Here 21...♗d3 wins easily, but at the board I worked out another variation that appealed to me: 21...♗xc3+ 22 ♕xc3 ♕xe4+ 23 ♕e3 ♕xg2 24 ♕xe6+ (the only move) 24...♔h8 25 ♕c6 ♕xc6 26 ♖xc6 ♗b7!, and Black wins a rook. Moreover, it is amusing that, if White tries to give up his rook as dearly as possible, after 27 ♖xh6+ gxh6 he is mated: 28 0-0 ♖g8 mate, or 28 ♖g1 ♗f3 and then ...♖d1 mate.

17 ... dxc3
18 bxc3 ♗xc3
19 ♕d6 ♖xa6

Of course, not 19...♗xa1 20 ♕xc6.

20 ♗xc6

If the rook had moved from a1, Black would have played 20...♘d4.

20   ...   ♗b4!

The concluding move of the combination. White loses his bishop at c6. 20...♗e5 was insufficient on account of 21 ♕e7.

21   ♕b8   ♖xc6
22   ♖ac1   ♗c5
23   ♖c2

Spassky aims for pressure on the c-file, but in White's position an Achilles' heel comes to light — at f2. Possibly he should have looked for counter-chances by moving his rook off the c-file, for example to d1.

23   ...   ♕a4
24   ♕b3

24 ♖fc1 was not possible on account of 24...♗xf2+.

24   ...   ♕f4

Here I considered two moves — 24...♕e4 and 24...♕f4.

I rejected 24...♕e4 in view of 25 ♖fc1 ♗b7 26 ♕xb7 ♗xf2+ 27 ♔f1! (not 27 ♔h1? ♖xc2) 27...♕d3+ 28 ♔xf2 ♖xc2+ 29 ♖xc2 ♕xc2+, when it is clear that the resulting queen ending

with an extra pawn for Black is an extremely minor achievement.

Therefore I switched my choice to 24...♕f4. Against 25 ♕b5 I was intending 25...♕d6, and if 26 ♖fc1 ♗a6, when 27 ♕a5 is not possible: 27...♗xf2+.

25   ♕g3

25 ♕f3 was better, and if 25...♕xf3 26 gxf3 e5 27 ♔h1! ♗b7 28 ♖b1 ♖b6 29 ♖xb6 ♗xf3+ 30 ♔g1 ♗xb6 31 a4, when the ending is still unclear.

Black, however, would not have exchanged queens, but could have played 25...♕d6 or 25...♕c7, retaining the advantage.

25   ...   ♕f5
26   ♖fc1   ♗b7
27   ♕f3

27 ♕b8+ ♔h7! (but not 27...♖c8 28 ♕xc8+ ♗xc8 29 ♖xc5, when it is White who wins) 28 ♕xb7 was not possible on account of 28...♗xf2+, but 27 h3 was more tenacious.

27   ...   ♕g5
28   ♕b3

If 28 ♕g3 the check at f2 is again decisive: 28...♗xf2+ 29 ♔xf2 (or 29 ♕xf2 ♕xc1+) 29...♖xc2+ 30 ♖xc2 ♕f5+.

28   ...   ♖c7
29   g3

On 29 ♕xe6+ Black would have won by 29...♖f7, while if 29 ♕g3 he again has the decisive 29...♗xf2+.

The only move not to lose immediately was 29 ♔h3.

29   ...   ♗xf2+
30   ♔xf2   ♕f6+

I played this in accordance with my preliminary calculations. 30...♕f5+ 31 ♔g1 ♕e4 wins more quickly.

31	♔e1	♛e5+
32	♔f1	

32 ♔d1 ♛d4+ 33 ♔e1 ♛g1+ and 32 ♔f2 ♖f7+ 33 ♔g1 ♛d4+ were equally bad.

32	...	♗a6+
33	♔g1	♛d4+
34	♔g2	♛e4+
35	♔g1	

If 35 ♔h3 ♖xc2 and then 36... ♗f1+.

35	...	♗b7
36	h4	♛h1+
37	♔f2	♖f7+
38	♔e2	♛e4+

White resigns: after 39 ♛e3 ♗a6+ 40 ♔d2 ♖d7+ he loses his queen.

WHAT WOULD YOU HAVE PLAYED?

No.7

White stands more actively, but how can he build up his initiative?

No.8

Although there are signs that the position is double-edged (in particular on account of the g-file), it is nevertheless clearly in White's favour. Black's king prevents his rooks from uniting, but what particular plan should White aim for? And how should it be carried out?

No.9

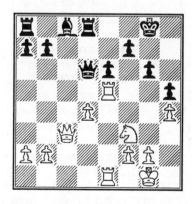

The h5 and g6 pawns are weak, as well as the whole complex of dark squares around the black king. Where should the first blow be struck?

3 The Assault Ratio

THE PLAYER WITH A LEAD IN development is obliged to attack, or risk losing this advantage. This is a chess truth, formulated back in the last century by Steinitz, repeated by other classic writers, and in the intervening century merely confirmed on thousands of occasions in practice.

Here is one single example:

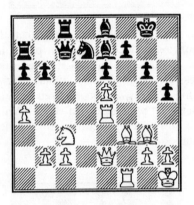

Geller-Korchnoi
Candidates Quarter-Final
Moscow 1971

White has every justification for taking decisive measures, and indeed 24 ♗xh5 gxh5 25 ♖f6! would have given him a very strong attack, for example: (a) 25...♕d8 26 ♕xh5 ♘f8 27 ♖h6 f5 28 ♖h8+ ♔g7 29 ♕h6+ ♔f7 30 ♖h4, or (b) 25...♘c5 26 ♖g4+ hxg4 27 ♕xg4+ ♔f8 28 ♖h6 ♗f6 29 exf6 ♘xf6 30 ♖xf6 ♔e7 31 ♖f4! True, a collective analysis later found an improvement here — 27...♔h7!!, and

there appears to be nothing more than perpetual check (28 ♘e4 ♘xf6 29 exf6 ♗f8).

M.T. But firstly, I am sure that even here White can strengthen his attack and should win, and secondly, by declining to attack he altogether concedes the initiative...

Indeed, after **24 h3 ♗f8 25 ♗h2 ♗g7 26 ♖e3 ♘c5 27 ♕e1 ♗c6 28 ♗xc6 ♕xc6 29 ♕h4 ♖d7** Black obtained a counter-attack.

White's cautious decision here was undoubtedly influenced by the fact that defence has changed fundamentally during this intervening century: the degree of resilience is commensurate with the previously unknown reinforced concrete, and defensive and counterattacking procedures have been found and systemised. Therefore a successful attack on the king is guaranteed only when an especially strong piece grouping can be created in the attack zone, when the power of such an assault exceeds for certain the defensive possibilities.

(see diagram next page)

The pieces of both sides are in a way polarised. But although "physically" White's pieces occupy squares on the kingside, for the moment they are not "looking" directly at the black king. In short, White cannot manage without strengthening his attacking force.

Kasparov-Marjanovic
Malta Olympiad 1980

17 ♘e4! ♗xb2 18 ♘g5!

White is already two pawns down, but now the concentration of his pieces clearly exceeds the defensive forces.

18...♕c6

Black cannot eliminate the most dangerous attacker: 18...♘e6 19 ♘d6, with numerous threats such as 20 ♘dxf7+, 20 ♕c2 and 20 ♕h5.

19 ♘e7 ♕f6 20 ♘xh7! ♕d4 21 ♕h5 g6 22 ♕h4

There is no way of saving the game, and the players each make an "unnecessary" move: Black, in the sense that he might well have not bothered to make one, and White, in that he can win "as he pleases".

22...♗xa1 23 ♘f6+

Black resigns: 23...♔g7 24 ♕h6+ ♔xf6 25 ♗g5 mate.

In the next diagram, Black's consistent pressure on c4 has proved successful. In order to defend his pawn, White would have to give up his outpost pawn at e5, by capturing 14 exd6 *en*

passant, but he can also sacrifice it, continuing his plan of concentrating his forces against the black king.

Kotov-Keres
Candidates Tournament
Budapest 1950

14 ♗b1!

White chooses the second alternative, the more crucial and only correct one. Besides, in the given instance his strategic idea is supported by concrete calculation.

14...g5

Of course, this is not a counterattack in the attack zone, but merely a defence, especially since 14...♗xc4 15 ♕c2 g6 16 ♗f6! followed by ♕d2 or ♕f2-h4 cannot be tolerated.

15 ♕c2 ♘g6

Black has eliminated the pin, and the attacking diagonal is blocked...

16 ♘f4!!

Now all White's forces (not including his rooks) are in the attack, aimed at one point.

16...gxh4

The alternative was to try and hold

the g6 square: 16...♕e8 17 ♘h5! ♕c6 (or 17...f5 18 exf6 gxh4 19 cxd5! exd5+ 20 ♔f2, and after regaining his piece — 20...♔h7 21 ♖e1, with the threat of 22 ♖e7 — White obtains a material advantage with an overwhelming position) 18 cxd5 exd5 19 ♗g3, with a decisive strengthening of the attack after the undermining move h2-h4.

17 ♘xg6 ♖e8 18 ♘h8!

While opening the way for the queen, the knight itself also remains in the attack.

18...♖e7 19 ♕h7+ ♔f8 20 f4 ♘xc4

It is not possible to evacuate the king: 20...♔e8 21 ♘xf7! ♖xf7 22 ♗g6 ♕e7 23 f5.

21 f5 exf5 22 0-0

The f-file is opened for the rooks, and the outcome is settled.

22...♗c8 23 ♗xf5 ♗xf5 24 ♖xf5 ♔e8 25 ♖xf7 ♔d7 26 ♕f5+ ♔c6 27 ♕f6+ ♔d7 28 e6+ ♔c6

Or 28...♔d6 29 ♖xe7, and 29... ♕xe7 is bad on account of 30 ♘f7+.

29 ♖xe7 ♕xh8 30 ♖xc7+! ♔b5 (30...♔xc7 31 ♕e7+ ♔b8 32 ♖f1) **31 ♕e7 a5 32 ♕d7+ ♔a6 33 ♖b1 Black resigns.**

The concentration of force before the final phase of the attack is often made by outwardly imperceptible piece movements far from the epicentre of the coming events (*see diagram next column*).

The material balance has been disturbed in favour of White. In the endgame this would be of decisive importance, but for the moment, exploiting in the full sense of the word his piece advantage, Black launches an assault on the kingside. In a certain sense he even has two "extra" pieces: after all, the bishops are of opposite colour.

Stein-Geller
Kislovodsk 1966

22...♗h4 23 ♖c2 ♖c7!

Black's last fighting unit, not ready for the assault, takes up an attacking position. Maximum concentration!

24 g3 ♗xg3! 25 fxg3 ♕g5 26 g4

The weakness of the king's pawn screen, the remoteness of the rook at a6, and, as a consequence, Black's decisive superiority in force leave White without any chances of saving the game. In the main variation 26 ♖g2 ♖e7 27 ♕d4 ♖e1+ 28 ♔h2 ♕c1 he also comes under a mating attack.

26...♖e7 27 ♕d4 ♕h4 28 ♖a1 ♖e1+ 29 ♖xe1 ♕xe1+ 30 ♔h2 ♕g3+ 31 ♔h1 ♕xh3+ 32 ♔g1 (or mate in three moves: 32 ♖h2 ♘g3+ 33 ♔g1 ♖f1+) **32...♘g3 White resigns.**

Here the rook was switched to the decisive part of the battlefield along the 7th rank (or, using the old descriptive notation, along the 2nd rank).

White most often uses the 3rd rank for the same aim, prudently avoiding pawn advances such as h2-h3, but sometimes making use of the move a2-a4. In this case the concentration of force in the attack zone can grow very quickly.

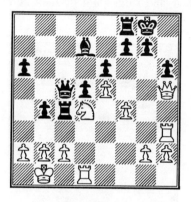

Kuzmin-Kondevsky
Krasnodar 1970

White has already transferred one of his rooks into a close attacking position along that 3rd rank. But with only two heavy pieces, the black king's defences cannot be smashed, and meanwhile his knight, splendidly placed in the centre and suppressing Black's counterplay on the c-file, is attacked.

If turns out that the knight can be ignored, if the mobilisation is continued!

21 ♖dd3!!
After thinking for an hour and a half (!), Black... overstepped the time limit. But neither after 21...♖xd4 22 ♖dg3 followed by the sacrifice on g7, nor in other variations such as 21...f5 22 ♖dg3 ♖f7 23 ♕xh6 ♔f8 24 ♕h8+ ♔e7 25 ♖xg7 ♖xg7 26 ♕xg7+ ♔d8

27 ♘xe6+ is there any way of saving the game.

By coincidence, it was on the same move that White's rook made a decisive entrance in the following game.

Yusupov-Kengis
Moscow 1983

21 ♖a3! ♔h8 22 ♖g3
An accurate choice of target, although White could also have won by 22 ♖h3 ♗f8 23 ♖g3 (with the threat of 24 ♘xh6 gxh6 25 ♕g4) 23...♕h4 (23...h5 24 ♘f6 g6 25 ♕xh5+) 24 ♘f6 and the black queen is trapped.

22...♖g8 23 ♘c4
Aiming, in passing, at the d6 square, which the same dark-square bishop is obliged to cover.

23...♗d5
Or 23...♗a6 24 ♕e4.

24 ♖h3 ♗f8 25 b3
Threatening simply 26 exd6.

25...♗xc4
This hastens the end, but what else can be suggested?

26 bxc4 dxe5 27 ♕xe5, and Black resigned, since after 27...f6 (otherwise

28 ♖xh6 mate) his position makes a pitiful impression.

I.D. There is also another procedure for preparing a decisive assault, which has never previously been considered in chess literature. My co-author has suggested calling it "launching"...

M.T. ... and in doing so I have no claims to authorship. This is pure plagiarism, since in ice-hockey this concept has existed since the game was born.* The point of it is that the puck ends up close to the goal, but no one knows what will happen with it next. Who will gain possession of the puck, who they will pass it to, in which direction it will fly. At any event, when I "launch" a piece close to the enemy king, I never aim it only at one point.

I.D. In your opinion, is such a stratagem objectively strong, or is it more a means of psychological pressure?

M.T. One cannot, of course, deny the effect of surprise, and often after such an escapade a mistake follows.

---

* It is a popular practice, particularly in Canadian ice-hockey, for a player to pass the puck not to a team member, but simply close to the opponents' goal, in the hope that one of his team will get to it first and will be able to shoot at goal. Similarly in chess, a piece may be moved close to the enemy king, but without any concrete aim, much depending on future developments, including the defence chosen. In the absence of any generally accepted English name for this practice, the term "launching" has been adopted, to convey its speculative nature (Translator's note).

But that also happens in any situation when there is a sharp turn in the play. But the main thing is that it is "normal" move, and the "launching" is in no way disproved. After all, this is one version of concentrating force, only without a clear and single aim planned beforehand.

Tal-Vasyukov
32nd USSR Championship
Kiev 1964/5

One senses a certain remoteness of the black pieces from the kingside, and White aims to exploit this factor.

15 ♘h5!

Typical "launching". Approaching the black king at the length of a drawn sword, the knight is looking both at f6, and at g7 — according to circumstances. For example, 15...♖ae8 can be met by 16 c4 ♘b4 (16...♘5f6 17 ♘xf6+ ♘xf6 allows White to set up a strong piece outpost in the centre with 18 ♘e5, when 19 ♗xf6 and 20 ♘d7 is already threatened) 17 ♗xh7+ ♔xh7 18 ♖xd7 ♕xd7 19 ♘e5 ♕d4 20 ♘f6+ gxf6 21 ♕h5+ with a quick mate. In the game itself the knight goes the other way.

M.T. Only one should not harbour any illusions: at the moment of "launching" the knight had already been allotted the role of a condemned man.

15...♔h8!

A useful move from all points of view. The threat of a possible sacrifice at h7 is not so terrible (without check!), and in the variation 16 c4 ♘5f6 17 ♘xf6 ♘xf6 Black is ready after a further exchange to play his rook to g8.

16 ♗e4 f6!

Again the best, and possibly the only move. If White has time to play 17 c4, his advantage over the entire board will become evident. 16...f5 was weaker in view of 17 ♗xd5 ♗xd5 18 ♘f4, when 18...♗c4 fails to 19 ♖xd7!

17 ♗h4

White might have been tempted to win a pawn by 17 ♗f4, but after 17...♘xf4 18 ♘xf4 ♕xf4! 19 ♗xb7 ♖ad8 20 ♕xe6 ♘e5! any real advantage would have evaporated instantly — 21 ♖xd8 ♖xd8 22 ♘xe5? is not possible on account of 22...♕xf2+!

17...♗d6

Very interestingly played. Black only needs to follow up with 18...♘c5, and he will seize the initiative. Therefore White's move is forced, but in fact it had already been planned in outline at the moment of "launching".

18 c4 ♗a6

How should White continue? Defending the pawn with the rook is inconsistent: after all, the pin is maintained. On 19 ♗d3 Black replies 18...

♘f4 20 ♘xf4 ♗xf4 21 ♕xe6 ♘c5. Drastic measures are required, but 19 ♗xh7 is insufficient in view of 19...♔xh7 20 ♕e4+ ♔h8! 21 ♕xe6 ♗xc4. Only one move remains:

19 ♘xg7! ♔xg7 (bad is 19...♘f4 20 ♕d2, or 19...♗xc4 20 ♘xe6) **20 ♘d4 ♘c5 21 ♕g4+ ♔h8 22 ♘xe6 ♘xe6 23 ♕xe6 ♖ae8 24 ♕xd5 ♗xh2+ 25 ♔h1**, and now the lesser evil for Black was 25...♕xc4! 26 ♕xc4 ♗xc4 27 ♖fe1, although the ending favours White.

But after **25...♕f4 26 ♕h5!** White retains a winning advantage in the event of **26...♖xe4 27 ♖d7**, and on **26...♕xe4** (the only move) he could have won immediately by 27 ♖de1.

M.T. We once talked about "launching" at one of the sessions of the school run by grandmaster Gipslis and myself for young Latvian players, and fairly soon I was gladdened by 17-year-old Alexei Shirov, who by that time was already World Junior Under-16 Champion.

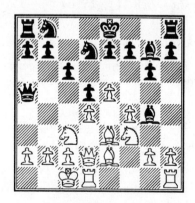

Shirov-Stangl
World Junior Ch., Tunja 1989

White needs to get rid of the one black piece that is preventing him from beginning an offensive on the kingside — the bishop at g4. With this aim, 11 h3 followed by g2-g4 and f4-f5 would have done, but a "launching" is even better.

11 ♘g5 ♗xe2 12 ♕xe2

Now the white knight supports the possible breakthrough 13 e6, and it is hard for Black to endure it close to his king.

12...h6 13 ♘xf7!

The goal has arisen of its own accord!

13...♚xf7 14 f5 gxf5 15 ♕h5+ ♚g8 16 ♖df1 e6 17 g4 ♕d8 18 gxf5 exf5 19 ♖hg1 ♕e7

Only White's knight is not participating in the attack, and his advantage in force suggests a solution.

20 ♖xg7+! ♚xg7

Had Black given up his queen (20...♕xg7 21 ♖g1) he would then have lost much more.

21 ♖g1+ ♚f8 22 ♗xh6+ ♖xh6 23 ♕xh6+ ♚e8 24 ♖g7 ♕b4

Forced: 24...♕f8 25 ♕e6+ ♚d8 26 ♖g8.

25 a3!

Elegantly removing the defence from f8 and forcing mate after 25...♕xd4 26 ♖g8+ ♚f7 27 ♕h7+ ♚e6 28 ♖e8. **Black resigns.**

In the next diagram too, White makes concrete gains by a "launching".

17 ♘g5!

The obvious aim is 18 ♘ge4, but there is also a reserve one that is not yet evident.

17...♘h5

Practically forced, since after

17...♖ad8 18 g4! Black altogether has a problem: what to move?

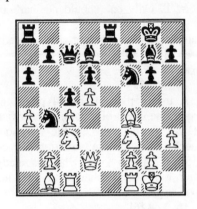

Balashov-Stein
39th USSR Championship
Leningrad 1971

18 ♗h2 f5 19 ♖fe1 ♗e5!?

The best chance — to remove his concerns over the d6 pawn. But...

20 g4! fxg4 21 ♘xh7!

Goal! Of course, talking in ice-hockey terms, the match is not yet won, but even after the most logical 21...♗f5 (bad is 21...♚xh7 22 ♕g5, and wins) 22 ♘g5 White has a clear advantage in view of the weakness of e6, to where his agile knight will soon find its way.

21...g3?! 22 fxg3 ♗f5

Here too the capture 22...♚xh7 23 ♕g5 ♗d4+ 24 ♚h1 ♘f6 25 ♕xg6+ ♚h8 26 ♖f1 ♗xh3 27 ♖xf6 ♗xf6 28 ♕xf6+ ♚g8 29 ♕h4 ♕d7 (or 29...♗c8) 30 ♘e4 would have given White an irresistible attack.

But in the game too, after the correct 23 ♘g5! he should have won "lawfully" — 23...♗xg3 24 ♖xe8+

Rxe8 25 Axf5 gxf5 26 Axg3 ♘xg3
27 ♔h2 ♘h5 28 Rg1, or 23...Axb1 24
Rxb1 Axg3 25 Axg3 ♘xg3 26 ♘e6
with a decisive advantage.

In fact, he went wrong with **23
Axf5?** (giving Black counterplay by
opening the g-file), and won only after
inaccuracies by both sides, during
which he was close to defeat.

M.T. Which in no way affects the
evaluation of the entire idea, begun on
the 17th move with the "launching".

Tal-Averbakh
USSR Team Ch. Semi-Final
Riga 1961
Ruy Lopez

1	e4	e5
2	♘f3	♘c6
3	Ab5	a6
4	Aa4	♘f6
5	0-0	Ae7
6	Re1	b5
7	Ab3	d6
8	c3	0-0
9	h3	♘a5
10	Ac2	c5
11	d4	♕c7
12	♘bd2	♘c6
13	dxc5	dxc5
14	♘f1	Rd8
15	♕e2	g6
16	♘e3	Rb8

Black's 14...Rd8 is clearly rather
provocative, since his f7 square is
deprived of its central defender. But if
White develops unhurriedly with Ad2,
Rad1 etc., as in many well known
games, Black's position will prove
quite satisfactory.

17 ♘g5

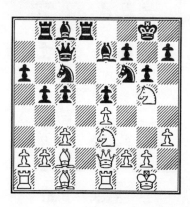

The knight does not threaten anything for the moment, but it clearly
intends to sacrifice itself at f7, or — in
some cases — at h7.

17 ... Af8
18 ♕f3

As though confirming his
"sacrificial mood" — now there is no
way back for the knight.

18 ... Ae7
19 ♘d5! ♕d6

After the capture on d5 the weakness of f7 would already have been felt
— 20...♘e7 is not possible.

20 Ae3 h6

It was difficult to tolerate the knight
any longer since 21 Rad1 was threatened, but now White begins a combination that he has calculated right to
the end.

21 ♘xf6+ Axf6

It would have been better to part
with a pawn after 21...♕xf6 22 ♕xf6
Axf6 23 ♘f3.

22 Rad1 ♕e7

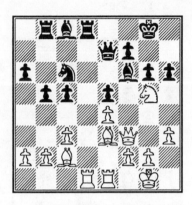

23	♗xc5!	♖xd1
24	♖xd1	♕xc5
25	♕xf6	hxg5
26	♗b3!	

This quiet move is the point of the combination. The black king loses its pawn protection and comes under the fire of all three remaining white pieces.

26	...	♖b7
27	♕xg6+	♔f8
28	♕h6+	

And in view of the variation 28...♔e7 29 ♖d5! ♕b6 30 ♕xg5+ ♔f8 31 ♕h6+ ♔e7 (31...♔g8 32 ♖d3) 32 ♕h4+, **Black resigned**.

WHAT WOULD YOU HAVE PLAYED?

No.10

Compared with familiar positions, in the opening Black has lost two tempi — this is too great a handicap. To what does it give White the right?

No.11

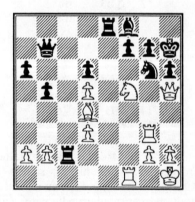

All five white pieces are aimed at the black king. Is some further strengthening required, or is it time to seek a combinational blow?

4 Invasion Trajectories

INVASION TRAJECTORIES ARE the diagonals, ranks and files that in fact make up the entire black and white arena of the chess battle. But initially they are blocked by pawn barriers, of both sides, and increasing the mobility of his pieces is essentially one of the main problems for each player. For this the pieces need clear trajectories. For such privileges a player has to battle, sacrifice pawns and pieces, or make positional concessions.

But let us nevertheless begin with some particular instances: the conclusions of attacks along trajectories that have already been cleared.

The idea of an attack along a weakened long dark-square diagonal is illustrated in pure form by the following example, from a ladies' competition.

Archakova-Andreyeva
Kaliningrad 1970

The position of the black king is quite badly compromised. White can choose between a piece attack on h6 and the advance of her h-pawn, which, however, does not completely rule out Black's defensive chances, associated in particular with 28...♕b4. But the latter preferred the mercenary **28... ♗xc5??**, after which the main line of attack became the a1-h8 diagonal.

29 ♕f6 ♖g8 30 ♖d8 ♕e7

So, has the diversion of the defender not succeeded? Has the attack been parried?

31 ♕h8+! Black resigns.

Kasparov-Korchnoi
Candidates Semi-Final, London 1983

In this, the first game of the match, the dark squares in the vicinity of the black king have been weakened, and although White no longer has his dark-square bishop, this weakening could and should have been exploited with the help of his knight, in spite of the piece sacrifice involved. After 21 ♘e5! the threat of 22 ♘g4 (and, in passing, 22 ♘c4) obliges Black to swim with the tide: 21...♖d8 22 ♕h4! ♖d5 23 ♘g4 ♖xb5, and now the interposition of 24 ♖ad1!, cutting off the king's escape to the queenside, forces him to find a way of neutralising the opponent's powerful initiative.

Thus, for example, 24...♘c6 is bad on account of 25 ♖d7!, while on 24... ♗d5 White has 25 c4 ♕xc4 26 ♖xd5! exd5 (otherwise the queen is lost) 27 ♕d8+ ♔g7 28 ♕f6+ ♔f8 29 ♖e1 ♕e4 30 ♕h8+ ♔e7 31 ♖xe4+ dxe4 32 h4, retaining the initiative.

Perhaps the only way to save the game is in the variation 24...♗d5! 25 c4 ♖d6! (the open file cannot be conceded, since 25...♖xd1, in the hope of 26 ♖xd1 ♘c6 27 ♖d7 ♕xd7! 28 ♘f6+ ♔g7 29 ♘xd7 ♖d8!, is refuted by the interposition of 26 ♘f6+!! ♔f8 — bad is 26...♔g7 27 ♘e8+, when Black can resign — 27 ♖xd1 with excellent attacking chances; in addition White has in reserve the drawing mechanism 27 ♕h6+ ♔e7 28 ♘g8+) 26 ♘f6+ ♔f8 27 ♕f4 ♖c6 28 ♕h6+ ♔e7 29 ♘g8+ ♔e8 30 ♘f6+, with a draw, which from the initial position is not a bad result for White. After all, his queenside pawns are organically weak, and in the game this factor led to his defeat after **21 ♘g5 h6 22 ♘e4 ♗xe4!**

In the next diagram the only open file has been firmly seized by White, and now his problem is to invade "deeper" and "wider", breaking up the defences around the black king.

34 ♖d6 ♘e8 35 ♖c6! ♕b7 36 ♗h4 ♘f6 37 ♖dd6 (the first stage) **37...**

♔f7 **38 ♕d1** (the second stage) **38... ♖g8.**

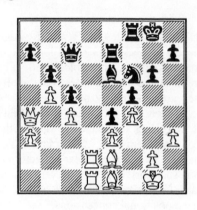

Ragozin-Lisitsin
12th USSR Ch., Moscow 1940

After 38...♖fe8 White could have changed the invasion trajectory with 39 ♕a1.

39 ♗xf6 ♔xf6 40 ♕d5, and in view of inevitable loss of material (40...♖ge8 41 ♖xe6+ ♖xe6 42 ♖xe6+) soon **Black resigned.**

But it happens much more often that attacking diagonals and files have first to be opened — and in a very fierce struggle!

Perhaps the most daring — and brilliant! — attempt to exploit the a1-h8 diagonal for attack, after first weakening it, was made in the following game (*see diagram next page*).

At that time this was one of the standard positions in the Sicilian Defence, where it was considered virtually obligatory for White to repeat moves: 12 ♕h6 ♗g7 13 ♕h4 ♗f6. But here he made a move that initially seemed fantastic, but then quite logical.

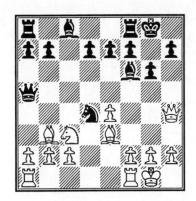

Nezhmetdinov-Chernikov
Rostov-on-Don 1962

12 ♕xf6!?!

The idea of the combination immediately becomes clear: with ♗d4, ♘d5 and ♖a1-d1-d3-f3 to set up powerful pressure on the f6 pawn, and after its fall — an attack along the diagonal.

12...♘e2+! (by diverting the knight, Black gains a tempo) **13 ♘xe2 exf6 14 ♘c3 ♖e8**

14...d5 seems better, in order after 15 ♘xd5 to continue 15...♖d8 or 15...♗e6, intending to get rid of the aggressive knight. But White too can try and save a tempo by continuing 15 ♗d4!?

15 ♘d5 ♖e6 16 ♗d4 ♔g7 17 ♖ad1 d6

On 17...♖xe4 White can interpose 18 ♗c3 and then 19 ♘xf6, while if 17...b5 18 ♗c3 ♕d8 19 ♘xf6 ♖xf6 20 ♖d6.

18 ♖d3 ♗d7 19 ♖f3 ♗b5 20 ♗c3 ♕d8 21 ♘xf6! ♗e2

Black loses after 21...♗xf1 22 ♘g4+ ♔g8 23 ♘h6+ ♔f8 24 ♘xf7 ♕e7 25 ♘g5+ ♔e8 26 ♘xe6, when

the only way to prolong his king's life is by giving up his queen.

22 ♘xh7+ ♔g8

Or 22...♔xh7 23 ♖xf7+ ♔h6 24 ♗d2+ g5 25 ♗xe6 ♗xf1 26 ♗f5 ♕h8 27 h4 ♗e2 28 ♗xg5+ ♔h5 29 f3 ♗xf3 30 gxf3 ♕d4+ 31 ♔g2 ♖h8 32 ♖f6, and the threat of 33 ♗g4 mate forces Black to part with his queen.

23 ♖h3 ♖e5

Alas, blocking the fatal diagonal (24 ♘g5 was threatened) does not prove possible.

24 f4! ♗xf1 25 ♔xf1 ♖c8 26 ♗d4

The hasty 26 fxe5 dxe5 27 ♗xe5 would have allowed Black a draw by perpetual check: 27...♕d1+. But now the knight again moves into a striking position.

26...b5 27 ♘g5 ♖c7

Black cannot also plug the neighbouring diagonal with 27...♖c4. White first captures both black rooks with his bishops(!), and then carries out the same "little combination" as in the game.

And if 27...♕f6 he wins by 28 ♗xf7+ ♔g7 29 ♖h7+ ♔f8 30 ♘e6+ ♔e7 31 ♗xg6+! ♔xe6 32 f5+.

28 ♗xf7+! ♖xf7 29 ♖h8+ ♔xh8 30 ♘xf7+ ♔h7 31 ♘xd8 ♖xe4 32 ♘c6 ♖xf4+ 33 ♔e2 Black resigns.

This is another example from the games of a player, who is not too well known in Europe, international master Rashid Nezhmetdinov...

M.T. ... Against whom, incidentally, I lost three of our official games, although I should have lost all four. And how I lost them!

I.D. Don't worry, we have already given one of them...

Nezhmetdinov-Kotkov
Russian Ch., Krasnodar 1957

The position of Black's king has certainly been weakened by the advance of his pawn to f5, but how can this factor be exploited? 17 ♘f4 is met by the simple 17...♘e5, and under the cover of this knight Black gradually completes his development.

17 ♘xc7!! ♕xc7 18 ♕d5+ ♔h8 19 ♖e8!

Of course, not 19 ♗xd6? ♘f6!, when the picture changes sharply.

19...♘f6 20 ♖xf8+ ♗xf8 21 ♗b2!

White plans — and carries out! — an invasion of the opponent's position along the a2-g8 diagonal, but in this he is helped by pressure and latent threats along the adjacent diagonal.

21...♗g7

After 21...♔g7 White realises his plan in pure form — 22 ♗c4, with the invasion at g8.

Black has a seemingly more tenacious, and certainly more cunning defence in 21...♕g7, when if White is tempted by the plausible and showy 22

♖e8 ♘xe8 23 ♕f7!!, he runs into 22... ♗e6! 23 ♖xf8+ ♖xf8 24 ♕xe6 d5 25 g4 fxg4 26 hxg4 h6 27 f4 g5, when Black gradually frees himself.

But instead of this, White had prepared in advance the essentially forced variation 22 ♕d4 ♘e4 (22...♘g8 is met by 23 ♖e8 ♕xd4 24 ♗xd4+ ♗g7 25 ♗c4, while if 22...♗e7 23 ♕e3 ♗f8 24 ♕g5) 23 f3 d5 24 fxe4 fxe4 25 ♕f2!, which Black can avoid only at the cost of a hopeless ending.

22 ♗c4! ♗d7 23 ♗xf6 ♗xf6 24 ♕f7 ♕d8

24...♗g5 is also insufficient: 25 g3 ♖c8 26 h4 ♗c6 27 ♖e8+ ♖xe8 28 ♕xc7, and White must merely avoid blundering into the mate after 28... ♖e1+ 29 ♔h2?? (29 ♗f1). The move in the game allows a pretty finish.

25 ♖e8+!!

Black resigns. He cannot simultaneously defend f6 and f8.

So that the timely opening of a diagonal brought the attacking side rich — and pretty, if they can be such — dividends.

It would be naive to think that a good friend of both authors, five-times Women's World Champion Nona Gaprindashvili, did not know about this attacking procedure...

I.D. The point is probably that knowledge comes in different forms. Some, that was once assimilated, is stored somewhere in the depths of the brain, and is soundly asleep...

M.T. Of course, no grandmaster, on sitting down at the board, repeats in his mind the entire range of chess knowledge, but for me a sign of good form is when it is all "spontaneously", as it were, available, and what is needed surfaces of its own accord at the required moment...

I.D. But how can this be attained?

M.T. Nothing, apart from constant training, has yet been thought up by mankind. Neither in science, nor in art, nor in chess...

Gaprindashvili-Vereczi
Belgrade 1974

Here White is attacking, Black is counterattacking, and it is not clear which is the more dangerous. It is White's move, and she has a draw in the rook ending (36 ♕f7+), but she has also discovered a mating motif.

36 h3!! ♖xf1+ 37 ♔h2

Here there is no point in giving any exclamation marks: White is merely continuing what has been begun. The threat is 38 hxg4+, with mate to follow, and 37...gxh3 allows 38 g4+ ♔h4 39 ♕xf6+, mating.

37...g3+ 38 fxg3 ♕e3

Black has taken control of the invasion square h6 and is herself threatening mate in one move. Therefore White

gave perpetual check — **39 ♕g4+ ♔h6 40 ♕g7+**, although she could have opened one more diagonal for a decisive attack. After 39 ♖xe5+ fxe5 40 g4+ ♔h4 the game would have been concluded by 41 ♕e7+, and if 41...♕g5 42 g3 mate. A finish, worthy of any textbook, in any era!

The opening of files is virtually the main motif in the majority of games where the target of one side is the enemy king. Lines can be cleared by exchanges, but more often — by sacrifices.

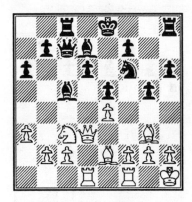

Geller-Vasyukov
USSR Spartakiad, Riga 1975

White has an advantage in mobilisation, and in the placing of his king. In addition Black's position has many weaknesses (the d6 pawn, the d5 and f5 squares, and the kingside pawns), but it is very difficult to approach them. Apart from one way...

16 f4! exf4 17 ♗xf4! gxf4 18 ♖xf4 ♘h7

At the cost of a piece White has opened lines on the kingside, exposed a glaring weakness at f7, acquired an outpost at d5, and his attack on the king becomes threatening.

19 ♘d5 ♛d8 20 b4 ♝a7 21 e5 ♝e6 (21...dxe5 is decisively met by 22 ♖xf7!) **22 exd6 ♖c6 23 ♝g4** (again aiming at f7) **23...♖xd6 24 ♝xe6 ♖xe6 25 ♘f6+ ♚e7 26 ♘d5+ ♚f8 27 ♖df1 ♘g5 28 h4 ♝b8 29 ♖c4 ♖e5 30 ♖d4 ♘e6** (30...♘e4!? came into consideration, creating counterplay) **31 ♛g6 ♛e8 32 ♖d3 ♖xd5 33 ♖xd5 ♘f4 34 ♛f6 ♖g8 35 ♖d8**, and Black played on for a further ten moves, only because it was a team event.

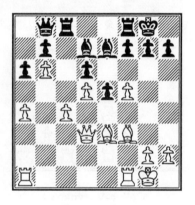

Kupreichik-Belyavsky
Chelyabinsk 1974

White has an enormous spatial advantage, and in addition virtually all the black pieces are practically stalemated. True, had it been Black to move, with a pawn sacrifice he could have gained a "gulp of air" — 23...e4 24 ♝xe4 ♝f6 25 ♝d4 ♝xd4+ 26 ♛xd4 f6 27 ♝d3 ♖fe8, and after White's "normal" move — 23 ♝e4, he could have tried to set up some defensive lines with 23...f6, which, however, would hardly be sufficient.

But White (and it is in fact him to move) is not inclined to defer his assault, and he resorts to a typical attacking device, opening the f-file and the b1-h7 diagonal.

23 f6! ♝xf6 24 ♝e4 ♚h8

Roughly the same variations would have occurred after the alternative 24...♖ce8.

25 ♖xf6! gxf6 26 ♝xh7 ♖g8 27 ♖f1 ♖g7 28 ♝e4 f5 29 ♝xf5 ♝xf5 30 ♖xf5 ♚g8

Here Black evidently breathed a sigh of relief...

31 ♝h6 ♖g6 32 ♖g5!

Exchanging one of the three attacking pieces for the only defender! After this the black king is completely exposed.

32...♚h7

Or 32...♖xg5 33 ♝xg5 ♖c5 34 ♝f6 ♚f8 35 ♛h7 ♚e8 36 ♛g8+.

33 ♖xg6 fxg6 34 ♛h3 ♚g8 35 ♛d7 Black resigns.

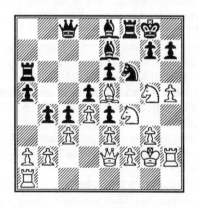

Kostina-Sammul
Tbilisi 1974

Every single white piece is ready, either immediately or within a couple of moves, to take part in the attack on the enemy king. But the latter has enough — or nearly enough — defenders, there are no serious weaknesses, and, most important, for the moment the position is a closed one.

Hence White's immediate task — to open lines!

24 ♘g6! hxg6

It would have been preferable to decline this Greek gift and to prevent the immediate opening of lines by 24...♗xg6 25 hxg6 h6, although even here after 26 ♘f7 ♖xf7 (evidently forced) 27 gxf7+ ♔xf7 28 ♗xf6 ♗xf6 29 f3 exf3+ 30 ♕xf3 followed by e3-e4 White stands clearly better.

25 hxg6 ♗xg6 26 ♖ah1 ♘h5 27 ♖xh5 ♗xh5 28 ♕xh5 ♗xg5 29 ♗xg7!

Not the only solution, but the most consistent: the pawn screen is completely destroyed, Black's king is "undressed" and, strictly speaking, she could already have resigned.

29...e5 30 ♕h7+ (other moves were also possible) **30...♔f7 31 ♗xf8+ ♔e8 32 ♗c5**, and White won.

It is usually another gift that is offered at g6, when the g-pawn, supported by its neighbour on the h-file or sometimes even unsupported, moves into a double attack.

However, this procedure is examined in detail in one of the illustrative games in this chapter (Tal-Mohrlok). For the moment here is another example of the opening of lines, and of how the pieces can exploit this.

There is nothing to herald a storm, except perhaps that one senses a rather abstract weakness of the a7-g1 diagonal. And yet...

Mititelu-Tal
World Student Team Ch, Varna 1958

17...♘g4!!

This is not a queen sacrifice, since 18 ♗xd8 ♘f2+ 19 ♔g1 ♘xd1+ 20 ♔h1 ♘f2+ 21 ♔g1 ♖exd8 gives Black both material compensation, and an attack. His idea was a different one, based, incidentally, on White's accurate reply.

18 fxg4 ♕xg5 19 exd5 ♗g4 20 d6 ♗xe2 21 ♘xe2 ♗xd6 22 ♖xd6 ♘b5 23 ♕d2 ♕g4 24 ♘c3 ♘xd6 25 ♕xd6 ♖cd8

Forcing play has led to Black's desired result. The disturbing of the material balance is nominally not in his favour, but on the other hand all the central files are open, and the black rooks are established on them. Strictly speaking, there is no attack as yet, but with every justification Black can count on one, as soon as his rooks advance, ideally onto the 2nd rank.

26 ♕c7 h5 27 ♖f1 ♖d7 28 ♕xa5 h4 29 gxh4 ♖d2

Black's idea is realised in pure form, although in passing he has to parry some counterthreats by the opponent.

30 ♗d5 ♔h8 31 ♕b4 ♕h3 32 ♕f4 ♖xh2+ 33 ♔g1 ♖c2!

Pawn-grabbing (33...♖xb2?) would have given White an important tempo for defence.

34 ♘d1 ♖e6 35 h5 ♖f6 36 ♕b8+ ♖c8 37 ♗g2 ♖xf1+

After this Black can "sadistically" remain the exchange up, or (after interposing a check) with an extra queen. **White resigns**.

Minasian-Miles
Moscow 1990

One senses that the black king has already endured some anxious moments, but... Now the tripled g-pawns hinder the approach to it, for example, 20 f3 gxf3 21 ♕xf3+ ♘f5, and the king is clearly destined for a long life.

But White nevertheless finds a way of opening both files and diagonals for the attack.

20 h3! gxh3 21 ♗xg6+!! ♔xg6 22 ♘f4+ ♔f7 23 ♕h5+ ♔g8 24 ♘xe6 ♕e8 25 ♖dg1!

Gaining a tempo for the decisive mobilisation of reserves.

25...♗f8 26 ♕xh3

There is no need to resort to drastic measures such as 26 ♖g6: Black has practically no useful moves.

26...♘f7 27 ♕f5 ♖c8 28 ♖xh8+ ♘xh8 29 ♘xg7! ♗xg7 30 ♗h6

There are many black pieces around the king, but none to defend it.

30...♖c1+ 31 ♔xc1! Black resigns.

Diagonals often have to be cleared not only of enemy pieces, but also of one's own. Here, as in play along the files, it can be useful to vacate a square for the piece that can occupy it to greatest effect. Time in attack is precious, and lines are normally cleared with gain of tempo, i.e. with a sacrifice.

Schmid-Kinzel
Siegen Olympiad 1970

A rook on the 7th rank is always an achievement, but in the given instance it has no particular prospects, and White also has to concern himself about his knight. He could, of course, try to set up a queen and rook battery along the h2-b8 diagonal, but is it not simpler (of course, knowing this procedure) to clear this diagonal.

24 ♖xb7+! ♛xb7 25 ♕e5+ ♚a8

Black has little choice: 25...♚c8 26 ♖c1+ ♚d7 27 ♕d6+ ♚e8 28 ♘c7+, and he loses his queen.

26 ♘c7+ ♚b8 27 ♘xe6+ ♚a8 28 ♘xd8, and White easily realised his material advantage.

White was also able to extend his attacking trajectories in the following game.

Uhlmann-Uitumen
Palma Interzonal 1970

White has the initiative for the pawn, but no direct strengthening of the attack is apparent. In addition the white queen is tied to the back rank. Of course, the black king could be approached by giving check on the a1-h8 diagonal, but the c3 square is under control.

27 b4!

Whether or not Black accepts the sacrifice, all the same one square, a1 or b2, is opened for the white queen.

27...♕xb4?

The only defence was 27...♕d8, in order to oppose the white queen from f6. But now Black loses.

28 ♗xe6

And it transpires that after 28...♗xe6 29 ♕a1+ the black king is unable simultaneously to defend the rook, the bishop and itself. Hence — **28...♕b1 29 ♕xb1 ♗xb1 30 ♘d2**, and a gradual loss for Black.

Vacating a file before one's strongest piece (usually the queen) moves onto it — this theme is well known from the following textbook pattern, which, however, occurs from time to time in practice with various modifications.

Both rooks are sacrificed at h8, and then comes ♕h1+ and ♕h7 mate.

Therefore we will restrict ourselves to one elegant example.

White's queen very much needs to reach g7, but both his own rooks are in the way. In addition he has to worry about the c2 square, where he may himself be mated.

Heemsoth-Heisenbutter
Germany 1958

White found a splendid solution.
1 ♖c5!!
Interrupting Black's counterattack for an instant, with gain of tempo White prepares also to dispose of his second rook — 2 ♖xh7+. In addition Black's queen is attacked, and he merely deferred his capitulation for the moment by defending his king — **1...♘e8 2 ♖xc4 ♖xc4 3 ♔xb2**.

It should be borne in mind that — mainly in the games of top players — one also sees another, rather rare form of vacating lines for attack — in this case ranks. This happens when the attack on the king is being mounted from the flank, or when an attacking piece has to be switched from flank to flank. One has to look hard for such a possibility: it is usually well camouflaged and... effective, as in the following example.

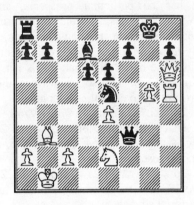

Karpov-Gik
Moscow University Ch. 1968/9

Both sides have been playing actively, but now it is only White who is attacking. His offensive, however, would appear to have come to a halt, since after 24 ♕xh7+ ♔f8 the black king escapes from the firing line, and the knight cannot be included in the attack: 24 ♘d4 ♕d1+ and 25...♕xd4.

Black's position proved to be hopeless only after the following far from obvious decision.

24 g6!!
Usually files are opened by such an advance, but here the white rook's scope is expanded, not only forward, but also to the side, along the rank. Its increased power proves decisive.

24...♘xg6 25 ♕xh7+ ♔f8 26 ♖f5!
Winning the queen and the game.

26...♕xb3+ 27 axb3 exf5 28 ♘f4 ♖d8 29 ♕h6+ ♔e8 30 ♘xg6 fxg6 31 ♕xg6+ ♔e7 32 ♕g5+!
Not allowing the rook across to the kingside.

32 ♔e8 33 exf5 ♖c8 34 ♕g8+ ♔e7

35 ♕g7+. Black resigns: the f-pawn will now advance.

Stein-Tukmakov
USSR 1972

This illustrates a similar idea, but much simpler. White gives up the pride of his position — his passed d-pawn, in order to open up the 7th rank.

38 d8=♕+! ♖bxd8 39 ♕e7+

The white queen has joined the attack, and **Black resigned**.

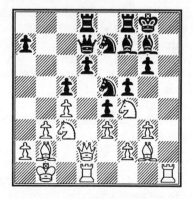

Larsen-Kavalek
Lugano 1970

The position is sharp and full of life. White is pressing on the half-open d-file, and the h-file has also been opened "in his favour". But Black too has his play: he is threatening to drive away the knight by ...g5 and establish a piece outpost at d3, attacking the important dark-square bishop.

The scales tip in favour of White only after his far from obvious clearing of the 2nd rank.

20 g4! ♘xg4 21 f3 exf3 22 ♗xf3

At the cost of a pawn the way for the queen to h2 has been opened.

22...♘e5

Switching to defence — 22...♘f6 23 ♕h2 ♖fe8 — is insufficient: 24 ♘b5 ♘c8 25 ♗xf6 ♗xf6 26 ♕h7+ ♔f8 27 ♗d5 and White wins (he threatens, in particular, 28 ♗xf7 ♕xf7 29 ♘xg6+).

23 ♕h2 ♗xc4!?

An interesting counterattack, for which, however, Black does not have enough resources. But pure defence would have led to variations similar to those given earlier.

24 bxc4 ♘xf3 25 ♕h7+ ♔f7 26 ♘cd5 ♖g8 27 ♘xe7 ♖b8 28 ♔a1 ♕xe7 29 ♕xg6+ ♔f8 30 ♘e6+ ♕xe6 31 ♗xg7+! ♔e7 32 ♗f8+!! ♖bxf8 33 ♖h7+

And in view of the variation 33...♖f7 34 ♖xf7+ ♕xf7 35 ♕xd6+ ♔e8 36 ♕d8 mate, **Black resigned**.

Holes in the Fortress Walls

Thematically linked to the attack along a weak diagonal is the attack along a whole complex of weak squares in the vicinity of the enemy king. This can arise with numerous pawn formations:

And in various other cases. But in principle there is a single attacking mechanism: pieces are established on the unprotected squares, and from close range they pursue the king, completely destroying its protection.

In the next diagram, the white bishop, which has just captured a rook, is clearly out of play, and there is no point in spending time on its recapture. It is much more effective to begin an attack on the dark squares, which for the moment have been left undefended.

Botterill-Tal
European Team Ch., Bath 1973

41...♗e3! 42 ♔g3

If 42 ♖a1 Black interposes 42...♗g1+, and only then plays 43...♕xa1.

42...♗g5!

This bishop has a great future: if 43 ♕f2, defending against the mate at f4, then 43...♗h4+, and taking the bishop allows mate on g5.

43 ♕c4

43 ♕g4 h5 44 ♕d4 is convincingly met by 44...♕e1+, and if 45 ♔h2 ♗e3, all on those weakened dark squares!

43...♕e3+ 44 ♔g4 ♗h4

Simultaneously creating two mating threats.

45 ♗e7

45 ♘xf7 is nicely refuted: 45...♕g3+ 46 ♔h5 ♗e8!

45...♗xe7 46 ♘xf7

Or 46 ♕xc6 h5+.

46...h5+ 47 ♔xh5 ♗e8 48 ♔g4 exf5+ 49 ♔xf5 g6+

M.T. Here Botterill smiled: evidently the finish appealed to him too...

50 ♔g4 ♗d7+

White resigns; this attack along the weak squares won Black the brilliancy prize at the European Team Championship.

Liebert-Tal
Skopje Olympiad 1972

In principle the theme is the same here, with the not especially important difference that the role of the g2 pawn is played by a bishop.

22...♘de5! 23 fxe5 ♗xe5+ 24 ♔g1 ♕g3 25 ♘f3 ♘h4 26 ♘xh4 ♕h2+ 27 ♔f2 ♗g3+ 28 ♔f3 ♗xh4

The first phase of the attack is complete. The white king has been drawn out into the open, and is "ready" to perish after the rook invasion at g3. Covering this square by 29 ♗f4 does not help, since all the same there follows 29...♖g3+.

29 ♗d4+ ♗f6 30 ♕f2

30 ♗xf6+ ♖xf6 31 ♕f2 would have given a respite, but only for an instant — 31...f4.

30...♗e5! 31 ♖h1

All the same the weak dark squares cannot be defended.

31...♕f4+ 32 ♔e2 ♕xd4 33 ♕xd4 ♗xd4 34 ♗f3 ♖g3

Alas for White, the theme of Black's entire play in this game remains unchanged to the end.

35 b3 ♗c5 36 ♖ef1 ♖e7+ 37 ♔d2 ♖e3 38 ♗d1 ♖g2+ 39 ♔c1 ♖c3+ 40 ♔b1 ♗a3 White resigns: dark-square strategy!

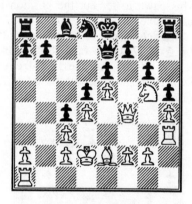

Damsky-Stefanov
Kazan 1962

White's superiority is determined by his spatial advantage and his invulnerable pawn outpost at e5, but most importantly — by the weakness of a whole complex of dark squares on the kingside, of which the white knight has already made "convenient" use. On the kingside, castling is practically impossible, on the queenside it cannot be done without losing the f7 pawn, and it only remains for Black to castle artificially under the cover of the blocked pawn centre.

16...♔d7 17 g4!

When lines are opened, the weakness of the dark squares will become a decisive factor.

17...hxg4 18 ♗xg4 ♔c6 19 ♖ah1 ♗d7 20 h5 gxh5 21 ♖xh5 ♖xh5 22 ♖xh5 ♖c8 23 ♖h7 ♗e8

Are attack and defence balanced? If 24 ♗h5 Black has the sufficient defence 24...♖c7, then ...b6 and ...♔b7. True, in reserve White has the advance of his pawn to f5, but the position is already ripe for a "little combination".

24 ♗xe6! ♘xe6 25 ♘xe6 ♕xe6 26 ♖h6 ♗d7 27 ♖xe6+ fxe6 28 ♕f6, and in view of the weakness of the e6 pawn, Black was unable to set up a "fortress".

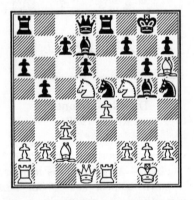

Kalinkin-Nezhmetdinov
Vologda 1962

All the indications suggest that it is White who is attacking. His minor pieces are actively placed, the dark squares around the black king are weakened, and, for example, in the event of 17...♗xh6 18 ♘xh6+ ♔f8 19 f4 ♘c6 20 g4 ♘f6 21 g5 this will soon

tell. But, it turns out, Black too has the preconditions for a counterattack — or attack? — and they too are based on exploiting the weak squares, which in the vicinity of the white king... do not yet exist!

17...c6! 18 ♘c7 ♘f4!

Of course, 18...♕xc7 19 ♗xg5 would have surrendered the complex of dark squares to White. But the exchange sacrifice enables Black to seize the initiative, which, however, would not have led to anything without the idea mentioned above.

By threatening the knight at f5, Black begins forcing play.

19 ♗xg5 ♕xg5 20 ♘g3 h5 21 ♘xa8 ♖xa8 22 ♕xd6 h4 23 a4

White does not even suspect any danger, especially since after 23...hxg3 24 hxg3 ♘h5 he, of course, was not intending 25 f4?? ♕xg3 26 fxe5 ♘f4 27 ♕d2 ♘h3+, when he has to agree to perpetual check, since 28 ♔f1 loses to 28...♗e6 29 b3 ♕h2 with the threat of 30...♕g1+ or immediately 30...♗g4. Instead, the simple 25 axb5 cxb5 26 ♗b3, with the threat of 27 ♖xa6, would have given him a material advantage and good prospects.

23...h3!!

It transpires that it is not the white knight that is attacked, but the securely defended g2 square, and — all the suddenly weakened light squares on the kingside. Surprisingly, White no longer has any satisfactory defence.

24 axb5 cxb5 25 ♖xa6

Desperation, but 25 ♗d1 hxg2 26 f3, not allowing the black bishop to go to g4, is refuted by the simple 26...♘fd3 27 ♖e2 ♗h3!

25...罝xa6 26 豐xa6 hxg2 27 奧d1 奧g4 28 豐a1 奧f3 29 豐a8+ 含h7 30 豐c8 奧xd1 **White resigns**.

The weakness of squares around the king is especially acute if their natural defender — the bishop — is no longer on the board. The attacking side may exchange it, but even more effective is an attack with the participation of an "opposite-colour" bishop, since in this case it does not have any worthy opponent.

I.D. In short, in the endgame opposite-colour bishops are a saving factor...

M.T. ... but it is no accident that between the opening and the endgame the Gods have created the middlegame.

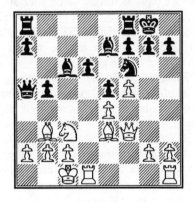

Sax-Hebert
Rio Interzonal 1979

The plans for the two sides are determined: after castling on opposite sides, mutual pawn storms are in prospect. To the usual principle in such cases of "who is quicker" is added here — and this is decisive — the factor of opposite-colour bishops.

Incidentally, White took this into account beforehand, when he aimed for this position.

14 奧g5! b4 15 奧xf6 奧xf6 16 ᵑd5 奧xd5 17 奧xd5 罝ac8

Contrary to the usual state of affairs, on this occasion simplification has favoured the attacking side: he has an "extra" piece. For the moment the counterattacking side does not have an "extra" piece — the bishop at f6 is rather passive. And the interposition of 17...奧g5+ does not help: 18 含b1 罝ac8 19 h4 奧h6 20 f6 g6 21 h5, and in principle Black can resign.

18 h4 含h8 19 含b1 豐c7 20 奧b3 a5 21 g4 奧e7 22 g5 f6

And immediately the idea takes shape of a mate at g8...

23 豐h5 奧d8 24 罝hg1 豐e7 25 罝g3 奧b6 26 罝d2 奧d4 27 罝dg2

Now the black bishop too can participate in the attack, but White has achieved more in the concentration of force.

27...a4 28 奧e6

No deviation!

28...罝b8 29 gxf6 豐xf6

The light-square bishop would also have triumphed after 29...gxf6 30 豐g4.

30 罝xg7 豐xg7 31 罝xg7 含xg7 32 豐g5+ 含h8 33 h5 罝b7 34 h6 奧c5 35 f6 罝ff7

Against 36 豐g7+ there is no other defence.

36 奧d5 罝bc7 37 豐g4 **Black resigns**.

In this last example we have seen the role that pawns can play in the offensive against a king. Apart from the fact that pawn advances open attacking lines and break up the walls of the king's fortress (about which more in detail in a later chapter), they also secure space for their pieces, and cramp the opponent's forces and the enemy king itself. Normally all this is at the cost of their own lives.

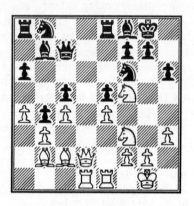

Geller-Gligoric
"Match of the Century"
Belgrade 1970

At first sight White appears to have no grounds for a pawn storm, and in addition Black is just one move away from being perfectly safe. Yet with the help of a sacrifice this becomes possible.

23 ♘xe5! ♖xe5 24 ♗xe5 ♕xe5 25 f4

White's idea, in launching this operation, is that the rapid advance of his central pawn pair will drive back the black forces to unfavourable positions.

25...♕e6

Here Black's queen comes under a further attack by the white f-pawn, but what can he do? After the "active" 25...♕c3 26 ♕f2 the queen would

simply be lost: 26...♘c6 27 e5 ♘e8 28 ♖e3 ♕b2 29 ♘xh6+ gxh6 30 ♗h7+.

26 e5 ♘e8

Trying to hold the position by tactical means, 26...♘e4, does not succeed: 27 ♖xe4! ♕xf5 28 ♖ee1 ♕e6 (or 28...♕h5 29 ♕d3) 29 f5, and the pawns continue their formidable advance.

27 ♘h4!

The most energetic. Now the weakness of Black's h7 becomes fatal.

27...♘c6 28 ♕d3 g6 29 f5

The culmination of White's entire plan. Now the black king is opened up, and the attack continues as though of its own accord.

29...gxf5 30 ♘xf5

Threatening mate: 31 ♘e7+ etc. Black's reply is forced, since after 30...♗g7 31 ♘xg7 ♔xg7 (31...♘xg7 32 ♕h7+ ♔f8 33 ♕h8+) 32 ♕h7+ ♔f8 33 ♗f5! the queen has no retreat - 33...♕e7 34 ♕h8 mate.

30...♕g6 31 ♕e2!

31 ♕d7 would also have won, but White wishes to deny his opponent any chances at all.

31...♕g5

This leads to the loss of the queen, but Black's position was already indefensible.

Thus after 31...♕e6 32 ♕e4 ♕g6 White has a pleasant choice between 33 ♖e3 ♘d8 34 ♖d5 ♗xd5 35 cxd5, and the sharper 33 ♖d7! ♗c8 34 e6 ♗xd7 (34...♕xe6 35 ♘e7+) 35 exd7 ♘g7 (or 35...♘c7) 36 ♘h4!

32 h4 ♕f4 33 g3

The queen is trapped: after **33...♕xe5 34 ♕g4+ ♕g7 35 ♘xg7** and a few further unnecessary moves, **Black resigned**.

Far-advanced pawns can also play a part in the endgame, if the pursuit of the king continues. They may take away squares from the enemy king and create a mating net.

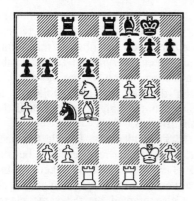

Tseshkovsky-Polugayevsky
Riga Interzonal 1979

Here the struggle has largely lost its sharpness. White has the advantage, but it becomes decisive only after Black underestimates the strength of the f5/g5 pawn pair and... the always potential weakness of his back rank.

25...罝e2+? 26 罝f2 罝xf2+ 27 曾xf2 匂xb2 28 奧xb2 罝xc2+ 29 曾e3 罝xb2

And so, Black is two pawns up, but the very next move is essentially the last one in the game.

30 罝c1!

M.T. Strictly speaking, the exclamation mark should have been attached much earlier, to White's entire plan. At the least, to his move 25 匂d5.

I.D. What was the mechanism of Black's mistake?

M.T. I think, the absence of the queens from the board. With the

queens on, even a player of a much more modest standard than grandmaster Polugayevsky would have kept his eyes on the white pawn pair, the strength of which is evident. But after the exchange of queens, even a top-class grandmaster can exclude this factor from his attention.

30...罝b3+ 31 曾e2 罝b2+ 32 曾e1 f6 33 g6

On 32...g6 there would of course have followed 33 f6.

33...罝a2 34 罝c8 罝a1+ 35 曾d2 罝a2+ 36 曾d3 罝a3+ 37 曾c2 罝a2+ 38 曾c3

Now the rook can even be allowed onto the e-file: 38...罝e2 39 匂f4 (with gain of tempo) and then 匂e6.

38...hxg6 39 匂e7+ 曾h7

It would be good to play 39...曾f7 40 匂xg6 奧e7, and if 41 罝c7 罝e2, but alas — 41 匂h8 mate!

40 fxg6+ 曾h6 41 罝xf8 罝e2

Black would have lost even more quickly after 41...罝xa4 42 h4 曾h5 43 罝h8+ 曾g4 44 h5 and then h5-h6. However, in the game itself White required only 10 more moves to realise his advantage.

In the next diagram there appears to be no sign of an impending tragedy. But when Black went in for this position, he overlooked the fact that the f5 pawn was too close to his king. True, for the moment it is alone...

28 奧xc6! 匂xc6 29 罝xb6 曾xb6 30 曾c4+ 曾h8 31 曾f7

The pawn has received "reinforcement" in the form of the queen, and in addition 32 奧f8 is threatened. Blocking the bishop's diagonal (by 31...匂b4) does not succeed: 32 f6 罝g8

33 fxg7+ ♖xg7 34 ♕f8+ and 35 ♕xb4.

Yusupov-A.Sokolov
55th USSR Ch., Moscow 1988

31...♖g8 32 f6 ♕d8 33 ♗e7 ♘xe7 34 fxe7

The white pawn has moved away from the king, but only in order to become a queen. This cannot be prevented.

34...♕d7 35 ♖d3 h6 36 ♖f3! ♖c8 37 ♕f8+ ♔h7 38 ♖f7 ♖c1+ 39 ♔g2 ♕c6+ 40 ♔h3 ♕e6+ 41 ♔h4 Black resigns.

Tal-Mohrlok
Varna Olympiad 1962
Sicilian Defence

1	e4	c5
2	♘f3	♘c6
3	d4	cxd4
4	♘xd4	♘f6
5	♘c3	d6
6	♗g5	e6
7	♕d2	♗e7
8	0-0-0	0-0

9	♘b3	♕b6
10	f3	a6
11	g4	♖d8
12	♗e3	♕c7
13	g5	♘d7
14	h4	b5
15	g6	

This pawn sacrifice is a fairly routine one, since it is obvious that White needs open lines for an attack on the black king, which for the moment has been deserted by its "subjects", in particular the knight from f6 and the rook from f8.

M.T. Incidentally, I made this sacrifice on two earlier occasions, but the game with Mohrlok is taken as the main one, for the reason that after it no one else granted me the same pleasure...

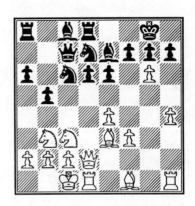

15 ...   fxg6

This was how the problem of the "impudent" pawn was solved by Boleslavsky in a game with Spassky (25th USSR Championship, Riga 1958). In a training game Tal-Koblenz (also in Riga, but a year earlier) Black eliminated the presumptuous infantryman in a different way: 15...hxg6.

M.T. I cannot deny myself the pleasure of giving the attack and combination that followed: 16 h5 gxh5 17 ♖xh5 ♘f6 18 ♖h1 d5 19 e5! ♘xe5 (19...♕xe5? 20 ♗f4 ♕f5 21 ♗d3 ♘e4 22 fxe4 and 23 ♕h2) 20 ♗f4 ♗d6 21 ♕h2 ♔f8 22 ♕h8+ ♘g8 23 ♖h7 f5 24 ♗h6 ♖d7 25 ♗xb5! ♖f7 (if 25...axb5 26 ♘xb5, 27 ♘xd6 and 28 ♗xg7+) 26 ♖g1 ♖a7 27 ♘d4 ♘g4 28 fxg4 ♗e5 29 ♘c6! ♗xc3 30 ♗e3! (with the threat of 31 ♗c5+) 30...d4 31 ♖gh1! (threatening 32 ♕xg8+) 31...♖d7 32 ♗g5 axb5 33 ♖1h6!, and against the concluding stroke 34 ♖f6+ there is no defence.

Finally, in a telegraph game Tal-Stoltz, 1959, in the diagram position Black declined the gift, and attempted in search of counterplay to strengthen his piece pressure on the queenside: 15...♘c5. But he too came under an attack — 16 gxf7+ ♔xf7 17 ♗h3! (aiming at the weak e6 pawn) 17...♘a4 18 f4 ♘b4 19 f5 e5 (it turns out that 19...♘xc3 20 bxc3 ♘xa2+ 21 ♔b2 is not possible) 20 ♘xa4! (White is not tempted by the win of the exchange — 20 ♘d5 ♖xd5 21 ♕xd5+ ♔f8 22 ♕xa8 ♗b7 23 ♕a7 ♖a8 24 ♘d4 exd4 25 ♕xd4, since then Black gains counterplay: 25...♗f6 26 ♕xd6+ ♕xd6 27 ♖xd6 ♗xb2+ 28 ♔b1 ♗xe4) 20...♘xa2+ 21 ♔b1 bxa4 22 ♘a5 ♖b8 (the sharpening of the play seems to be not unfavourable for Black, since if 23 ♔xa2 he has 23...♖b5, but...) 23 ♕d5+! ♔f8 24 ♔xa2 ♕xc2 (or 24...♖b5 25 ♕c6 ♕xa5 26 f6) 25 ♖d2! ♖xb2+ 26 ♔a1 ♕c3 27 ♕d3!, and Black resigned.

16	h5	gxh5
17	♖xh5	♘f6
18	♖g5	♘e5
19	♕g2	♗f8
20	♗e2	♘c4
21	♗xc4	bxc4
22	♘d4	♖b8
23	♖h1	♖b7
24	♖h6!	

A difficult move. On 24...g6 White had prepared 25 ♖hxg6+ hxg6 26 ♖xg6+ ♔f7 27 ♕g5 ♘h7 28 ♕h5 ♘f6 29 ♖xf6+ ♔xf6 30 ♘f5!!, and against the threat of ♗g5+ there is no defence.

24	...	♔f7
25	♖h4	♕b6
26	♘d1	♕c7
27	f4	h6
28	♖g6	♖e8
29	f5	e5
30	♘c3!	

Threatening 31 ♖xf6+.

30	...	♕d8
31	♘c6	**Black resigns**

Torbergsson-Tal
Reykjavik 1964
King's Indian Defence

1	d4	♘f6
2	c4	g6
3	♘c3	♗g7
4	e4	0-0
5	f4	d6
6	♘f3	c5
7	d5	e6
8	♗e2	exd5
9	exd5	b5!?
10	♘xb5	

If 10 cxb5, Black would have continued 10...a6, in analogy with the Benko Gambit.

10	...	♘e4
11	0-0	a6
12	♘a3	

This then is the idea of Black's sac-rifice! The knight at a3 occupies a most unfavourable position, and Black has time to concentrate his forces in the centre. Perhaps White should have returned the pawn with 12 ♘c3.

12	...	♖a7!

Black finds a "clear road" to trans-fer his rook to the centre.

13	♗d3	♖e7
14	♘c2	♖fe8
15	♖e1	

It is now clear that White has diffi-culties in developing his queenside.

15	...	♘d7
16	♘e3	♘df6
17	♕c2	♘h5

White has not found the best plan, and is already obliged to parry con-crete threats.

18	g3

. This move is a success... for Black. But 18 ♘f1 would have been very strongly answered by 18...♘g5!

18	...	♗d4
19	♘xd4	cxd4
20	♘g2	♘g5!
21	♖xe7	♘h3+
22	♔f1	

If 22 ♔h1 Black has 22...♕xe7 23 ♗d2 ♘f6 24 ♖e1 ♘g4.

22	...	♖xe7

The natural 22...♕xe7 after 23 ♗d2 would have given White a tempo for the defence - 24 ♖e1.

23	♗d2	♘f6
24	♘h4	

24 ♖e1 is decisively met by 24... ♘g4 25 ♖xe7 ♕xe7! 26 ♘h4 ♘e3+.

24	...	♘g4
25	♘f3	

On 25 ♔g2 Black had prepared the following variation: 25...♕e8 26 f5 ♖e2+ 27 ♗xe2 ♕xe2+ 28 ♔xh3 h5 29 ♖h1 ♘f2+ 30 ♔g2 ♘xh1+.

25	...	♖e3
26	♔g2	♕e7
27	♖e1	

M.T. Here Black could have carried out two interesting combinations. I spent a long time considering 27... ♖xe1 28 ♘xe1 ♗f5 29 ♘f3 ♕e3 30 ♗xe3 ♘xe3+ 31 ♔h1 ♗xd3! 32 ♕d2 ♗e4 33 ♕e2 g5 34 g4 h5, and wins. Unfortunately, the combination is not forced. After 29 ♕d1 I could not see any way to win, and so I chose the second possibility.

27	...	♘xf4+!
28	gxf4	♖xe1
29	♘xe1	♕h4
30	♗c1	

Obviously the only move.

30	...	♕xe1
31	h3	

This loses very quickly, but even after the superior 31 f5 ♘e5 Black has an irresistible attack.

31	...	♞h6!
32	f5	♞xf5
33	♗f4	

Now comes the concluding combination.

33	...	♞h4+
34	♔h2	♞f3+
35	♔g2	♗xh3+!
36	♔xf3	

36 ♔xh3 loses to 36...♛h4+ and 37...♞e1+.

| 36 | ... | ♛g1! |

With the threat of 37...♗g4+ 38 ♔e4 f5 mate. If 37 ♗h6, then 37...♗g4+ 38 ♔f4 ♗h5 is decisive.

37	♗xg6	♛g4+
38	♔f2	♛xf4+
39	♔g1	hxg6

White resigns

Tal-Donner
Beverwijk 1968
French Defence

1	e4	e6
2	d4	d5
3	♞c3	♗b4
4	e5	c5
5	a3	♗xc3+
6	bxc3	♛c7
7	♞f3	b6
8	a4	♗a6
9	♗xa6	♞xa6
10	♛e2	♞b8

In solving the problem of his "French" bishop, Black is forced to pay for it in terms of tempi. Thus the knight is obliged to return home, since on 10...cxd4 there would have followed 11 ♛b5+ ♔d8 (or 11...♔f8 12 ♗a3+ ♞e7 13 ♛xa6 ♛xc3+ 14 ♔e2 ♛xc2+ 15 ♞d2 and 16 ♖hc1) 12 ♛xa6 ♛xc3+ 13 ♔e2, and 13...♛xa1 is not possible in view of the bishop check at g5. But since the black pieces have retreated to their initial positions, White needs to open as many files and diagonals as possible for the attack.

| 11 | a5! | bxa5 |

If 11...cxd4 12 0-0!, and White achieves his aim. Nevertheless 11...♞d7 was more circumspect, but Black had not anticipated his opponent's 14th move.

| 12 | ♗a3 | ♞d7 |

Perhaps Black should have given up a pawn to gain a tempo — 12...♞e7 13 ♗xc5 ♞d7.

| 13 | dxc5 | ♞e7 |
| 14 | c6! | |

A consistent continuation of the same tactics.

14	...	♛xc6
15	0-0	♛xc3
16	♖fd1	♞c6

First 16...♛c4 was rather more accurate. But Black wants with gain of tempo (the e5 pawn!) to reposition his knights, such that they block the open files on the queenside.

17	♗d6	♛c4
18	♛e3	♛e4
19	♛b3	♞b6
20	c4!	

M.T. The white rooks need the c-file! Hence this new intuitive sacrifice of what is now a third pawn. Moreover, in my calculations I established that neither 20...♞xc4 21 ♛b7, nor 20...dxc4 21 ♛b5 ♖c8 22 ♖xa5 is possible. The counterattacking attempt 20...a4 is parried by 21 ♖xa4! (21 ♛b5? ♛xc4) 22...dxc4 22 ♛xb6!

axb6 23 罝xa8+ ♞d8 24 罝c8, when there is no defence against 25 ♗c7 or 25 罝c7.

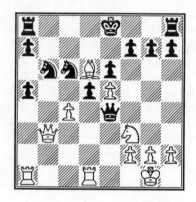

20	...	營xc4
21	營a3	營a6
22	罝ac1	罝c8
23	♞d2!	

Aiming for c5.

| 23 | ... | f6 |

After the game 23...♞d4 was suggested, and if 24 罝xc8+ 營xc8 25 營xa5 營d7, but White can play more elegantly and strongly: 24 ♚h1! ♞f5 25 罝xc8+ 營xc8 26 罝c1 營d8 27 ♗c5 f6 28 營xa5 fxe5 29 營xa7 ♞d7 30 ♗a3 ♞e7 31 罝c7, when the threats of 32 ♞f3 and 32 ♞b3 are irresistible.

| 24 | exf6 | gxf6 |
| 25 | 營f3 | ♚d7 |

25...♚f7 is insufficient on account of 26 營h5+ ♚g7 27 罝c3, while if 25...♞d7 the following variation, while somewhat "cooperative", is not without its logic: 26 營g4 (with the threat of 27 營g7) 26...♚d8 27 營xe6 罝e8 28 營xd5 營e2 29 ♞c4 營e6 30 ♞xa5 營xd5 31 ♞b7 mate.

| 26 | 營xf6 | 罝he8 |

Or 26...♚xd6 27 ♞e4+ ♚c7 28 ♞c5 營e2 29 營g7+ ♚d6 30 ♞b7 mate.

| 27 | ♞e4 | ♞e7 |

27...dxe4 28 營g7+ ♞e7 29 ♗xe7+ ♞d5 30 ♗f6+ leads to mate.

28	♞c5+	罝xc5
29	♗xc5	♞c4
30	♗xe7	

Black resigns: 30...罝xe7 31 罝xd5+.

WHAT WOULD YOU HAVE PLAYED?

No.12

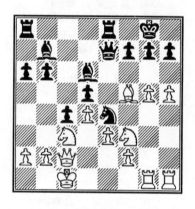

In this position from our classical heritage, reckoning that after 18 h6 Black would block the position by 18...g6, and after 18 g6 by 18...fxg6 19 hxg6 h6, White began the concluding attack with **18 ♗xh7+ ♚xh7 19 g6+ ♚g8 20 ♞xe4 dxe4 21 h6! f6** (or 21...exf3 22 gxf7+ 營xf7 23 hxg7) **22 hxg7 exf3 23 罝h8+ ♚xg7 24 罝h7+,** and soon won. We will say straight away — a possible solution. But is it obligatory?

No.13

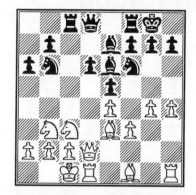

White carried out a similar plan in this position: **13 h5! ♞c4 14 ♝xc4 ♜xc4 15 g5 ♞d7 16 ♜dg1 ♛c7 17 g6 ♜c8**. How can Black's defences be further broken up? (After all, he himself has prepared counterplay with 18...♜xc3.)

No.14

The impression is that on the kingside Black has been playing not chess, but draughts (checkers). At any event, the pawn formation here resembles the jaw of an old man, who not once in his life has been to the dentist. Naturally, the light squares have already been occupied by the white pieces. But what next?

No.15

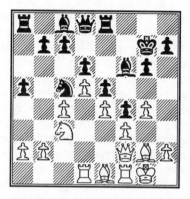

For the moment Black has managed to forestall the opponent's activity on the queenside and to gain the initiative on the kingside, as, however, often happens in the fianchetto variation of the King's Indian Defence. But now White is threatening by 21 h4 to block all the lines here, and then to begin play on the opposite side of the board, where he is stronger. And after 20...h5 21 gxh5 gxh5 22 ♔h1 there is no possibility of Black creating an attack on the g-file...

5 Lines of Communication

IT IS ON HOW THE PIECES behave on the communication lines — files and diagonals — that the success or failure of an attack depends. There is nothing surprising about this: for 200 years no one has cast doubts on Napoleon's aphorism: "War is communications". How to clear and use them was the subject of the previous chapter. But for victory this is sometimes not enough. Not only to give your own pieces scope, but to close lines to the opponent's men: this is the task of any player who sits down at the chess board. Intuitively everyone senses this, but strangely enough, in practice such attacking procedures and plans are not regularly encountered. Evidently our subconsciousness needs to be reinforced by consciousness, based on knowledge — and then your opponent's pieces will often be too late in reaching the decisive part of the battlefield. Too late, because of you!

The Barrier

In the theory of chess this is a new concept. The authors define it in the first instance as a non-material barrier, through which either one piece, or a whole group of pieces, is unable to pass. In short, it is a communication line under close-range fire, and the creation of one is usually a basis for future success.

It was this motif that prompted White's decision in the following game, the final one of the match.

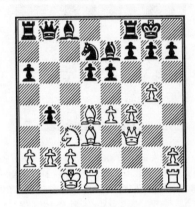

Tal-Larsen
Candidates Semi-Final, Bled 1965

16 ♘d5! exd5 17 exd5
The piece sacrifice is a positional one, since it has been used to erect an invisible barrier on the e-file. A number of squares on it (e5, e6) are controlled by white pawns, and a white rook will soon be moved to e1. By contrast, Black's pieces (queen, rook, bishop and to some extent his knight) are bunched together on the queenside and cannot easily come to the aid of their king. Now White is threatening the routine combination with bishop sacrifices at h7 and g7, against which Black cannot defend without making positional concessions. If 17...g6 White can continue his attack either by 18 h4, or the more active 18 ♕h3! So Larsen aims to cover his h7 with the other pawn.

17...f5

But now White's dark-square bishop is too strong.

18 ♖de1

Here Black has an unpleasant choice: he can either defend the bishop with his rook from f7, but this will then allow the white pawns to open up the kingside with gain of tempo (g5-g6!), or else move yet another piece away from the kingside. On 18...♗d8 the following very curious variation was possible: 19 ♕h5 ♘c5 20 ♗xg7! ♘xd3+ 21 ♔b1 (not 21 cxd3? ♕c7+) 21...♘xe1 (21...♘xf4 22 ♕h6) 22 g6 ♔xg7 23 ♕xh7+ ♔f6 24 g7 ♖f7 25 g8=♘ mate!

18...♖f7 19 h4 ♗b7 20 ♗xf5

M.T. But this can be attributed to competitive considerations. Had this position not been reached in the last game of the match, I would undoubtedly have played more sharply: 20 g6 hxg6 21 h5 g5 22 ♗xf5 (weaker is 22 h6 g4 23 hxg7 ♗f6, or 23...♘f6 24 ♖xe7 gxf3 25 ♗xf6 ♖xe7) with very dangerous threats. E.g., 22...♖xf5 23 ♖xe7 ♘e5 fails to 24 h6! ♘xf3 25 h7+ ♔f8 26 ♖xg7 with inevitable mate. But at this point I wanted to make absolutely sure, and at the board I was unable to find a forced win after 22...♗f6 23 ♗e6 ♕f8! (not 23...♗xd4 24 fxg5 and g5-g6). That there was a win, I was sure (just as I am sure now), but the experience of the preceding game warned me against spending time on the calculation of long, complicated variations — I might end up in time trouble, particularly since after the move made my position remains very favourable.

20...♖xf5

If 20...♘f8 White can simply intensify the pressure, by defending the bishop with his queen and renewing the still-present threat of ♗xh7+.

21 ♖xe7 ♘e5

After the passive 21...♖f7 Black is crushed by 22 ♖xf7 ♔xf7 23 g6+ hxg6 24 h5, when his king is completely exposed. The Danish grandmaster tries to seize the initiative by tactical means, but White is prepared for this.

22 ♕e4 ♕f8! 23 fxe5! ♖f4 24 ♕e3 ♖f3

After this move White wins without any great difficulty. The main variation of the combination begun with 20 ♗xf5 was 24...♗xd5 25 exd6 ♖xd4 (after 25...♗xh1 26 ♖xg7+ Black's scattered pieces are helpless) 26 ♕xd4! (weaker is 26 ♖e1 ♕f4!) 26...♗xh1 27 b3. Here Black probably does best to return the piece immediately by 27...♗f3 28 ♕c4+ ♔h8 29 ♖f7 ♕xd6 30 ♖xf3, with some chances of saving the game. The attempt to maintain his material advantage is hopeless — the white h-pawn, on reaching the 6th rank, lands the decisive blow. The exchange of rooks after 27...♖e8 also loses to 28 ♕e5 ♖xe7 29 dxe7 ♕e8 30 ♕e6+ ♔h8 31 h5 ♗f3 32 h6, or 31...♗c6 32 g6 with the irresistible threat of 33 ♕f7.

25 ♕e2 ♕xe7

No better is 25...♕f4+ 26 ♕d2 ♖f1+ 27 ♖xf1 ♕xf1+ 28 ♕d1, or 25...♗xd5 26 exd6.

26 ♕xf3 dxe5 27 ♖e1 ♖d8

The ending after 27...♖f8 28 ♖xe5 ♕xe5 29 ♕xf8+ ♔xf8 30 ♗xe5 gives

White an easy win — Black has no time to take on d5 in view of 31 ♗d6+.

28 ♖xe5 ♕d6 29 ♕f4!

With this simple bit of tactics (29... ♗xd5 30 ♖e8+) White keeps his two extra pawns. The finish is straight-forward.

29...♖f8 30 ♕e4 b3

There is nothing better.

31 axb3 ♖f1+ 32 ♔d2 ♕b4+ 33 c3 ♕d6 34 ♗c5!

Not altogether necessary (there were many ways to win), but an amusing concluding combination.

34...♕xc5 35 ♖e8+ ♖f8 36 ♕e6+ ♔h8 37 ♕f7 Black resigns.

A similar idea was carried out by White in the following game, with the "slight" difference that a real sacrifice proved unnecessary, and the barrier, cleaving Black's position, was erected not even for free, but with the win of a pawn...

Shishkin-Karasev
Leningrad 1989

13 ♘d5! ♕d8 14 ♘f5! exf5 15 ex-f5 ♔h8

The threat of ♖e4-h4 does not even leave Black time for 15...♖e8.

16 ♘xe7 ♗xg2 17 ♕h6!

The quickest way to win.

17...♘d7 18 ♘g6+ ♔g8

Alas, after 18...fxg6 19 fxg6 not one of Black's pieces is able to come to the aid of his king - partly on account of the barrier erected by White.

19 ♘xf8 ♕xf8 20 ♕xf8+ ♔xf8 21 ♔xg2, and **Black resigned**.

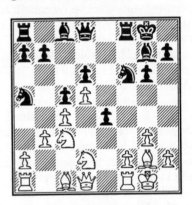

Geller-Velimirovic
Havana 1971

In this position the role of the bar-rier is partly played by the pawn chain a2/b3/c4/d5. It is practically keeping one black knight out of the game, but that is only part of the matter. White's plans include active play on the king-side, from which will be excluded the remaining black pieces, in particular the queen's rook. This is possible only if he can establish control over the "transit" square e7, from which the black queen could carry out the great-est number of functions — of defence and counterattack.

Hence the fantastic and unusually audacious plan — to sacrifice a rook! Instead of 14 ♗b2 e3 15 fxe3 ♘g4, for which Black was hoping, there came a clap of thunder.

14 ♘dxe4!! ♘xe4 15 ♘xe4 ♗xa1 16 ♗g5 ♗f6

Black cannot avoid the coming pin, since, if he moves his queen, the bishop at a1 is lost, and with material almost equal (a pawn for the exchange) White gains a powerful attack.

17 ♘xf6+ ♖xf6 18 ♕a1 ♔f7 19 ♖e1

Despite being a rook down, in the main thrust of the attack White has a superiority in force. It is difficult for Black to bring his queenside pieces into play, since simple developing moves do not work. For example, on 19...♗f5 or 19...♗d7 there follows 20 ♕c3! (with the threat of 21 ♗xf6 ♕xf6 22 ♕xa5) 20...b6 (the only defence) 21 ♖e6! and White wins, since the forced 21...♗xe6 leads to the opening of the long light-square diagonal — 22 dxe6+, and loss of material for Black.

19...♖b8

The alternative defence was 19...h6, but it would not have saved the game after the simple reply 20 ♗xh6. For example: 20...♗f5 21 ♗g5 ♖c8 22 g4 ♗xg4 23 ♖e4 ♗f5 24 ♖h4, or 20...♕h8 21 ♗g5 ♗d7 (if 21...♗f5 22 ♕c3 b6 23 ♖e6, whereas now in this variation Black has 23...♖f5) 22 ♖e4! ♖f5 (otherwise 23 ♗xf6 ♕xf6 24 ♖f4, while on 22...♖f8 there would have followed 23 ♖h4 ♕g7 24 ♗h6 ♕g8 25 ♗xf8 ♕xf8 26 ♖h7+ ♔e8 27 ♕e1+ ♔d8 28 ♕xa5+) 23 ♖e7+ ♔g8 24

♕xh8+ ♔xh8 25 ♗d2, with a decisive advantage.

20 ♖e3 b6

Defending the knight, which, as we have seen, was "hanging" in several variations. No better was 20...♗f5 21 h3! h5 22 g4 hxg4 23 hxg4 ♗xg4 24 ♖e4 ♗f5 (24...♗h5 25 ♖e6) 25 ♖h4.

21 ♖f3 ♗f5 22 g4 ♕h8 23 ♗xf6

The simplest solution: White transposes into a won ending. 23 ♗h3 is not altogether clear in view of 23...♖g8.

23...♕xf6 24 ♕xf6+ ♔xf6 25 gxf5 gxf5 26 ♖e3

An important link in the plan for realising White's advantage. The frontal attack on the f5 pawn, 26 ♗h3, would have allowed Black to maintain equality: 26...♖g8+ 27 ♔f1 ♖g5. But now the white rook penetrates into the heart of Black's position.

26...♘b7 27 ♖e6+ ♔f7 28 ♗f3

The threat of a bishop check at h5 finally disrupts the coordination of the black pieces.

28...♖g8+ 29 ♔f1 ♔f8

Black cannot hold the h5 square: 29...♖g5 30 h4.

30 ♗h5 ♖g5 31 ♖e8+ ♔g7 32 ♖e7+ ♔h6 33 ♖xb7 ♖xh5 34 ♖xa7 ♖xh2 35 ♖d7, and White won easily in the rook ending.

Interference

Closely approaching the "barrier" theme, first formulated here, as an effective attacking procedure, is so-called "interference" — a purely tactical blow, which also has the aim of cutting off the opponent's forces from the defence of some key or simply important point. But whereas the barrier is lowered for a long time and acts rather as part of a strategic plan, interference is instantaneous and operates immediately.

Klovans-Tolush
Leningrad 1962

Only the black queen is guarding the mating point g7, and the interference move **37 ♖c7!** is immediately decisive: if 37...♗xc7 38 ♕d4+, forcing mate.

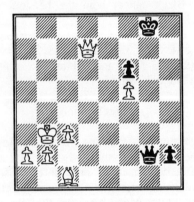

Simagin-Bronstein
Moscow 1947

Must White force perpetual check? The answer would have been yes, had he not noticed the thunderous **51 ♗g5!**, when Black must either go into a lost queen ending after 51...♕xg5 (if 51...fxg5 52 f6, forcing mate) 52 ♕d8+ ♔g7 53 ♕c7+ and 54 ♕xh2, or else accept the fact that both(!) his queens are cut off from the king's residence. He preferred the latter: **51... h1=♕**, and after **52 ♕e8+ ♔g7 53 ♕g6+ ♔f8 54 ♕xf6+ ♔g8 55 ♕d8+ ♔g7 56 ♕e7+ ♔g8 57 ♕e8+ Black resigned** in view of mate in three.

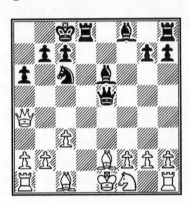

A.Petrosian-Panchenko
Odessa 1973

After incorrectly accepting a pawn sacrifice in the opening, White is markedly behind in development. True, he has no weaknesses, and at first sight it is not clear how Black can approach the white king still in the centre.

The solution to the problem lies in a far from obvious interference move.

14...♗b4!!

The threat of 15...♗xc3 leaves White no time for 15 ♘g3, and after his forced reply his queen loses control of the 4th rank, from which the assault on his king intensifies.

15 cxb4 ♗c4 16 ♘g3

After 16 ♘e3 ♗xe2 17 ♔xe2 ♘d4+ White loses the right to castle, and he is left with simply nothing to move (18 ♔e1 ♖he8, with the threats of 19...♕h5 20 ♕d1 ♕xd1+ or 19...♕e4). But now he hopes, by returning the material, to take his king to safety.

16...♗b5! 17 ♕a3

Otherwise the black knight comes into play with gain of tempo.

17...♖d3! 18 ♗f4 ♕e6 19 b3

And once again the queen's path to the centre of the battle is blocked.

19...♖xg3 20 0-0 ♖xg2+ 21 ♔xg2 ♗xe2 22 f3

In parrying the deadly check at g4, White is prepared to part with his gains, but for Black this is not enough.

22...♖f8 23 ♗g3 ♕e3 24 ♕c1 (24 ♖f2 ♘d4) 24...♗xf3+ 25 ♖xf3 ♕xf3+ 26 ♔g1 ♖e8, and with a continuing attack Black now has a material advantage. He soon won.

It was this attacking procedure that was at the basis of a deeply-calculated variation in the following game.

M.T. To be honest, I recalled it with pleasure during the illustrative game that we selected for this chapter.

Botvinnik himself admitted that he went in for this position, assuming that after 22 axb3 ♖b7 Black would not have any serious difficulties.

22 ♖d1!

In this somewhat paradoxical way White ensures the invasion of his rook onto the 8th rank. But it would not have brought any dividends, had he not

had "in reserve" his murderous 25th move...

Ragozin-Botvinnik
Moscow 1945

22...♖a8

Bad is 22...♖b7 23 ♖d8+ ♔h7 24 ♗d3+ f5 25 ♖xc8 ♘d4 26 ♗a6, when Black can resign; 22...♘c1 loses to 23 ♖d8+ ♔h7 24 ♗d3+ ♘xd3 25 ♗xb8.

23 ♖d8+ ♗f8

This leads to a mortal pin on the 8th rank, but there is no choice. If 23...♔h7 24 ♗d3+ g6 25 cxb3! (after 25 ♗e5 ♗b7 26 ♖d7 ♘c5 27 ♖xf7+ ♔g8 28 ♗c4 ♗a6! or 28 ♗xg6 ♖d8! 29 h4 ♖d1+ 30 ♔h2 ♘d7 Black holds on) 25...♗b7 26 ♗b8 a5 27 a4, with the threat of 28 ♗c4. If Black tries to free himself by tactics: 27...♗c3 (threatening 28...♗e5, and if 28 ♖e8 ♗d4, threatening 29...♗a7), then 28 ♗c7, and after 28...♖xd8 29 ♗xd8 ♔g7 30 f3 White would appear to have a decisive advantage in the endgame, in view of Black's weak queenside pawns.

24 axb3(?)

Here this "automatic" capture

"towards the centre" is a serious inaccuracy, spoiling a splendid idea.

24...♗b7

So, is the activity of the white rook curtailed? After all, it cannot be kept on the 7th rank after 25 ♖d7 ♗c8.

25 ♗b8!

The crux of White's plan. On the main part of the battlefield he retains an advantage in force.

25...a5 26 f3

Alas, after the correct 24 cxb3 White could now have stalemated the black pieces by 26 a4!, when equally bad for Black are 26...♗a6 27 ♗xa6 ♖xa6 28 ♗d6, and 26...c5 27 ♗c7, winning the a5 pawn, and 26...g6 27 ♗c4 ♔g7 28 ♗e5+ and 29 ♖d7. True, he still retains an advantage.

26...a4 27 bxa4 ♖xa4 28 ♔f2 (28 ♗d6 ♖a8) **28...c5 29 ♔e3 ♗c6 30 ♗d3 ♖a8**, and now, by continuing 31 ♗e4!, White could well have hoped to win, e.g. 31...♖a3+ 32 ♔f4 g5+ 33 ♔e5 ♗xe4 34 ♔xe4 ♖a6 35 ♔d5, threatening the thematic 36 ♗d6.

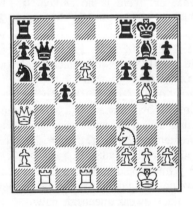

Kasparov-Pribyl
Skara 1980

After the quiet 20 ♗f4 White would have retained sufficient compensation for the pawn. But with a piece sacrifice he excludes the enemy queen from the defence of the weakened kingside, thereby gaining the opportunity to mount an attack with superior forces.

20 d7! fxg5 21 ♕c4+ ♔h8 22 ♘xg5 ♗f6

A weighty argument in favour of White's entire plan would have been 22...♗d4 23 ♖xd4! cxd4 24 ♕xd4+ ♔g8 25 ♘e6.

23 ♘e6 ♘c7

There is nothing else: if 23...♘b4 24 ♕f4 ♘c6 25 ♘xf8 ♖xf8 26 d8=♕ ♘xd8 27 ♖xd8.

24 ♘xf8 ♖xf8 25 ♖d6 ♗e7 26 d8=♕!

Seemingly paradoxical, but consistent and strong. Now d7 is needed for the attack along the 7th rank, and the black queen is still out of play.

26...♗xd8

Or 26...♖xd8 27 ♖xd8+ ♗xd8 28 ♕f7 ♕d5 (defending against the mate at f8) 29 ♕xd5 ♘xd5 30 ♖d1, and White wins.

27 ♕c3+ ♔g8 28 ♖d7 ♗f6 29 ♕c4+ ♔h8 30 ♕f4

The piece is regained, and the ending after 30...♗g7 31 ♕xc7 ♕xc7 32 ♖xc7 ♗d4 33 ♖f1 must be won for White. But...

30...♕a6? 31 ♕h6 Black resigns.

Obstruction

There is also another typical "mine", or more precisely, a typical barricade, that can be erected in the path of the enemy forces: the well known obstructive sacrifice. If a game takes a normal, even course, to gain a lead in development, giving the basis for an attack, is difficult, if at all possible. One has to resort to radical measures, which nevertheless follow a common pattern. This is normally a pawn sacrifice, that in one way or another disrupts the quiet course of the game.

The effectiveness of such a procedure — given an inadequate counter to it — is seen in the following example.

Spielmann-Landau
Amsterdam 1933

1 e4 ♘f6 2 ♘c3 d5?! (not the best reaction to White's move) 3 e5 ♘fd7 (after 3...♘g8 Black is very far behind in development) 4 e6! fxe6 5 d4 ♘f6? 6 ♘f3 c5 7 dxc5 ♘c6 8 ♗b5 ♗d7 9 0-0 ♕c7 10 ♖e1 h6 11 ♗xc6 bxc6 12 ♘e5, and White won quite easily.

An excellent illustration is provided by the following game.

Kasparov-Andersson
Tilburg 1981

At this point Black was happy with his position. He plans ...d5, after which his backward c-pawn will be weak only nominally, rather than in actual fact. In addition, the wretched white bishop at b2 will provide compensation.

The evaluation is changed by an obstructive sacrifice planned in advance by White.

14 d5! exd5 15 ♗g2

Now it is very difficult for Black to develop his kingside, and strategically the outcome of the game is already decided. A rare case of such an instant return from this type of sacrifice.

15...c6 16 0-0 f6

Black begins artificial castling, but this entails weakening a whole complex of light squares on the kingside, which spells disaster. White merely has to open lines for his rooks with e3-e4.

17 ♖e1!

A useful preparation. The immediate 17 e4 dxe4 18 ♗xe4 ♗f7! would have enabled Black to "plug" the light-square holes for the time being, although even so after 19 ♕g4 it is hard to offer any good advice.

17...♗e7 18 ♕g4 ♔f7 19 h5 ♗h7 20 e4 dxe4 21 ♗xe4 ♗xe4 22 ♘xe4 ♘c8

The aim of this seemingly strange manoeuvre is to defend the f5 square after ...d5 and ...♘d6. The need for this is apparent in the variation 22...♖e8 23 ♕g6+ ♔f8 24 g4, when against the threat of ♘g3-f5 there is no defence. And the natural continuation of the artificial castling manoeuvre, 22...♖f8, runs into 23 ♖ad1 (provoking a weakening of e6) 23...d5 24 ♘xf6!, mating.

23 罝ad1 罝a7 24 ②xf6!

Another typical sacrifice with this type of pawn structure: the king is deprived of its shelter.

24...gxf6

It all ends even more quickly after 24...奧xf6 25 瞥g6+ 當f8 26 奧xf6 gxf6 27 罝e6.

25 瞥g6+ 當f8 26 奧c1 d5 27 罝d4!

This is more accurate than the immediate 27 奧xh6+ 罝xh6 28 瞥xh6+ 當g8 29 罝d4 奧f8 30 罝g4+ 罝g7 31 罝xg7+ 奧xg7 32 瞥g6 ②e7, when for the moment Black can hold on.

27...②d6 28 罝g4 ②f7 29 奧xh6+ 當e8 30 奧g7 Black resigns.

For the h-pawn he has to give up his rook, and, what's more, immediately.

Here we see a similar idea:

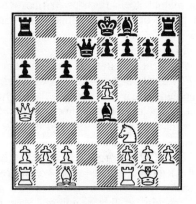

Keres-Schmid
Bamberg 1968

Seemingly, Black's bishop pair and sound pawn centre should allow him to face the future with confidence, but White finds an interesting possibility of increasing his lead in development.

12 e6!

An excellent sacrifice, obstructing the development of Black's kingside.

12...瞥xe6

Totally cheerless is 12...fxe6 13 ②e5, and wherever the queen moves to (13...瞥d6 14 奧f4), White, relying on his powerful piece deployment, creates very strong pressure.

13 ②g5 瞥g6

After 13...瞥d7 14 ②xe4 dxe4 15 瞥xe4 Black's queenside is broken up, but even so this looks the lesser evil.

14 ②xe4 dxe4 15 奧f4 f5 16 瞥c4!

Rather than the tempting 16 瞥b3, with the threat of 17 瞥b7, White prefers the consistent obstruction of the enemy forces: again 16...e6 is not possible. meanwhile, his plans include doubling rooks on the open d-file, adjacent to the black king.

16...c5

Opening a retreat for the queen; Black has no objection to 17 瞥xc5 瞥e6 followed by ...當f7 and ...g6.

17 罝ad1 瞥c6 18 f3

An extra file for the attack will do no harm, although 18 罝d2 is also sufficient, threatening after the doubling of rooks to invade Black's position.

18...h6

Alas, here too the "normal" 18...e6 runs into 19 罝d6! 奧xd6 20 瞥xe6+ 當d8 21 罝d1, and Black can resign.

19 fxe4

19 罝fe1 looks even stronger, and if 19...exf3 20 罝e5 with decisive threats.

19...瞥xe4 20 瞥xc5 e6 21 瞥c7 奧e7 22 罝d7! 奧d8 23 罝xd8+ 罝xd8 24 瞥xg7

Black's position has collapsed, and since 24...瞥d4+ 25 瞥xd4 罝xd4 fails to 26 奧e5, it is essentially all over.

24...♖f8 25 ♗xh6 ♕d4+

There is nothing else: 25...♖f7 26 ♕g8+ ♔e7 27 ♗g5+.

26 ♕xd4 ♖xd4 27 c3!

A precise little move: for the moment the d2 square is under control.

27...♖d6 28 ♗xf8 ♔xf8 29 ♖e1, and White realised his great material advantage.

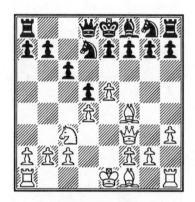

Kasparov-Lutikov
Minsk 1978

White has a lead in development, but under the cover of his central pawn chain Black hopes gradually to neutralise it. Therefore White's obstructive sacrifice is more than justified.

9 e6! fxe6 10 ♗d3 ♘gf6 11 ♕e2 g6 12 ♕xe6 ♗g7 13 0-0

"The opponent's defences will not be cracked by crude pressure down the e-file; operations on one of the flanks are also required. I already had in mind the general idea of a pawn offensive on the queenside, and so I decided to hide my king away on the opposite wing" (Kasparov). But queenside castling followed by the advance of the g- and f-pawns was also possible.

13...♘h5 14 ♗g5 ♘f8

Preparing to take the king to its "usual" place. After 14...♗xd4 15 ♖fe1 ♗f6 16 ♗xf6 ♘hxf6 17 ♘a4 intending c2-c4 White has good play.

15 ♕g4 ♘f6 16 ♕e2 ♕d6 17 ♖ae1

Planning to open up the game by f2-f4-f5.

17...e6 18 ♘a4 ♔f7 19 b4 b6

White has too many threats after 19...♕xb4 20 ♘c5.

20 ♕d2 ♖e8 21 ♗f4 ♕e7 22 b5 ♕a3 23 ♘c3 c5 24 ♘b1! ♕a4 25 dxc5 bxc5 26 c4!, and since after 26...d4 the black queen remains out of play, the opening of the centre is inevitable and White's unhurried attack continues. It was begun, as you will recall, by the obstructive pawn sacrifice.

In order to seal the opponent's forces in their initial positions, more generous offers can be made, as in the following game. True, here the obstructive sacrifice also plays the role of a powerful pawn outpost.

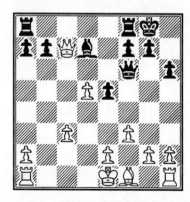

Beylin-Lipnitsky
Yurmala 1950

15...e4!

And immediately it becomes clear that White's extra pawn, his passed pawn in the centre, and his attack on the black bishop do not compensate for his lack of development. For the moment, the sacrifice is not a real one: the threat of 16...罝ac8 does not leave White time for anything, apart from

16 罝c1 罝ac8!

Nevertheless!

17 豃xd7 e3!

The apotheosis of Black's idea. First, the opponent is now playing without his kingside pieces, and second, the white king is almost encircled.

18 豃a4

Further "pawn-grabbing" — 18 豃xb7 — is punished by 18...罝xc3 19 豃b2 罝fc8 20 罝xc3 罝xc3 21 g3 罝b3!!

18...罝xc3 19 罝d1 罝fc8 20 g3 罝c1 21 奡h3 罝xd1+ 22 豃xd1 豃c3+ 23 奡f1 豃d2! 24 奡g2

I.D. I asked Mikhail Beylin, who was playing White, whether he felt reassured at this point, and received a reply in the affirmative...

M.T. Really? Black's concluding blow is not so complicated, although this does not make it any less pretty. Besides, Black clearly must have anticipated it six or seven moves earlier.

24...罝c1!

White resigns, since after 25 豃xc1 豃xe2+ 26 奡g1 he is mated by 26...豃f2.

Even so, the obstructive sacrifice is usually of a more local nature, and usually prevents the king from being defended by the advance of one of the pawns sheltering it. The pawn is blockaded on the square where it

stands, and for this aim a long-range piece is usually used.

I.D. The first combination of my co-author to appear in print was of this type. Did you keep the cutting from the magazine?

M.T. No, but I liked it.

I.D. What exactly?

M.T. Both the combination, and its publication.

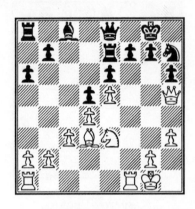

Tal-Leonov
Riga 1948

28 罝f6!

Now Black does not have the defensive advance 28...f5, and "in passing" the threat of 29 罝xh6 is created. At the same time, the rook is taboo: 28...gxf6 29 奡xh7+ 奡xh7 30 奡g4 豃f8 31 奡xf6+ 奡h8 32 罝f1, and against the manoeuvre 罝f4-g4 there is no satisfactory defence.

28...豃f8 29 罝f4 奡d7 (here 29...f5 no longer works on account of the immediate 30 g4) **30 奡g4!** (the pressure intensifies) **30...奡e8 31 奡f6+ 奡xf6 32 exf6 罝c7 33 fxg7 奡xg7 34 豃e5+ Black resigns.**

A similar and even more concrete situation developed in the next game.

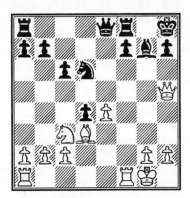

Fischer-Benko
USA Championship 1963/4

Black's h7 is weak, but the direct attack on it, 19 e5, is parried by 19...f5. Hence the natural — and only good — continuation of the attack.

19 ♖f6! ♚g8

After 19...♗xf6 20 e5 there is no defence against the mate.

20 e5 h6 21 ♘e2

A quiet reply, emphasising the hopelessness of Black's position. Against mate in a few moves there is no defence, and so **Black resigned**.

White had to conduct a much more complicated attack in the following game, but at its basis was the same device of obstruction.

Black is threatening most of the attacking pieces, but at the decisive moment he is unable to make a saving pawn move.

1 ♘xg7! ♚xg7

The gift cannot be declined: 1...♘cxd3 2 cxd3 ♘xd3 3 ♘h5, and

the threat of 4 ♗xd8 and 5 ♘f6+ is more than unpleasant.

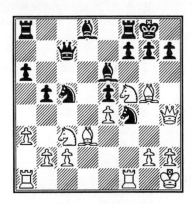

Ravinsky-Ilivitsky
Riga 1952

2 ♖xf4! exf4 3 ♕h6+ ♚g8 4 ♗f6!!

The black bishop is lured to f6, where it blocks the f7 pawn.

4...♗xf6 5 e5 ♘xd3 6 exf6

Black has avoided the mate at h7, but now there is a threat of mate at g7!

6...♘f2+ 7 ♚g1 ♘h3+ 8 ♚f1!

Capturing the knight would have allowed Black perpetual check.

8...♗c4+ 9 ♘e2 ♗xe2+ 10 ♚e1!

The checks are at an end, and so **Black resigned**.

Aronson-Tal
24th USSR Ch., Moscow 1957
Dutch Defence

I.D. Strictly speaking, the procedure examined in this chapter was employed here by Black in a counterattack, since at one point he simply overstepped the mark, and in general the famous "sense of danger" of the young, even very young Tal was still virtually in its embryo state...

M.T. Well, of what significance is this? Interference — it is the same, both in attack, and in counterattack.

1	d4	e6
2	c4	f5
3	♘f3	♘f6
4	♘c3	♗e7
5	g3	0-0
6	♗g2	d6
7	0-0	♕e8
8	♖e1	♕g6
9	e4	fxe4
10	♘xe4	♘xe4
11	♖xe4	♘c6

The unprotected state of the white rook is clearly illusory: after 11...♕xe4?? 12 ♘h4 the centralised black queen is trapped.

12	♕e2	♗f6
13	♗d2	e5

At just the right time: had he allowed the white bishop to go to c3, Black would have been cramped.

| 14 | dxe5 | dxe5?! |

Black deliberately weakens his position for the sake of complicating the play. The "normal" 14...♘xe5 15 ♗c3 ♘xf3+ 16 ♕xf3 ♗f5 17 ♖e3 and ♖b8 would have led to approximate equality and a more than probable draw.

M.T. But it wasn't for the sake of such tedium that Black moved onto "Dutch rails" from those of, say, the Orthodox Defence.

15	♗c3	♗f5
16	♘h4	♗xh4
17	♖xh4	♖ae8
18	b4!	

A natural and powerful reaction to Black's antipositional play. His pieces

have abandoned the queenside, and it is here that White begins his offensive.

18	...	♕f6
19	♕e3	h6

In search of tactical chances, associated with the one current drawback of White's position — the restricted position of his king's rook.

20	b5	♘d8
21	♗d5+?	

The simple 21 c5 would have seized a mass of space, opened a path for the rook along the 4th rank, and White's advantage would have grown markedly. But now the greater part of his advantage is lost, since his bishop at d5 is not only an attacker, but is also the target for a counterblow.

| 21 | ... | ♔h8 |

Of course, not 21...♔h7?, when after the exchange of bishops (22 ♗e4) Black's chances of counterplay would have been close to nil.

| 22 | f4? | |

Now the character of the position changes sharply, and the main role begins to be played by the dynamics of the pieces — and Black's are developed at least as well, and are better coordinated.

Of course, trying to win the exchange by 22 ♗b4? would also not have succeeded: 22...g5 23 ♗xf8 ♖xf8 24 ♖e4 c6 (here it is, the vulnerable position of the bishop at d5) 25 ♖xe5 cxd5, and the threat of 26...♘f7 leaves White no time for 26 cxd5.

But even so, 22 c5 would have retained for White slightly the more pleasant game after 22...c6 23 bxc6 ♘xc6 24 ♖e1.

| 22 | ... | exf4! |

23 ♕d2 ♕b6+!

By luring White's bishop to d4 and thereby weakening his control of e1, Black already has in mind the start of his counterattack.

24 ♗d4 ♕g6
25 ♕xf4

On 25 ♖xf4 Black would have continued simply 25...♘e6, but now this does not work in view of 26 ♖xh6+. In addition, the c7 pawn is attacked.

25 ... ♔h7
26 ♕xc7

This looks the logical continuation of his preceding play. Besides, 26 ♖f1 runs into 26...♗h3!, when the white king faces an unpleasant journey. But now too a surprise - the theme of this chapter - is awaiting him.

26 ... ♗b1!!

By shutting out the white rook from the defence of the back rank, Black ensures the invasion of his heavy pieces into the opponent's position.

27 ♗e5 ♘e6
28 ♕d6 ♕f5
29 ♗f4

White is even prepared to give up material — 29...g5 wins a piece, but Black prefers to continue his attack.

29 ... ♘g5
30 ♕b4 ♗e4

At last White's rook can come to the aid of his king, but it is too late: he loses one of his strong bishops, and all Black's pieces have already taken up attacking positions.

31 ♗xe4 ♖xe4
32 ♖f1 ♖e2
33 ♕d6

With a last hope of catching Black in a trap: 33...♘h3+?? 34 ♖xh3 ♕xh3 35 ♕d3+ and 36 ♕xe2.

33 ... ♖xa2

Of course, not in order to win a pawn, but to allow the queen onto the 2nd rank in front of the rook.

34 ♕d5 ♕c2
35 c5 ♖d8!!

A very fine move, but more important, an instructive one. The attacking side does not have the right even for a second to forget about the opponent's potential threats. Thus if here, instead of the text move, Black had played the "natural" 35...♖e8, with the threats of ...♖e2 or ...♖e1, White would have had available the winning 36 ♖xh6+!!, e.g. 36...gxh6 37 ♕d7+ ♔g6 38 ♕xe8+ ♔h7 39 ♕e7+! ♔g6 (or 39...♔g8) 40 ♗d2!

36 ♗d6 ♖e8

Now, when the bishop has stopped "looking at" the black king, this invasion of Black's third major piece decides the game in his favour.

White was "saved" from capitulation only by the flag on his clock falling.

WHAT WOULD YOU HAVE PLAYED?

No.16

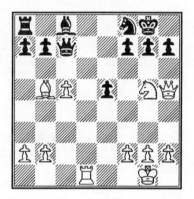

For the moment f7 and h7 are defended. How can the attack be intensified?

No.17

After **23 ♕h6 Black resigned**. Of course, his bishop and rook are attacked, and if 23... ♗e7 there follows mate at g7. But, after all, there is the simple 23...♖xg3, and if 24 ♕xf8+ ♖g8. So was his capitulation was premature?

No.18

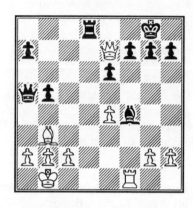

An attack on f7 is imminent, and the white bishop has its "X-ray" sights set on the black king. But where is that last straw that, so to speak, is capable of breaking the camel's back? After all, if 21 g3 ♕c7!, defending everything...

No.19

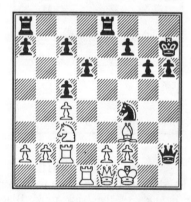

How can Black continue his attack? If 1...♕h3+ 2 ♔g1 ♖e5 3 ♘e4, or 1... ♘h3 2 e3, while if 1... ♖e5 2 ♘e4 ♖h5 3 ♘f6+. So does he have to be content with perpetual check?

6 Outposts

MILITARY DICTIONARIES give a single interpretation of the concept of an outpost: "a well defended fortification in an advanced position". In the Middle Ages they could have been bulwarks in front of the bridge, not allowing an enemy to begin an immediate assault on some nobleman's castle. Later these were flèches and redoubts at Borodino, Waterloo, Port Arthur...

Chess has added another meaning to the word "outpost". On the board too it is a securely defended fighting unit, only not with the aim of defence, but for attack. Being advanced, beyond the demarcation line, even within the heart of the opponent's position, the outpost cramps the enemy forces, hinders manoeuvres aimed at bringing up pieces to the main part of the battlefield, and finally, controls various squares. Relying on the outpost, the attacking side assembles his forces and prepares a decisive assault, in which the outpost piece also usually plays a part.

This is why not every advanced and securely defended piece has the right to "call" itself an outpost.

In the next diagram it is clear that White's "interests" are by no means limited to the queenside, and therefore the role played by the white knight can be called anything you like, only not that of an outpost. Essentially it is merely covering the black passed pawn, and this is too modest, too thankless a role for it. After all, White is a pawn down, and to achieve any

kind of dynamic balance he must revive his dying initiative.

The move sealed by him was an excellent one!

Makarychev-Kholmov
Frunze 1989

41 ♘d8!

At the cost of two tempi White transfers his knight to e6, creating a genuine outpost, and its role in the attack on the king very soon becomes apparent.

41...b4 42 ♖xa4 ♕xa4 43 ♘e6 ♕a3

After the seemingly more consistent 43...b3 White has the prosaic defence 44 ♘xc7 ♕a2 45 ♗c1.

44 ♕f2 ♕a2 45 ♗d2 b3 46 ♕c5 ♕xd2 47 ♕xc7 ♘e8 48 ♕xc4! b2 49 ♕c6, and instead of allowing perpetual check after 49...b1=♕ 50 ♕xe8 followed by ♘g5-f7, Black preferred to give it himself: **49...♘f6 50 ♕b7**

♘g4+ and then ...♘f2-g4.

A far from obvious plan for setting up an outpost was carried out by White in the following game.

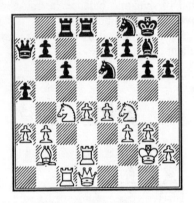

Barcza-Panno
Amsterdam Olympiad 1954

Naturally, White can increase his activity only by the break d4-d5, followed by occupying the central file that is then opened. But he discovers a potential weakness in Black's position and begins creating it.

26 ♘e2 ♖c7 27 ♗c3! b6

The c6 point has been weakened, and the breakthrough now has the aim not of opening files, but of establishing an outpost.

28 d5! cxd5 29 exd5 ♘c5 30 ♗xg7 ♔xg7 31 ♘c3 ♕b7 32 ♘e5 b5 33 ♘c6 ♖a8

The black rook has been denied the d8 square. But even more important is the fact that the knight outpost on the queenside is aimed in particular at e7, and this is close to the black king.

34 ♘e2 ♕b6 35 ♕c2 ♘b7 36 ♕c3+ f6

This creates fresh weaknesses in the king's pawn screen, but there is nothing to be done: 36...♔g8 37 ♕e5 ♖e8 38 ♕f4 ♔g7 39 ♘d8! is no better.

37 ♘f4 ♘d6 38 ♕d3 ♖e8 39 ♖e1

40 ♘e6+ ♖xe6 41 ♖xe6 is threatened, when the pressure on e7 (with the active participation of the outpost!) becomes unbearable. Black's desperate attempt to free himself runs into a little combination.

39...e5 40 dxe6! ♖xc6 41 e7 ♘f5 (otherwise White invades at g6) **42 exf8=♕+ ♖xf8 43 ♕d7+ ♖f7**

The outpost has done its work. White has broken into the opponent's position and the simplest now would be to give mate by 44 ♕xf7+ ♔xf7 45 ♖d7+. In fact he satisfied himself with the exchange — **44 ♘e6+ ♖xe6 45 ♕xe6**, and won on the 53rd move.

For a model example of a piece outpost in the centre, the authors have chosen (though not unanimously, one being "for", and one abstaining) the following game.

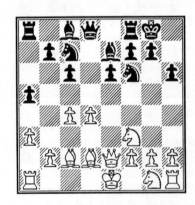

Tal-Speelman
Subotica Interzonal 1987

It is sufficient to say that the black knight reached c7 not in two moves (...♞b8-a6-c7), but in four (...♞b8-d7-b6-d5-c7)! Therefore White is obliged energetically to exploit his lead in development.

14 ♞e5!

The price for this eternal knight in the centre is very modest.

14...♛xd4 15 ♗c3 ♛d8 16 ♞gf3

The alternative was 16 ♖d1 ♛e8 17 ♛d3, with the threat of ♞g4.

16...♞ce8 17 g4! b5 18 g5!

This is not stronger, but it is more pleasant than 18 ♞xc6 ♛c7 19 cxb5.

18...hxg5 19 ♞xg5 ♖a6 20 ♛f3 b4 21 ♛h3 g6

Otherwise mate.

22 ♗xg6! bxc3

Or 22...fxg6 23 ♞xg6 ♔g7 24 ♛h7 mate.

23 ♞exf7 ♛d2+ 24 ♔f1 ♖xf7 25 ♗xf7+! ♔g7 26 ♖g1

Aiming not at Black's queen, but at his king — 27 ♞f3+ ♔f8 28 ♛h8+ ♔xf7 29 ♞e5 mate.

26...♛xg5 27 ♖xg5+ ♔xf7 28 bxc3!

The last precise move: after 28 ♛xc3 ♞e4 29 ♛f3+ ♞8f6 White would lose the exchange on account of the threatened check at e2.

28...e5, and after dejectedly making this move, **Black resigned**.

Here we saw nearly all the functions of a piece outpost: the support and organisation of a flank offensive, and the landing of a decisive blow. That these actions are typical is confirmed by numerous practical examples, such as the following.

14 g4! ♗b7 15 g5 ♞d5

Keres-Petrov
Estonia v. Latvia 1939

The rook is immune: 15...♗xh1 16 gxf6 ♗xf6 17 ♞d7 ♛c6 18 ♞xf6+ gxf6 19 ♛g4+ ♔h8 20 ♛h4 f5 21 ♛f6+, when White mates as he pleases.

16 ♖hg1!

This is stronger than 16 ♞d7 ♛c7 17 ♞xf8 ♞f4 with counterplay.

16...♛c7 17 ♖g4

With the help of his outpost White prepares a powerful attack. He is already threatening 18 ♗xh7+, with mate in a few moves.

17...g6 18 ♖h4!

Renewing the threat against h7, but now with the rook.

18...♗d6 19 ♞g4

A weakening around the black king has been provoked, and the knight outpost itself joins the attack.

19...♖fc8 20 ♔b1

Though not without its uses, this prophylaxis against a check at f4 is nevertheless unnecessary. However, White has no reason to hurry.

20...b5 21 ≡g1 ≙e7?

White was threatening 22 ♘f6+ ♘xf6 23 gxf6 followed by the un-avoidable 24 ≡xh7 ♔xh7 25 ♕h5+, but why lose immediately? 21...♕e7 was more tenacious, when White con-tinues 22 ≙e4, threatening 23 ≙xd5 and 24 ♘f6+.

22 ♘h6+ ♔f8 23 ♘xf7 ≙c5 24 ≡xh7 ≙d4 25 ♕xe6, and soon **Black resigned**.

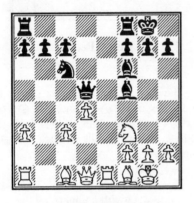

Tal-G.Garcia
Yurmala 1983

With his last move (14...≙e7-f6) Black has prevented the advance of the white pawn centre, which was possi-ble, for example, in the event of 14... ≙g6 15 c4 ♕d7 16 d5 (Karpov-Por-tisch, Lucerne Olympiad 1982). But now White gains the opportunity to put into operation another plan: to create a piece outpost at e5 and with the help of a flank pawn attack to drive back the black pieces to unfavourable positions.

15 ≙f4 ≡ac8 16 ≡e3 ♘a5 17 ♘e5 c5 18 g4! ≙g6 19 ≙g2 ♕d8 20 dxc5!

The threat of moving the white out-post a further step forward, to d6, and the fact that 20...≡xc5 is not possible on account of 21 ♘d7, force Black to spend a tempo on capturing the c5 pawn and restoring material equality. But during this time the attack on his king comes to a head.

20...≙xe5 21 ≡xe5 ♕f6 22 ≙g3 ♘c4 23 g5! ♕a6 24 ≡e7

The first achievement!

24...≡xc5 25 ♕d4!

The tempo for mobilising White's queen's rook is more precious than pawns — his at b5 and Black's at b7.

25...≡xg5 26 h4 ≡a5 27 ≡ae1 h6 28 ≙f1 b5 29 ≡e8!

Against the mate on the 8th rank there is no defence (29...♕b6 30 ≡xf8+ ♔xf8 31 ♕d7 ♔g8 — 31...f5 32 ♕c8+ with mate in three moves — 32 ≡e8+ ♔h7 33 ♕c8 ≙c2 34 h5), and so **Black resigned**.

When a player has an outpost in the centre, with its help he can plan and carry out flank attacks not only with pawns, but also with pieces.

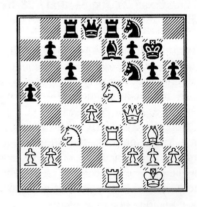

Keres-Kurajica
European Team Ch, Kapfenberg 1970

White exploits the strength of his advanced knight to the full.

23 ♕xh6+! ♚g8

If Black takes the queen, he remains two pawns down with a bad position. White could again have forced this by continuing 24 ♕h8+, but he now has a better alternative.

24 ♗h4 ♞8h7 25 ♞xg6!

And in view of the mate after 25... fxg6 26 ♕xg6+ ♚f8 27 ♖g3, **Black resigned**.

Ivkov-Kolarov
Wageningen 1957

From this position the game did not last long. White played **1 a4**, and after **1...bxa4 2 ♖xa4 ♕d7!!** he **resigned**, since whatever he does the rook at f7 is "freed" and gives mate at f1. The weakness of the back rank certainly told here, but firstly, Black's occupation of the f-file was assisted by his outpost, and secondly, the white rooks were so cramped by the black bishop that the attempt to free them can be considered obligatory.

White's position in the following diagram is strategically superior thanks to his occupation of the c-file and the two bishops.

Kasparov-Butnoryus
USSR Spartakiad, Moscow 1979

Therefore Black's tactical attempt **15...♕g5 16 f4 ♕g6 17 fxe5 ♞c5 18 ♗g3 ♞xa6** would have been quite justified, had it not allowed White to create a powerful piece-pawn outpost.

19 ♞f5! ♖ae8

Naturally, 19...exf5 20 ♕xd5 would have been practically equivalent to capitulation, the white bishop being so much stronger than the black knight.

20 ♞d6 ♖e7 21 ♖f4!

Threatening in passing 22 ♖g4 ♕h6 23 ♗f4 ♕h5 24 ♖xg7+, White creates decisive pressure on f7, begun by the knight manoeuvre to d6.

21...h5 22 e4 ♗a8 23 ♗h4 ♖d7 24 ♖c3 ♕h6 25 ♕f1 ♞c7 26 ♖cf3! f5

There is nothing else, since on 26... ♕g6 there would have followed 27 ♗f6, with the threat of 28 ♖g3.

27 exf6!

"The Moor has done his duty..."

Sacrificing both his outpost, and a piece, White begins a concrete variation.

27...☐xd6 28 f7+ ☗h7 29 ♗e7 e5 30 ♗xf8 exf4 31 ♗xd6 ♛xd6 32 ♛d3 ♛e7, and here 33 ♛d7 ♛xd7 34 f8=♘+ would have won for White, as would **33 ♛c4 ☗h6 34 f8=♛ ♛xf8 35 ♛xc7 g5 36 ☐d3**.

He in fact chose the more complicated **34 ☐xf4 ♘e6 35 ♛c8 ♛d6 36 ♛h8+ ☗g6 37 f8=♘+ ♘xf8 38 ♛xf8 ♛d1+ 39 ☗f2 ♛d2+ 40 ☗g3 ♛e1+ 41 ☗h3**, and since 41...♗xe4 fails to 42 ♛e8+, **Black resigned**.

As a rule, the deeper the attacking side is able to establish his outpost in the opponent's territory, the greater the difficulties it causes the opponent. The defending pieces become even more cramped, the proximity to the king becomes even more dangerous...

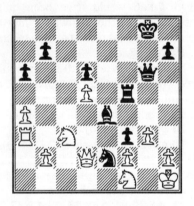

Bakinskaite-Voronova
Vilnius 1985

The role of outpost is being equally shared by the black knight and the f3 pawn. They are taking away squares

from the white king, and this could have been exploited by the forcing manoeuvre 1...♛h5 2 ♘xe4 (other replies do not change anything) 2...♛h3 3 ♘e3 ♛xh2+ and 4...☐h5 mate.

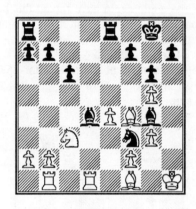

Suba-Tal
Tallinn 1983

M.T. In the opening for some reason my opponent allowed me to make a knight move, about which there is a warning in all books on the King's Indian Defence. Black's position has immediately become the more pleasant, but it is too early to exchange mind for matter: 20...♗xf2 21 ☗g2 ♗b6 22 ♗e2 ♘e5 23 ♗xg4 ♘xg4 24 ☐d7, and White's active rook compensates for all his losses. Besides, it was tempting to continue the pursuit of the king, which even without the queens is perfectly possible: along the h-file!

20...h6! 21 gxh6 ♗xc3!

Essential, otherwise after 21...g5 22 ☐xd4! ♘xd4 23 ♗xg5 it is altogether unclear who stands better.

22 bxc3 g5 23 ♗c7 ☐ac8 24 ♗d6

Keeping this square for the rook —
24 ♖xb7 ♖e6 25 ♖d6 does not succeed: 25...♖xc7.

24...♖e6 25 h7+ ♔xh7 26 ♔g2 ♖h6 27 ♗d3

There is no other square for the bishop.

27...♖xd6

Not 27...♖h2+ 28 ♔f1 ♖h1+ 29 ♔g2! ♖xd1 30 ♖xd1 ♘h4+ 31 gxh4 ♗xd1 32 hxg5, when it is White who has the attacking prospects.

28 e5+ ♖xd3 29 ♖xd3 ♗f5 30 ♖xf3 (30 ♖h1+ ♘h4+) **30...♗xb1 31 ♖xf7+ ♔g6 32 ♖xb7 ♗xa2 33 f4** (33 ♖xa7 ♗d5+ 34 ♔f1 g4, and White can resign) **33...gxf4 34 gxf4 ♖a8**, and some 50 moves later Black eventually converted his advantage into a win.

For the creation of such a powerful outpost one must sometimes be prepared to pay an appropriate price.

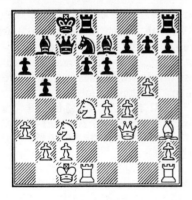

Tal-Gligoric
Moscow 1963

This position had occurred frequently in practice, and had been handled in different ways. The Yugoslav

grandmaster himself, for example, against Fischer in the 1959 Candidates Tournament, tried here to exploit the positioning of the white bishop and black king on the same h3-c8 diagonal with 15 f5, which is perfectly feasible.

I.D. Why did you reject a well-tried and promising idea?

M.T. Least of all because the author of it was Gligoric, and not at all for the reason that at the start White makes a very small sacrifice — a piece for two pawns. I was attracted by the power of the white knight at e6 and realised that with the help of such a knight the remaining white pieces would be capable of anything.

15 ♗xe6! fxe6 16 ♘xe6 ♕c4

16...♕b6 must be considered the lesser evil, although even then after 17 ♘d5 ♗xd5 18 exd5 White has sufficient compensation for the piece.

17 ♘d5!

This is the whole point. On his 15th move White had no intention of exchanging two pieces for a rook and two pawns, but was intending to demonstrate that the splendid knight at e6 is worth more than the fat and unwieldy rook at d8.

17...♗xd5 18 exd5 ♔b7

Forced, since 19 b3 was threatened, and 18...♘c5 is bad on account of 19 b3 ♕e4 20 ♕c3, when Black is unable to parry both 21 b4 and 21 ♖he1.

19 b3 ♕c8 20 ♖d3 ♘b6 21 ♖c3 ♕d7 22 ♖c7+

The white knight has after all done its duty.

22...♕xc7 23 ♘xc7 ♔xc7 24 ♕c3+ ♔b8 25 ♕xg7 ♘c8 26 ♖e1

White has a material advantage. In

addition it is very difficult for Black to coordinate his pieces and bring them out into play. The outcome of the game is decided, and an illustration of this is the possible variation 26...罝hg8 27 營xh7 罝h8 28 罝xe7!

26...罝dg8 27 營d4 兔d8 28 罝e6 罝f8 29 h4 h6 30 g6 罝hg8 31 h5 罝f5

In the event of 31...罝xf4 32 營xf4 兔g5 33 營xg5 hxg5 34 h6, in place of one queen White quickly acquires another.

32 營e4 罝xh5 33 罝e8 罝xe8 34 營xe8 兔f6 35 c4! bxc4 36 bxc4 罝h3 37 會d2 兔c3+ 38 會c2 兔d4 39 f5 罝xa3 40 c5! dxc5 41 d6, and after giving a few checks, **Black resigned**.

Until now the diagram positions have mainly shown piece outposts. The other type — pawn outposts, are even more common. Their existence is determined even by opening theory: for example, in the French Defence a white pawn is established at e5, and the evaluation of many variations depends on whether Black can destroy this outpost or will be forced to endure its pressure.

Moreover, it should be borne in mind that a classic piece outpost, supported by a pawn, has the property that it can be transformed into a pawn outpost, with all the attendant consequences.

In the following diagram Black has no weaknesses, but he also has little breathing-space, mainly on account of the powerful piece outpost in the centre. With his next move White further strengthens it.

15 f4 營e7

After the exchange 15...仑xe5 16 dxe5 the piece outpost is transformed

into a pawn outpost, which in turn secures White control of d6, and after 16...營e7 17 罝xd8 營xd8 (alas, forced, otherwise the a7 pawn is lost) 18 罝d1 White, after seizing the only open file, creates a new outpost at d6.

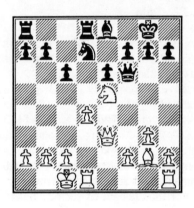

Spassky-Donner
Leiden 1970

With the move in the game Black begins a battle against the e5 outpost, planning ...f6. But this creates a weakness at e6, which means that White's outpost has done its job.

16 h4! f6 17 仑f3 兔h5 18 兔h3 兔xf3 19 營xf3 仑f8 20 罝he1 營f7 21 兔f1 罝d6 22 兔c4 罝ad8 23 f5! 罝xd4 24 fxe6 罝xd1+

The blockade of the white pawn does not succeed: 24...營e7 25 營a3! c5 26 營xa7 罝xd1+ 27 罝xd1 罝xd1+ 28 會xd1 仑g6 29 營xb7!

25 罝xd1 罝xd1+ 26 營xd1 Black resigns (if 26...營e7 27 營d8).

The next diagram is another typical transformation of an outpost — and its fruits.

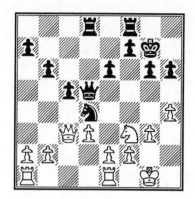

Larsen-Tal
Leningrad Interzonal 1973

After further strengthening his outpost by **19...e5**, and at the same time removing the pin on the knight, Black invites his opponent to give a reply to the eternal question - "what to do?"

20 ♘xd4

After 20 ♘d2 White would have had to reckon with the flank attack 20...g5, again under cover of the outpost in the centre.

20...exd4 21 ♕c4 ♕h5 22 ♕a4

The lesser evil was 22 e3 dxe3 23 ♖xe3, and although Black would have immediately restored his outpost with 23...♖d4, nevertheless the unpleasant pressure of the black d4 pawn would have disappeared. But now this outpost also plays the role of a barrier, cutting off the white queen from the kingside.

22...♖fe8 23 ♕xa7 ♖d6

Not so much to defend the b6 pawn, as to attack f2.

24 b4 ♖f6

24...cxb4 was also good, but the position is ripe for a forcing variation.

25 bxc5 ♕f5!

Inducing a serious weakening, since 26 ♖f1 loses immediately to 26...♖xe2.

26 f3 ♕h3 27 ♕c7 ♖f5!

A quiet move with an irresistible threat. As soon as Black places one of his rooks at e5, the white king will be absolutely defenceless.

28 cxb6 ♖fe5

Or 28...♖ee5 29 g4 ♕g3+ 30 ♔h1 (30 ♔f1 ♖xf3+) 30...♖h5!, which would also have won.

29 e4

The main variation of Black's attack was 29 ♕xe5+ ♖xe5 30 g4, hoping with rook against queen to exploit the strength of the b-pawn.Then he can continue 30...♕g3+ 31 ♔h1 (after 31 ♔f1 ♕h2! White cannot do anything, since on 32 b7 there follows 32...♖b5, when 33 ♖b1 is not possible, while if 32 a4 the attack can be continued by 32...h5!, e.g. 33 b7 ♖e7 34 ♖ab1 hxg4 34 b8=♕ g3) 31...h5! 32 b7 ♖b5 33 ♖eb1 hxg4! 34 ♖xb5 ♕h3+ 35 ♔g1 g3.

29...♕xg3+ 30 ♔h1 ♕xh4+ 31 ♔g2 ♖g5+ 32 ♔f1 ♕h3+ 33 ♔e2 ♖g2+ 34 ♔d1 ♕xf3+ 35 ♔c1 ♕f2 White resigns.

Even in the concluding attack the pawn outpost at d4 played its part, taking a square away from the white king.

A pawn outpost, even more than a piece outpost, gains in strength the more advanced it is. On the 6th rank the pawn is not only close to its queening square, but — in the context of our attacking theme — it usually becomes virtually the main component of the mating net around the enemy king. This is so obvious that it will be sufficient to give one single example from "girls'" chess...

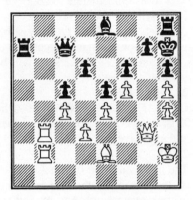

Ziedinya-Auzinya
Riga 1980

A part is undoubtedly played by the inadequately defended back rank, but the chief credit in the mate: **1 ♕g6+! ♗xg6 2 hxg6+ ♔g8 3 ♖b8+** nevertheless goes to the pawn outpost at g6.

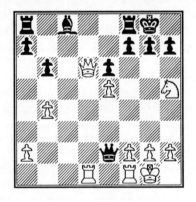

Levenfish-Ryumin
Moscow 1936

And now here is one example from

"men's" chess, where such an opportunity was missed.

White has a clear advantage: better development, outpost at e5, occupation of the open file, and a knight that has been "launched" into the vicinity of the black king. All this could have been realised instantly — 27 ♘f6+! gxf6 28 exf6, when the f6 pawn "guarantees" one of the two mates — 29 ♕g3+ or 29 ♕xf8+. But after the lame **27 ♘g3?** Black was able to save the game: **27...♕b5 28 ♖fe1 ♗b7** etc.

And now another slightly exotic example of how dangerous it is to allow the opponent to set up a bind with a pawn outpost in the centre...

Kaila-Kivi
Helsinki 1949

1 e4 c6 2 d4 d5 3 exd5 cxd5 4 c4 dxc4 5 ♗xc4 e6 6 ♘c3 ♘d7? 7 d5 e5 8 ♘f3 a6 9 0-0 ♘gf6 10 d6 ♘b6 11 ♗xf7+ ♔xf7 12 ♕b3+ ♔g6 13 ♘xe5+ ♔h5 14 ♘e2 (bringing up the assault cavalry) **14...♕e8 15 ♕f3+ ♗g4 16 ♕xg4+ ♘xg4 17 ♘g3+ ♔h4 18 ♘f3 mate**.

This game should not be taken too seriously, but as the saying goes, "in every joke there is a grain of truth".

A pawn outpost contains an additional, latent strength, when it is not blockaded and retains its mobility.

In the next example, in full accordance with opening theory, back on move 11 Black advanced his pawn to f4, and with energetic play he has made more progress on the kingside, than White on the queenside. But to "get at" the king is not so simple: if 39...♖h1 40 ♕g4, and he has to reckon with the thematic 🛇c8.

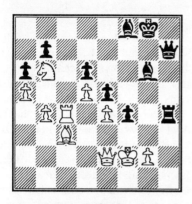

Najdorf-Gligoric
Mar del Plata 1953

Everything is decided by the energy of the pawn outpost, whose main function has already been fulfilled.

39...f3! 40 ♕e3 (all three captures lead to the loss of the queen!) **40...♖f4 41 gxf3**

But now the king is completely exposed, and the attack on it proceeds from both the flank and the rear.

41...♕h2+ 42 ♔e1 ♕h1+ 43 ♔e2 ♗h5 44 ♔d2 ♖xf3! 45 ♕g5+ ♗g7 46 ♔c2 (another check would not have changed anything - 46 ♖c8+ ♔h7) **46...♖f2+ 47 ♗d2 ♕d1+ 48 ♔c3 ♕a1+**, and in view of the inevitable mate (49 ♔d3 ♗e2+ 50 ♔e3 - or 50 ♔c2 ♗d1+ 51 ♔d3 ♕b1+ - 50...♖f3+ 51 ♔xe2 ♕f1 mate) **White resigned**.

The above ideas were as though synthesised in the following example.

Black would appear to have achieved a great deal, but... While still on the way to this position, White had planned to eliminate the enemy out-post, realising that the basis for creating his own had already been laid.

Chekhov-Pähtz
Lvov 1983

23 ♖fxe3! fxe3 24 ♕xe3 ♕g6 25 ♘e4!

No deviations from the general course, such as 25 ♘xe5...

25...♖ae8

The knight could have been prevented from going any further by 25...h6, but then 26 ♕h3 with a very strong attack on the light squares (♗h5).

26 ♘g5 ♔h8 27 ♘e6 ♖f5

Returning the exchange by 27...♖xe6 would have simply meant losing the e5 pawn.

28 ♗f3 ♖g8 29 g3 ♖f7

Evidently 29...♕f7 would have been slightly more tenacious.

30 ♕e2! ♕h6 31 ♗h5 ♖f5 32 ♗g4 ♖f6 33 ♘xe5! ♗c8

The pawn has been captured at just the right time, since on 33...♘xe5 34 ♕xe5 ♖xg4 35 ♖f1 ♖gg6 36 ♖xf6 ♖xf6 White wins by 37 ♕b8+. Here too the e6 outpost plays a decisive role.

34 ♘xd7 ♗xd7 35 ♕e5! ♗xe6

The white bishop is still immune, but now the piece outpost is transformed into a pawn outpost — or a far-advanced passed pawn!

36 dxe6 ♖xg4 37 ♖f1 ♕g5

If 37...♔g7 or 37...♖gg6 the simple 38 e7 wins.

38 ♕xf6+ ♕xf6 39 ♖xf6 ♖e4 40 ♔f2 ♔g7 41 ♔f3 ♖e1, and simultaneously with this move **Black resigned**.

Polugayevsky-Tal
Riga Interzonal 1979
English Opening

M.T. This game was played exactly ten years after, in September 1969, in the 2nd round of the 37th USSR Championship, Polugayevsky had opened the score in our personal encounters. That game received wide recognition, and found its way into the theory books.

And now it was September 1979, again the 2nd round (the events, it is true, were different); naturally, this sort of association did nothing for my frame of mind, and besides, in the intervening decade Polugayevsky had increased the score to 5-1. But... that is the way the pairings came out!

1 ♘f3   c5!

Of course, an exclamation mark is attached to this move not because it is the strongest, the best. Simply, I did not want to allow my opponent the possibility of repeating the opening of the first game won by him, an extract from which is given in the chapter *Breakthrough in the Centre*.

2   c4   ♘f6
3   ♘c3   d5
4   cxd5   ♘xd5
5   e4

The move 5 e4 has enjoyed its "ebbs" and "flows". According to the latest theoretical conclusions, it casts doubts on the 3...d5 variation. Incidentally, the game Timman-Tal (Montreal 1979) developed in the same way. Black played 5...♘xc3, and after 6 dxc3 he ended up in a difficult position. Only then did I realise that the offer to exchange queens here is by no means synonymous with an offer of a draw.

Possibly 5 e4 is not such a terrible move for Black. In particular, three months later this was demonstrated by Vaganian in a game with me in the USSR Championship in Minsk. After 5...♘xc3 6 dxc3 ♕xd1+ 7 ♔xd1 the Yerevan grandmaster played the much stronger 7...♘c6 8 ♗e3 b6 9 a4 ♗b7 10 ♘d2 0-0-0 11 ♔c2 ♘a5, and achieved a perfectly acceptable position.

But at any event, in September I did not yet know this game, and neither did Polugayevsky.

5 ...   ♘b4

This is considered the most critical move. As it transpired only after the tournament, my opponent had specially prepared this variation for his game with me. And it so happened that my trainer and I had also specially examined this very continuation before the game with Polugayevsky.

6   ♗c4

The bishop check at b5, which has recently been fashionable, achieves little after 6...♘8c6 7 d4 (this is much stronger than 7 a3, as Poutiainen played against me in Tallinn 1977, or 7 0-0, the continuation employed against me by Tukmakov, 45th USSR Championship, Leningrad 1977) 7...cxd4 8 a3, and here the simple 8...♗d7, if there is nothing better, secures Black a practically equal game.

6 ...   ♗e6

The whims of chess fashion! — I suspect that 50 years ago this continuation would have shocked its legislators. But now it is considered the strongest, and virtually the only move. Black allows the doubling of his pawns on the e-file, obtaining in return only one compensating factor, but an attractive one: his knight ensconces itself at d3, but whether its residency will be temporary or permanent, depends on the opponent.

7   ♗xe6   ♘d3+
8   ♔f1   fxe6
9   ♘g5

So far this is a standard variation. Until quite recently it was thought that Black could achieve an excellent game

here by continuing 9...♘c6 10 ♘xe6 ♕d7 11 ♘d5 ♖c8 etc. But in the game Timman-Stean from the Amsterdam Zonal Tournament (1978) the Dutch grandmaster prepared a significant improvement: instead of 11 ♘d5 came the simple, but nevertheless unexpected 11 ♘xc5!, and it transpired that after 11...♘xc5 12 ♕h5+ g6 13 ♕xc5 Black has an initiative that might compensate for one pawn, but two pawns in this position is too high a price for it. In short, mind gave way to matter. This game was widely reported, and searches for an improvement in Black's play began. Players reverted to the plausible 9...♕d7, and 9...♘c6 was tried. And in the game Sekey-Palatnik (Frunze 1979) Black employed the experimental 9...♘a6. True, from this game it is not possible to give a real assessment of the move, since immediately after 10 ♕a4+ ♕d7 the players agreed a draw. But at any event the position had become problematic, and one of the attempts to solve this problem was the move employed in the present game.

9 ...   ♕b6!?

I am not inclined to overrate the strength of this move, but in the given instance the experiment fully justified itself. During a training session three of us analysed this position: Kapengut, Koblenz and I. And the following move, made by Polugayevsky, was suggested by Koblenz.

10   ♕e2

Other continuations would seem to be more dangerous for Black. In particular, 10 ♕c2, 10 ♕f3, or 10 ♘a4. However, analysis in one's study is one thing, playing in a tournament is another. It seems to me that only the latter can serve as a true criterion.

10 ...   c4

11 b3

This move is the idea behind White's plan. His primary task is to deprive the advanced knight of support, since it is perfectly evident that nearly all Black's remaining pieces are still occupying their "god-given" positions.

But, strangely enough, Black nevertheless succeeds in consolidating his grip on the "enemy beach-head". Jumping ahead I should mention that the knight holds its ground at d3 almost to the end of the game.

11 ...   h6!

The point is that White's forces too are not well placed. The knight at g5 is his only active piece. With his last move Black drives it back, and at the same time prepares to develop his queenside. He does not fear the check at h5, since after 12 ♕h5+ ♔d7 his king moves to safety, while in certain cases the position of the enemy queen at h5 even gives him a tempo for the developing move ...g6.

12 ♘f3

It is important that the attempt at an immediate attack does not succeed, since after 12 ♘a4 ♕d4 (12...♕c6 is also possible) 13 ♘xe6 ♕xa1 14 ♕h5+ g6! (14...♔d7? 15 ♕d5+ ♔c8 16 ♕d8 mate) 15 ♕xg6+ ♔d7 no decisive continuation is apparent.

It is probable that 12 ♘h3, covering f2, was slightly more accurate, but in this case, I think, there can be no question of the variation being refuted.

12 ...   ♘c6

13 bxc4   0-0-0

White's first sortie has not succeeded. The black knight has not only held on to d3, but has even, it could be said, established itself more comfortably.

The evaluation of the plan chosen by Black depends largely on the sharp variation 14 ♘d5!? But during the game both players established that after 14...exd5 15 ♕xd3 Black can interpose the strong move 15...♘b4!, when White's plan is essentially refuted. For example: 16 ♕b1 dxc4, 16 ♕d4 ♕xd4 17 ♘xd4 dxe4, or 16 ♕c3 dxe4 17 ♘e5 g5 18 ♘f7 ♗g7 19 ♕xg7 ♘d3, and the other black knight settles in at the sacred d3 square.

14 ♗a3 was also examined. In the event of 14...♕a5 15 ♘b5 a6 16 ♘d6+ exd6 17 ♕xd3 ♘e5 18 ♕b3 ♘xf3 19 gxf3 ♕xd2 20 ♖b1 White has a good game, but Black was planning to answer 14 ♗a3 with 14...g5.

Perhaps some consideration should be given to the positional piece sacrifice 14 ♘d5 exd5 15 cxd5 ♘ce5, although White does not appear to gain a great deal in compensation.

Be that as it may, but White's rather phlegmatic development leads to a very difficult position. Black only needs to bring into play his bishop and then to occupy the half-open f-file, and his attack will become very powerful.

14 g3   g5

15 ♔g2

The exchanging operation 15 ♘d5 exd5 16 ♕xd3 ♗g7! 17 e5 (17 ♖b1 dxc4!) 17...♖hf8 holds little promise for White. Now he is ready to "smoke out" the knight from d3 by ♘e1, and therefore, rather than the natural development of the bishop at g7, Black prefers the following move, which proves very effective.

15 ...   ♕c5!

If now 16 ♘e1, simply 16...♕xc4, and instead of the knight a much "heavier" piece establishes itself at d3.

16 ♖b1   ♗g7

Perhaps only now can one confidently state that White's position is very difficult. Sensing this, Polugayevsky attempts a counterattack, but it proves insufficiently justified.

17 ♘b5   ♕xc4

Active defence (18...♘f4+ is threatened). Of course, not 17...a6? 18 ♗a3 ♕xc4 19 ♘a7+! (19...♘xa7 20 ♖hc1).

18 ♕e3   ♖hf8

Black's threats are the more immediate: 19...♖xf3 and 19...g4. Therefore White is forced to cover f2.

19 ♖f1   g4

Strictly speaking, now 19...a6 was not at all bad, but simply Black had worked out a fairly clear-cut variation.

20 ♘h4   ♘xf2!
21 ♘g6

21 ♖xf2 ♖xf2+ 22 ♔xf2 ♖f8+ or

22 ♕xf2 ♕xe4+ is quite unacceptable for White. Polugayevsky was probably pinning some hopes on the interposition 21 ♘g6, although after it the white king is too alone.

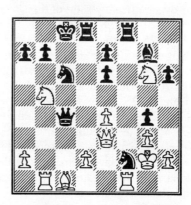

21 ...   ♖d3!

In this game the d3 square has proved to be something of a staging post for Black. 21...♖f3 would have been much weaker, since after 22 ♘xa7+ ♘xa7 23 ♕xa7 ♕xe4 White has 24 ♘xe7+ ♔c7 25 ♕b6+ ♔d7 26 ♕xb7+. Here it is important that the e4 pawn is not captured with check. Thus now this variation does not work, since after ...♕xe4+ Black gives mate.

22 ♘a3

Another interposition. 22 ♕e1 ♖df3 would have led positions similar to those in the game.

For Black there is naturally no point in considering variations where the queens are exchanged — his main aim is to maintain the attack on e4. Therefore his next move suggests itself.

22 ...   ♕a4
23 ♕e1   ♖df3

Now there is nothing to prevent the

black knight from returning to the fatal (for White) square, and what's more, with much greater effect than earlier. To complete the picture it should be added that by this time White was already significantly short of time.

24 ♘xf8   ♘d3
25 ♕d1

Not without its piquancy is the variation 25 ♕e2 ♘d4 26 ♕d1 ♕xd1 27 ♖xd1 ♖f2+ with mate after 28...♘f3.

Here too 25...♖f2+ was very strong, but for some reason I did not want to allow White the possibility of sacrificing his queen, although, of course, this would not have saved him. I chose the continuation in the game, only because I had planned it beforehand.

25 ...   ♕xe4
26 ♖xf3   gxf3+
27 ♔f1   ♕f5
28 ♔g1   ♗d4+
White resigns

WHAT WOULD YOU HAVE PLAYED?

No.20

The attempt to set up a piece outpost at d6 does not succeed: if 19 c3 or 19 ♗c3 Black immediately replies 19... ♘c5, exchanging knights. But White already has a pawn outpost at e5...

No.21

Taking account of what has been said, there are at least three reasons that allow Black to play... what?

No.22

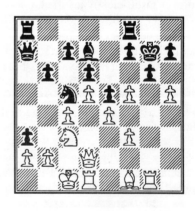

This position, where it is White to move, should not cause any problems.

7 Eliminating Defenders

DEFEND TO THE LAST MAN! — such was the order usually given by commanders of fortresses under siege, after they themselves had received similar dispatches from their superiors. It is another matter that attitudes have changed to such exalted and threatening words, thereby saving precious human lives. And besides, what could objectively be done by a dozen or so remaining defenders against a much greater enemy force?

In chess — a wonderful model of our everyday life — things are different. The dimensions are different, and the role of the single lone "soldier" is also different. Even on his own, he is sometimes capable of holding a dubious game, or saving a position that, as they say, is at death's door. Therefore the most important task in any attack is to eliminate those defenders that stand in the way to the king, even if a considerable price has to be paid.

However, there are several ways of eliminating a particular piece, that is the mainstay of the enemy defences. The most convenient for the attacking side is to do this, so to speak, for free — by forcing its exchange.

As usual in positions with the type of pawn formation in the following diagram, the main defender of the dark squares is the bishop of the corresponding colour, and it is this piece that White begins pursuing.

21 ♗g5! ♘d4 22 ♕e3!

White is prepared to tolerate the knight at d4 for a time, and to give up the exchange: 22...♘c2 23 ♕f4 ♗xg5 24 ♘xg5 ♖f8 25 ♘g4!, so long as the dark squares become a gaping wound in the opponent's position. Black can no longer avoid the exchange.

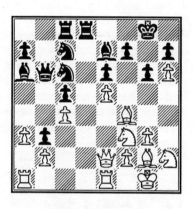

Fischer-Feuerstein
USA Ch., New York 1957/8

22...♗xg5 23 ♕xg5 ♘e8 (the functions of the bishop are taken on by the knight) **24 ♘g4 ♘f5 25 ♖ac1**

The position is not the sort where you have to burn your boats in making a swift attack. Besides, in passing the weakness at b3 can also be harassed.

25...♕c7 26 ♘d2 ♖d4 27 ♘xb3 ♖xc4 28 ♖cd1!

Leaving the black bishop unemployed for the time being.

28...♖a4 29 ♖e4 ♗b5 30 ♖c1! ♕b6 31 ♘d2

The white pieces return to the main part of the battlefield.

31...Exe4 32 ♘xe4 ♗d3 33 ♘gf6+ ♔h8 34 g4

Now both black knights lose control over g7, and White wins easily: **34...♗xe4 35 ♗xe4 ♘d4 36 ♘xe8 ♕d8 37 ♕xd8 Exd8 38 ♘d6**, and soon **Black resigned**.

However, more often the exchange of a defender is achieved by sacrificial means, the material losses being more than compensated by the fact that the squares being defended are fully or partly taken over by the attacker. By giving up a more valuable piece for the defender, the attacking side greatly increases the energetic potential of his offensive. There is no opponent, and hence there is no counter to the attack on a particular part of the battlefield.

Ubilava-Timoshchenko
Chelyabinsk 1974

Black has just attacked the white queen, but for this he has incautiously used the sole defender of his weak dark squares. Its disappearance from the board is equivalent to defeat for Black, especially since a new master of the

dark squares appears.

14 ♕xe5!! dxe5 15 Exd8+ ♔xd8 16 ♗g5+ ♔e8

16...♔d7 is pointless, while after 16...♔c7 17 ♗f6 and 18 ♗xe5+ Black is a pawn down in a hopeless ending.

17 ♗f6 Eg8 18 Ed1 ♗d7 19 ♘a4 Eb4

It is easy to see that there is no other defence. For example, 19...c5 20 ♘xc5 ♗b5 21 a4, and after taking on a6 the white knight gives check at c7.

20 ♘c5 Ed4 21 Exd4 exd4 22 h4!

The domination of the dark squares must be consolidated: if now 22...g5 23 h5, and the black rook is still shut in.

22...e5 23 f3 ♗e6 24 b3 a5 25 g4 h5 26 g5 ♗h3 27 ♔f2 (the white king heads for the queenside, and it is all over) **27...Ef8 28 ♔e2 Eg8 29 a4 Ef8 30 b4 axb4 31 a5 ♗c8 32 ♔d3 Eg8 33 ♔c4 Black resigns**.

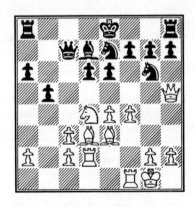

Tal-Suetin
Tbilisi 1969/70

In the opening Black has taken too many liberties. He has left his king in the centre and exchanged his dark-square bishop, and his knight at g6 is badly placed. In addition, without hindrance White has "launched" (cf. Chapter 3) his queen into Black's "goal area". He now begins a decisive attack, by helping the opponent to obtain an excellent "central" defender, and — by planning in advance its elimination.

16 f5! exf5 17 exf5 ♘e5 18 ♘e6! ♗xe6 19 fxe6 g6

Clearly, 19...0-0-0 20 exf7 ♖df8 21 a4 with a crushing attack is not a realistic alternative. But now after 20 exf7+ ♘xf7 21 ♕h4 0-0 22 ♖df2 ♘c6 Black is somehow able to hold on, thanks in particular to his knight at e5.

20 ♕xe5! (immediately resolving the problem of the defender and of the defence in general) **20...dxe5 21 exf7+,** and **Black resigned**, rather than face the piquant variation 21... ♔d7 22 ♗f5+ ♔c6 23 ♗e4+ ♘d5 24 ♗xd5+ ♔d7 25 ♗xa8+ ♔e7 26 ♗g5+ ♔f8 27 ♗h6+ ♔e7 28 f8=♕+ ♖xf8 29 ♗xf8+.

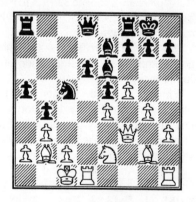

Gereben-Geller
Budapest 1952

After castling on opposite sides, pawn storms on the principle of "who is quicker" are a standard procedure, and therefore instead of the possible 17...♗d7 Black preferred not to waste a tempo, since for a start he had a quite specific aim, after, of course, the opening of lines.

17...a4! 18 h4

For the moment it is bad to accept the gift: 18 fxe6 fxe6 19 ♕g3 ♗h4 20 ♕h2 ♖f2 21 ♖he1 ♗g5+, and Black wins.

18...axb3 19 axb3 ♖a2! 20 fxe6 fxe6 21 ♕e3 ♕a5 22 c4 ♖xb2!

Removing one defender...

23 ♔xb2 ♕a3+ 24 ♔b1 ♖a8 25 ♘c1 ♕a1+ 26 ♔c2 ♖a2+!

And now a second, which had come to the aid of the king. After this the gathering in of the "harvest" begins.

27 ♘xa2 ♕xa2+ 28 ♔c1 ♘xb3+ 29 ♕xb3 ♕xb3

Black now has a material advantage, and his attack continues. When the bishop joined in, **White resigned**.

Very often the main defensive functions are entrusted to a knight (remember the aphorism: "bishops for attack, knights for defence"), but on open or half-open files they can typically become a target for the attacker's long-range rooks (*see diagram next page*).

Contrary to the aphorism just mentioned, White's attack is supported by his knight, but in addition the black knight is the only (for the moment, at any event, until ...f6 is played) defender of f6. And it is from this square that the black king can be invited to go for a walk.

Nezhmetdinov-Romanov
Arkhangelsk 1950

25 ⧉xd7! ♗xd7 26 ♕f6+ ♚h6 27 ⧉f5!

27 ⧉f3 was not dangerous in view of 27...♗xg4, but now against mate by ⧉h5 there is no defence. Unless Black prefers 27...♗xf5 28 ♘xf5 mate.

27...♕a7+ 28 ♚g2 Black resigns.

Keres-Szabo
USSR v. Hungary 1955

Here we have a position of so-called

dynamic equilibrium. White's play is on the kingside, whereas Black's is on the b-file and against the e5 outpost, which is insufficiently supported. Therefore everything depends on the energy of the two players and — an accurate choice of goal.

18 ⧉xd7!!

Realising that the black knight was ready to act as the sole defender of the kingside (from f8), White gains time for his attack and acquires an advantage in force on the required part of the board.

18...♗xd7 19 ♗d3 h6

Parrying the main threat of 20 ♕g5 g6 21 h5 with a crushing attack and, perhaps, secretly hoping for 20 ♕xh6? ♕xe5 21 ♕h7+ ♚f8 22 ♕h8+ ♚e7 23 ♕xg7 ♕xg7, which would suit Black perfectly well.

20 ♕f4 ♚f8 (defending against 21 ♕f6) **21 ⧉xg7!**

Now the white pawn outpost will have its say.

21...♚xg7 22 ♕f6+ ♚f8 (or 22...♚g8 23 ♕xh6 f5 24 exf6) **23 ♗g6**, and in view of 23...⧉e7 24 ♕h8 mate **Black resigned**.

The next diagram shows a slightly more complicated implementation of a similar theme.

White's standard threats on the h-file are strong. But he does not have time to double heavy pieces by 1 ♕h4 on account of 1...♕e3+ and 2...♕h6, when on 3 ⧉h5 Black can interpose 3...♘xg6. And the typical defence elimination 1 ⧉xf8+ is parried by 1...♚xf8! (1...⧉xf8 2 ⧉h8+ ♚xh8 3 ♕h5+ and 4 ♕h7 mate) 2 ⧉h8+ ♚g8, when the game is still alive.

Kosten-Sanz
Hastings Challengers 1978/9

But from the defending knight White can first remove the defending king!
1 罝h8+!! 含xh8 2 罝xf8+ 罝xf8 3 營h5+ Black resigns.

Vasyukov-Durasevic
Belgrade 1961

White already has a material advantage, which he could increase with the simple 1 罝xb7, when Black cannot even escape from the pin by 1...營c6 on account of 2 罝b6.

But the ideal position of White's rook (on the 7th rank) and bishop (on the long dark-square diagonal) demands that he look closely at the point where their "glances" intersect — the g7 square. True, it is defended three times(!) and very securely. Securely?

1 罝xe6! (the first defender is eliminated) **1...營xe6 2 營xf8!** (and now the second) **2...罝xf8 3 罝xg7+** (the third is powerless) **3...含h8 4 罝xg6+!** (the most precise), and **Black resigned**, as 4...罝f6 fails to save him on account of 5 罝xf6, when the queen has nowhere to hide on a completely open board.

The elimination of defenders around the king can be the theme of the most unexpected operations.

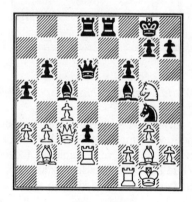

Saigin-Tal
Match, Riga 1954

M.T. It can be considered unexpected only as regards its ultimate aim, since in general the black pieces are ideally placed, the rook invasion at e2 is threatened, and there are also other motifs in the air...

25...♘e3! 26 fxe3 ♗xe3+ 27 ♔h1 ♗xd2 28 ♕xd2 ♖e2 29 ♕c3 ♖xg2!

This is the point of Black's idea. By leaving the white king without its last defender, Black intends to combine the advance of his passed pawn with an attack on the light squares, that are no longer controlled. For example, 30 ♔xg2 d2 31 ♖d1 ♗g4 32 ♘f3 ♕d3!

Therefore **White resigned**.

Spassky-Petrosian
World Championship, Moscow 1969

Any player with the slightest experience will immediately judge Black's position to be very dubious. Indeed: White has open files for his attack, the number of pawns sheltering the black king has been reduced, all the light squares around it are weak — and all this for one single pawn. But...

Firstly, the key point g7 is securely defended. Secondly, the light-square bishop cannot be switched to the b1-h7 diagonal, where together with the queen it could begin an attack on the light squares. Thirdly, there is no dark-square bishop to be sacrificed on the

traditional h6 square, and it is not evident how one of the knights can be moved across with this aim. As for the manoeuvre ♖f1-f3-h3xh6, it is both lengthy, and it leaves open the question: what next? Finally, Black has the possibility of defending his weakness at e6 a third time and of including his queen's rook in the defence along the 5th rank.

Therefore the means by which White eliminates the main defenders of the black king must be considered typical.

21 e5!! dxe5 22 ♘e4! ♘h5

The essence of White's manoeuvre lies in the variations 22...♘xe4 23 ♖xf8+ ♖xf8 24 ♕xg7 mate, and 22... exd4 23 ♘xf6 g5 24 ♕h3 ♖e7 25 ♖xg5 ♗g7 26 ♖xg7, mating. But now too the additional defence of the g7 squares proves insufficient.

23 ♕g6! exd4

After 23...♘f4 another motif would have worked: 24 ♖xf4! exf4 25 c3! and — an attack on the light squares after ♗c2 and ♘f6.

24 ♘g5!

The most energetic, and in view of the forced variation 24...hxg5 25 ♕xh5+ ♔g8 26 ♕f7+ ♔h8 27 ♖f3 **Black resigned**.

Sometimes a defender cannot be eliminated even at a high price — it is too securely defended. But in such cases one must consider: can it perhaps be diverted?!

In the next example Black appears to have been the more successful: he has a material advantage, and the white queen, that has broken into his position, is restricted by the bishop, which cannot be advantageously eliminated.

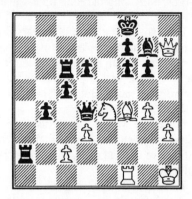

Spassky-Geller
Candidates ¼-Final, Sukhumi 1968

36 ♗h6! ♗xh6

An exchange? But what to do after 37 ♕xh6+ ♔e7 38 ♘xf6 ♕xf6 39 ♖xf6 ♔xf6? — the black rooks are clearly stronger than the white queen!

37 ♕h8+! ♔e7 38 ♘xf6!

After luring away the defender of the f6 pawn, White continues his attack, although he is now a rook down.

38...♗f4?

Black keeps his material advantage, but loses the game. By 38...♗f8, blocking White's main line of attack, he could have held the balance: 39 ♖e1+ ♕e5 40 ♖xe5+ dxe5 41 ♘d5+ ♔e6.

39 g5 ♔e6 40 ♕e8+ ♔f5 41 ♕xf7 ♖c7 (41...♔xg5 42 ♘e4+) **42 ♕xc7 ♔xg5**

The defence planned by Black on his 38rd move — 42...♖a1 43 ♕c8+ ♔e5 (43...♔xg5 44 ♘e4+ ♕xe4+ 45 dxe4 ♖xf1+ 46 ♔g2 leads to the loss of the bishop) 44 ♘g4+ ♔d5 would

have lost to the problem-like 45 c4+!

43 ♕e7! (now the black king is unable to escape from the firing line) **43...♕e3**

If 43...♕xf6 White wins the queen, or gives mate: 44 ♖g1+ ♔f5 45 ♕e4.

44 ♘e4+ ♔h5 45 ♕h7+ ♗h6 46 ♕d7

In order to answer 46...♗g5 with 47 ♕g4+ ♔h6 48 h4 ♗e7 49 ♖g1, when g6 cannot be defended.

46...♗f4 47 ♘f6+ ♔g5 48 ♘d5 Black resigns.

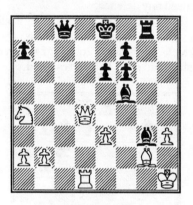

Gurieli-Wu Ming Qien
Women's Interzonal
Zheleznovodsk 1985

Both kings are rather unfavourably, if not badly placed. True, neither can be approached directly, and therefore at first sight Black's next move does not appear particularly good.

23...e5!?

Certainly, the h3 pawn is now attacked, but the important d6 square is also weakened, and it is immediately occupied by White.

24 ♕d6

Threatening the deadly 25 ♗c6+. If 24...♗d7 White has the extremely unpleasant 25 ♘c5, while after 24...e4 25 ♕xf6 ♗xh3 26 ♗xe4 the bishop check at c6 is again on the agenda.

But not only White is attacking, and the bishop at g2 is not only a striker, but also the central defender.

24...♗e4!!

Black diverts the bishop from the defence of the h3 pawn, simultaneously opening the diagonal for the queen. White no longer has any attack, nor indeed any defence.

25 ♔g1 ♗h4 (25...♗h2+ would have won more quickly) **26 ♘c5 ♗xg2** (and here 26...♖xg2+ forces mate), and soon **White resigned**.

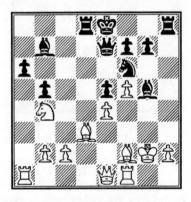

Gurgenidze-Sergievsky
USSR 1962

Strictly speaking, here too neither king feels altogether comfortable. One has been deprived of its pawn shelter, while the other is still in the centre. But whereas Black's king is not threatened by a single enemy piece, all his forces without exception are aimed

directly or indirectly at the white king: there is pressure both along the g- and h-files, and along the long light-square diagonal.

Even so, at first sight it appears that White can hold on. As yet there is no immediate threat against h2, and e4, the key point of his position, is quite securely defended. But suddenly...

27...♗d2!! 28 ♕xd2

Forced to worry about his knight, White's queen is diverted from the defence of e4, and everything promptly collapses.

28...♘xe4 29 ♕e3 ♕g5+!

Paradoxically, this is stronger than winning the queen after 29...♘g5+ 30 ♔g3 ♖h3+.

30 ♕xg5 ♘xg5+ 31 ♔g3 ♖h3+ 32 ♔g4 ♗f3+ 33 ♔xg5 ♖h5 mate.

Tal-Dvoretsky
42nd USSR Ch., Leningrad 1972
King's Indian Defence

1	d4	♘f6
2	c4	g6
3	♘c3	♗g7
4	e4	d6
5	♗e2	0-0
6	♘f3	e5
7	♗e3	c6

M.T. I cannot claim to have had much experience of this variation, but here either 7...♘c6 or 7...♘bd7 has been played against me. For a time 7...♕e7 was also popular. As Dvoretsky admitted after the game, at literally the last minute he glanced in Boleslavsky's book, and discovered that the author recommends the modest pawn move 7...c6. For the moment

Black refrains from developing his queen's knight. After some thought, I could find nothing better than castling, but perhaps White should play 8 d5!?

8 0-0 exd4
9 ♗xd4

The position after 9 ♘xd4 ♖e8 10 f3 d5 11 cxd5 cxd5 12 ♗b5 ♗d7 or 10 ♗f3 ♘bd7 does not promise White any advantage, but the capture with the bishop is also fairly harmless.

9 ... ♖e8
10 ♕c2 ♘bd7

Possibly Black should not have been in hurry to make this move. The direct 10...♕e7 11 ♖fe1 c5 came into consideration, when White has either to give up his bishop, or a pawn: 12 ♗e3 ♘xe4 13 ♘xe4 ♕xe4 14 ♕d2, for which he gains some compensation.

11 ♖ad1 ♕e7
12 ♖fe1 ♘e5

If 12...♘c5, which looks more purposeful, White had prepared 13 b4, when it transpires that the threat to the e4 pawn is illusory: 13...♘cxe4 14 ♗d3 d5 15 cxd5 cxd5 16 ♗xf6! Black could have continued 13...♘e6 14 ♗e3 ♘g4 with a complicated game. After the move played, White at least no longer has to worry about his e4 pawn.

13 h3 ♗h6

An interesting move, essentially forcing White to go in for complications, which, however, turn out to be in his favour. After other moves he would have had time for the regrouping ♗e3 and ♕d2, with positional pressure.

14 b4!

The threat of 14...c5 was rather unpleasant.

14 ... b6

15 c5!

As we have already indicated, this is forced, but... also good.

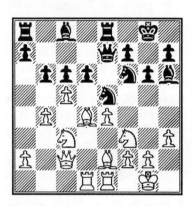

15 ... bxc5

M.T. After the game the dejected Dvoretsky said that he had simply forgotten about the transposition of moves that occurred in the game. For my part, I thought for a long time before making my next move.

16 ♘xe5

M.T. Since I was quite happy about the main variation (after 15...♘xf3+ 16 ♗xf3) 16...bxc5 17 bxc5 dxc5 18 ♗e3 ♗xe3 19 ♖xe3: for the pawn White has more than sufficient compensation, I hesitated, wondering whether I shouldn't be content with this. But then I decided that White could gain a more appreciable advantage.

16 ... dxe5

Better chances were probably offered by 16...cxd4 17 ♘xc6 ♕b7.

17 ♗xc5 ♕b7

White has a clear positional advantage, but this is only the first stage.

18 ♘a4

Aiming at the blockading square c5.

| 18 | ... | ♗e6 |

18...♗f8 was more tenacious.

19	♗d6	♘d7
20	♘c5	♘xc5
21	bxc5!	

The point is that now a transformation of advantages has taken place: instead of pressure on the weak c6 pawn and occupation of c5, White has acquired another, significantly more important advantage — undisputed (as long as the bishop at d6 is "alive") possession of the b-file.

| 21 | ... | ♗f8 |

21...♕b4 was perhaps more active, in order to answer 22 ♖b1 with 22...♕a3. True, White has 22 ♗a6, forcing the black queen to guard the b7 square.

M.T. The move in the game sets a clever trap. At first I began examining interesting variations such as 22 ♗xe5 ♗xa2 23 ♗a1 ♕b3 24 ♕d2 ♗xc5 (bad is 24...♖xe4 25 ♗f3 ♖xe1+ 26 ♖xe1 ♗g7 27 ♗xg7 ♔xg7 28 ♖a1!) 25 ♕g5. The variations appeared convincing enough, but, after some hesitation, I decided against opening the floodgates for the black pieces. And I was right: on 22 ♗xe5 Black had prepared 22...♗b3!, not only securing opposite-colour bishops, but also regaining his pawn!

| 22 | ♖b1 | |

White sticks to his overall plan.

| 22 | ... | ♕d7 |
| 23 | ♖ed1 | |

For the moment all White's pieces are directed against the queenside.

| 23 | ... | ♗xd6 |
| 24 | cxd6! | |

Another transformation. The point of White's play is his quiet 27th move.

| 24 | ... | ♖ab8 |
| 25 | a4 | |

A new trump comes into play. The advance of this pawn to a6 followed by the invasion at b7 is bound to decide the game.

| 25 | ... | ♖xb1 |
| 26 | ♕xb1 | ♕d8 |

It only remains for Black to play 27...♕b6, and his position will be tenable, but...

| 27 | ♕c2! | |

If now 27...♕b6 White has the decisive 28 ♖b1. The black queen is obliged to revert to its cheerless occupation of blockading the d6 pawn.

| 27 | ... | ♕d7 |
| 28 | ♕c5 | f6 |

Clearly, 28...♗b3 29 ♖b1 ♗xa4 30 ♖a1 is bad for Black.

29	a5	♔g7
30	♖b1	♖d8
31	a6	♔h6

Now White could have played 32 ♖b7 ♕xd6 33 ♕xa7, when the a-pawn must decide the game, but it was time to think also about the black king!

| 32 | ♕e3+ | |

More accurate than 32 ♖b7 ♕xd6 33 ♕e3+ g5 34 ♕f3 ♗d7, when all the same White is "forced" to capture the a7 pawn.

32	...	g5
33	♕f3	♕f7
34	♖b7	♖d7

(*see diagram next page*)

| 35 | ♗c4! | |

By diverting the defender of the f5 square, White wins by force.

| 35 | ... | f5 |

Clever, but insufficient. The acceptance of the sacrifice leads to mate:

35...♗xc4 36 ♖xd7, and if 36...♕xd7
37 ♕xf6+. Black also loses after 35...
♔g7 36 ♗xe6 ♕xe6 37 ♕f5. But now
misfortune strikes from the other side.

36   exf5

The c6 pawn is still weak! On
36...♗xc4 there follows 37 ♕xc6!

36   ...   ♕xf5
37   ♗xe6   Black resigns

WHAT WOULD YOU HAVE PLAYED?

No.23

White, to move, is one of the kings
of chess.

No.24

Again the player with White is a
former World Champion.

No.25

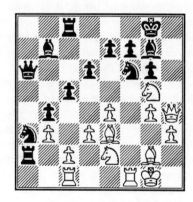

There is no way to defend the key c2
pawn, whereas Black's bishop and
knight are covering the approaches to
his king. Does this mean that the scales
have tipped in his favour? Even if the
turn to move is with his opponent, also
a former World Champion?

8 At the Royal Court

IF IT IS ACCEPTED AS AN AXIOM that the white and black troops are led by their kings, the royal court must be taken as the two extreme ranks at either end of the board, the 1st and 2nd, and the 7th and 8th. As in life, other pieces aim to come here for an audience, but in contrast to life — with evil intentions. After all, an invasion of the opponent's residence is both an aim, and a highly effective means of attack, and by the very nature of chess the pieces most suitable for this are the "straightforward-moving" rook and queen. Their "thoughts" are usually also straightforward: either to give mate on the back rank (if the king has no escape square, or if it is insufficiently open), or to drive the king via the escape square out of his residence into the open field, where it will come under the fire of the other pieces.

For the moment we are talking only about the very back rank, of which a detailed discussion invariably takes place in any lesson for beginners, and which is present in every chess primer. Nevertheless, variations on this theme are encountered from time to time even by the most famous of grandmasters...

(see diagram next column)

If World Champion Garry Kasparov were asked to find a win for White in this position, he would be unlikely to require more than five seconds of thought.

Kasparov-Ribli
World Cup, Skelleftea 1989

Yet he himself offered a draw, when after the obligatory 26 ♖xb5 ♗xe3 he could have played the very pretty and not especially complicated 27 ♖d8!! ♕xb5 (27...♖xd8 28 ♖d5!) 28 ♕d6 ♗xf2+ (28...♖e8 29 ♕e7 ♗xf2+ 30 ♔g2! ♕c6+ 31 ♔f1 ♕h1+ 32 ♔xf2 ♕xh2+ 33 ♔e1 ♕xg3+ 34 ♔d1! ♕g1+ 36 ♔d2, and the checks come to an end) 29 ♔xf2 ♕f5+ (or 29...♖e8 30 a4! ♕xa4 32 ♕xa6!) 30 ♔g2 ♕e4+ 31 ♔h3 ♕f5+ 32 g4 ♕f1+ 33 ♔g3 ♕g1+ 34 ♔f3 ♕f1+ 35 ♔e3 ♕h3+ 36 ♔d4! (36 ♔d2?? ♕h6+ 37 ♔d1 g6) 36...e5+ 37 ♔d5 ♕g2+ 38 ♔c5 ♕g1+ 39 ♔c6 ♕c1+ 40 ♔b7 ♕b1+ 41 ♔a7 ♕g1+ 42 ♔xa6, and Black can resign.

M.T. Kasparov overlooked this opportunity, but in the following game I did not miss the chance to allow a mate in two moves.

F.Olafsson-Tal
Alekhine Memorial, Moscow 1971

Here one might well ask the question — "What would you *not* have played?", and the overwhelming majority of players would give the correct answer. But...

21...♖c8?? 22 ♕xc8+ and, greatly surprised at what had happened, **Black resigned**.

I.D. In Kasparov's case it was all more or less understandable. The World Champion was "lulled" by the leisurely course of the game, without any particular tension, with exchanges, and, inwardly reconciled to a draw, at the last moment he simply did make the effort once more to check how well the 8th rank was defended. But what happened in your case? What was the mechanism of your blunder?

M.T. It was also purely psychological, as, evidently, is invariably the case. We know so much about tragedies on the back rank, that we simply forget about them. That is, these threats exist somewhere in theory, set apart, as it were, from our positions on the board. For me this game as though united them, if not for ever, then for a long time. And for probably ten years, in each game that I played, when the type of middlegame had been determined, I would spend a second, in order at almost every step to inspect my back rank. This would seem to have helped, and no more surprises of this type occurred.

I.D. But grandmaster Samuel Reshevsky was less lucky. It is well known that three times(!), at intervals of exactly eleven years, he overlooked stalemating combinations by his opponents. But things were also no better with the theme of our present conversation. Here are just two examples; there were also others.

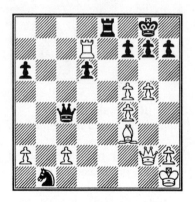

Unzicker-Reshevsky
Munich Olympiad 1958

For the moment White's extra pawn does not mean anything, since the f4 and a2 pawns are both "hanging", and, more important, a rook check at e1 is threatened.

White is saved by the eternal theme of the back rank.

27 ♕e2!! ♕c8 (after the exchange of queens White would have increased his material advantage) **28 ♖c7! ♕d8 29 ♕c4**

The black queen has been driven back, and the game is decided.

29...d5 30 ♗xd5 ♘d2 31 ♕c6 ♖f8 32 ♖xf7 ♖xf7 33 g6 hxg6 34 fxg6 ♔f8 35 gxf7 ♘e4 (mate in three moves was threatened: 36 ♕c5+ ♕e7 37 ♕c8+) **36 ♕e8+ Black resigns**.

Reshevsky-Fischer
Palma de Mallorca Interzonal 1970

White's attack on f7 has reached its peak and would seem bound to be crowned by success, since after **29...♕d4+ 30 ♔h1** Black's rook is attacked, and if 30...♖e7 he loses an important pawn — 31 ♕xd6. But is this obligatory?

30...♕f2!, and **White resigned** (31 ♖g1 ♖e1), because in the heat of the battle he completely forgot about the weakness of his back rank.

But things are not limited to these typical cases. In attacks on the back rank the heavy pieces are often helped by minor pieces, and sometimes the invasion of the back rank is merely a subsidiary factor, strengthening other attacking motifs.

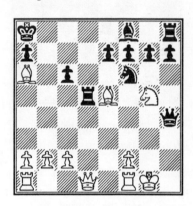

Rossolimo-Livingston
New York 1961

The black king is in a mating net, woven in particular by the white bishops, and White's entire subsequent play pursues just one aim: that of invading the 8th rank. This is not easy to achieve.

18 c4!! ♕xg5+ 19 ♗g3 ♖xd1 20 ♖axd1 ♘d5

20...♕a5 is less tenacious: 21 b4! ♕b6 22 c5 ♕xa6 23 ♖d8+, mating.

21 cxd5 c5 22 b4 c4 23 ♖d4

All the same, Black is unable to keep the files closed.

23...e5 24 dxe6 ♗xb4 25 ♖d7 ♖b8

Defending against 26 ♗b7 mate.

26 ♖fd1

White renews this threat: 27 ♗b7+ ♖xb7 28 ♖d8+, and mates.

26...♗e7 27 exf7 c3

On 27...♕f6 White would have won by 28 ♗xb8 ♔xb8 29 ♖b1+.

28 f8=♕

The diversion of the black rook or bishop leads to mate. **Black resigns**.

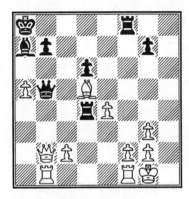

N.N.-Rossolimo
Paris 1944

In this game of the future grandmaster, the "sights" of Black's bishop and rook at f8 intersect at f2, which for the moment is defended. For the moment!

1...♖d1!!

Exploiting an additional nuance of the position — the overloading of White's queen's rook, Black creates irresistible threats both along the first, and the second (f2) ranks. White could already resign.

2 ♗xb7+ ♔b8 3 c4 ♖xf2!

This is much quicker than 3...♗xf2+ 4 ♕xf2 ♖xf2 5 ♖fxd1 ♕c5 6 ♗d5+ ♔c8 7 ♔h2, although here too matters end in a mating attack — 7...♖f6.

4 ♕xb5 ♖fxf1+ 5 ♔h2 ♖h1 mate

In this last example we had a glimpse of the diversion theme (of the queen's rook from the defence of the queen), which in principle is the main device in the attack on the back rank. Classic examples of this theme (Adams-Torre, New Orleans 1920, and Bernstein-Capablanca, Moscow 1914) are well known, and so we will restrict ourselves to three others, that create an unusually strong emotional impression.

Levitsky-Marshall
Breslau 1912

Despite being a piece down, White is clearly intending to take the initiative: after placing his rook on the 7th rank next move, he will create mating threats, and then, after the black knight moves, he will capture the rook on h3. True, Black already has a drawing mechanism in place: 23...♘e2+ 24 ♔h1 ♘g3+ 25 ♔g1 ♘e2+.

But he found what was perhaps the most beautiful move in the history of chess, emphasising the vertical and diagonal harmony of all the black pieces, attacking the king.

23...♕g3!! White resigns

Mate at h2 is threatened, and the

black queen is immune: 24 hxg3 ♘e2 mate; 24 fxg3 ♘e2+ 25 ♔h1 ♖xf1 mate; 24 ♕xg3 ♘e2+ 25 ♔h1 ♘xg3+ 26 ♔g1 ♘xf1 or 26...♘e2+, and Black remains a piece up.

This has something in common with the next game, where the blow struck by Black was equally spectacular, and as a manifestation of diagonal-vertical interaction was perhaps even more difficult to find.

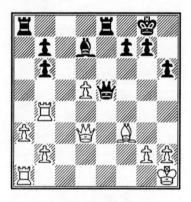

Mikenas-Bronstein
33rd USSR Ch., Tallinn 1965

White appears to stand not at all badly. He has the better pawn formation on the queenside, a passed pawn in the centre, and an active rook on b4, while the possible invasion by Black of his back rank — 24...♕e1+ is parried by the simple 25 ♕f1.

But his shrewd opponent had seen that the black queen on the long dark-square diagonal was aiming not only at the b2 pawn, which is securely defended, but also — "X-ray" fashion - at the unprotected rook on a1.

This means that it would be good to

divert the b2 pawn, and if not it, then the queen from the defence of f1, and if not it, then the rook from the back rank... And this was how Black conceived an amazing move, rivalling the concluding stroke in the previous example.

24...♖xa3!!

This attack on a three-times(!!) defended pawn, noticed moreover by "peripheral vision" on the edge of the board, led to White's capitulation.

The two preceding examples are chess classics, well and widely known. But here is one from more recent times.

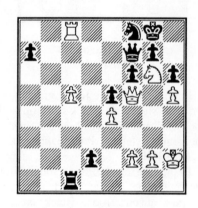

Kengis-Gufeld
Moscow 1983

All White's pieces have invaded the opponent's position, the price being the right for Black to have an extra (second!) queen. But after the immediate 45...d1=♕ 46 ♖xf8+ ♕xf8 47 ♕e6+ ♔h7 48 ♘xf8+ ♔h8, firstly, the number of queens becomes equal, and secondly (and most important) White promptly makes a new invasion — 49

♛e8!, with the threat of a "discovered mate".

Black therefore decided to play the diverting **45...ℋxc5**, hoping after 46 ℋxc5 d1=♛ 47 ℋc8 ♛d6 to advance his a-pawn and thereby divert the white rook or obtain a queen ending with an extra pawn. But here the strength of a rook in the opposing king's residence is fully revealed.

46 ♛e6!!

That's it! Black has no choice — 46...♛xe6 allows mate in two, and he could have spared himself the last few moves: **47 ♞e7+ ♚h7 48 ♛xf7 ♞e6 49 ♞xc8 d1=♛ 50 ♞e7 ♛d8 51 ♛xe6**.

But even if there is no direct mate, pieces invading the 8th rank can attack the opponent's king from the rear, and land unexpected blows in places that are inaccessible from "in front".

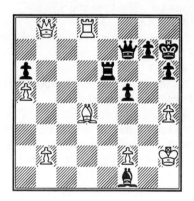

Geller-Tukmakov
50th USSR Ch., Moscow 1983

The game had a curious finish: **35 ℋh8+ ♚g6 36 ♛g3+ ♚h5 37 ♛g5 mate!**

This only became possible because the white rook was pinning the h6 pawn.

In the following game the then World Champion overlooked a similar possibility.

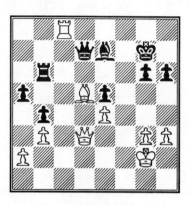

Karpov-Hübner
Montreal 1979

After driving the king onto a light square — 39 ℋg8+ ♚h7, White could have vacated the g8 square with gain of tempo for a "discovered check" to the queen and won a pawn — 40 ℋxg6 (he could also have won by 40 ♛e3, and if 40...ℌd8 41 ℋh8+!).

Instead he switched his rook to the 7th rank by **39 ♛c4 ℋf6 40 ℋc7**, which in this case proved insufficient for a win.

But usually, even a lone rook that has broken into the royal residence is a terrible force. The opposing pawns are initially arranged along the 7th rank, and in addition the enemy king is in the immediate vicinity. But when two pieces penetrate, and there is also support at hand...

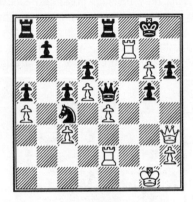

Ditman-Balanel
Erfurt 1955

If he picks up two pawns, White risks losing the game: 29 ♕xh6 ♔h8 30 ♕xg5 (30 ♖h7 ♕f6, and White has nothing better than to repeat moves, e.g. 31 ♖f2 ♕xc3!) 30...♖e5. But after all, he commands the cherished 7th rank!

29 ♕d7! ♘b6 30 ♖f8+! and mate next move. A typical idea: one attacking piece makes way for another, that is capable of more.

It is interesting that 29...♕h8 30 ♖h7 ♕f6 would have led to a mirror variation — 31 ♖h8+!

In the next diagram Black's rook has not only already penetrated into the opponent's position, but from the 2nd rank it is also ready to land a blow on the 1st rank — with the help of the other pieces, of course.

41...♘f3+! 42 ♔f1

A "step to the right" — 42 ♔h1 looks more dangerous, and this impression is confirmed by fantastically beautiful variations such as 42...

♗xe3!! 43 fxe3 ♖dxg2!! 44 ♘xg2 ♖g3, mating, or 43 ♘e6 ♖xf2 44 gxf3 ♖f1+ 45 ♔h2 exf3! 46 ♘xg5 ♗f4 mate.

Sunye-Kasparov
World Junior Team Ch., Graz 1981

However, the "step to the left" also leaves the white king under fire.

42...♗xe3!!

Joining the sights of both rooks on the g2 pawn.

43 fxe3

Naturally, 43 ♕xe3?? would have allowed mate on the 1st rank.

43...♖dxg2!

A rare instance, when the second rook does not aim for the 2nd rank. But here Black needs to create the threat of 44...♘d2+.

44 ♕c3 ♖h2 45 ♘e2 ♔h7!

Parrying the threat of perpetual check from c8 and f5, Black plans the "normal" invasion ...♖gg2.

46 ♕c8?!

46 ♕b4 was better, but even then Black would have won after 46...f5 47 ♕b5 f4! 48 ♕b4 ♘d2+! 49 ♕xd2 (or

49 ♔e1 f3 50 ♔xd2 ♖xe2+ 51 ♔c3 ♖xe3+ 52 ♔d4 f2) 49...♖h1+ 50 ♔f2 f3!

46...♖h1+ 47 ♔f2 ♘d2!

And **White resigned** in view of the forced 48 ♘g3 ♖h2+ 49 ♔e1 ♘f3+ 50 ♔f1 ♖xb2, when further resistance is pointless.

Spassky-Tal
25th USSR Ch., Riga 1958
Nimzo-Indian Defence

1	d4	♘f6
2	c4	e6
3	♘c3	♗b4
4	a3	♗xc3+
5	bxc3	c5
6	e3	♘c6
7	♗d3	e5

Even at that time Black knew perfectly well that the usual 7...0-0 8 ♘e2 b6 9 e4 ♘e8 leads to a complicated game, pleasant enough for him. But what if it was in this variation that White had prepared something? And so — Black deviates!

I.D. One of the favourite sayings of my co-author has always been: "When the tram-driver seeks new paths, the tram goes off the rails"...

M.T. But not this time!

8 ♘e2

On 8 d5 Black had "devised" 8...e4, when he stands well after either 9 ♗e2 ♘e5, or 9 dxc6 exd3 10 cxd7+ ♕xd7.

8	...	e4
9	♗b1	b6
10	♘g3	♗a6
11	f3	

The only real alternative was 11 ♘xe4 ♘xe4 12 ♗xe4 ♗xc4 13 f3.

The line recommended by Keres after the game, 11 ♕a4 ♘a5 12 ♘xe4, is less convincing, since Black quickly restores material equality by 12... ♘xe4 13 ♗xe4 ♖c8, with good play.

11 ... ♗xc4

"Pawn-grabbing" is punished: 11... exf3 12 ♕xf3 ♗xc4 13 ♘f5 0-0 14 e4, and White has a powerful initiative.

12 ♘f5!

In the variation 12 fxe4 d6 13 ♕f3 0-0 14 e5 dxe5 15 ♕xc6 exd4 it is Black who has a strong attack on the enemy king stranded in the centre.

12 ... 0-0

There is nothing else, but nothing else is required.

13	♘d6	♗d3
14	♗xd3	exd3
15	♕xd3	cxd4
16	cxd4	♘e8!
17	♘f5	d5

White's pawn centre has essentially been blocked, and Black can be happy with the result of his opening experiment.

18	a4	♘d6
19	♘xd6	

Of course, not 19 ♗a3 ♘xf5 20 ♗xf8? ♕g5, with numerous threats.

19	...	♕xd6
20	♗a3	♘b4
21	♕b3	a5
22	0-0	♖fc8
23	♖ac1	♕e6

Here Black offered a draw, having worked out the "long" variation 24 ♗xb4 axb4 25 ♔f2 ♕d6 26 ♔g1 ♕e6.

24	♗xb4	axb4
25	♔f2	♕d6

26 h3

White, naturally, avoids the objectively strongest continuation, since the tournament situation demanded that he play only for a win, but now after 26...h5, with the idea of ...h4, the initiative would have passed to Black.

M.T. But he played a routine move!

26	...	♔f8?
27	♖c2!	♖xc2+
28	♕xc2	g6
29	♖c1	♕d7
30	♕c6	♕xc6
31	♖xc6	♖a6

More accurate, of course, was 31...♖xa4 32 ♖xb6 ♔e7 with a quick draw. But now the game reverts... to the middlegame.

| 32 | a5 | b3 |

Here 32...♖xa5 33 ♖xb6 would have left White a pawn up.

33	axb6	b2
34	b7	b1=♕
35	♖c8+	♔g7
36	b8=♕	

The new queens have appeared on the same file, and in addition all the pieces are in the opponent's rearguard.

An unusual state of affairs!

36	...	♖a2+
37	♔g3	♕e1+
38	♔h2	♕xe3
39	♖g8+	♔f6

The draw that Black needed would have been more simply achieved by 39...♔h6 40 ♕f8+ ♔h5 41 ♕xf7 ♖xg2+!, forcing perpetual check.

40	♕d6+	♕e6
41	♕f4+	♕f5
42	♕d6+	♕e6
43	♕g3	

The position has radically changed. The white king is now in safety, whereas Black's is completely exposed to the elements.

| 43 | ... | ♕e3 |
| 44 | h4 | ♖e2! |

The tempting 44...♖a1 45 ♕d6+ ♕e6 46 ♕f4+ ♕f5 47 ♕h6 is weaker, since Black's pieces lose their coordination, and his king is in jeopardy.

45	♕d6+	♕e6
46	♕f4+!	♕f5
47	♕h6	

With the same idea.

47	...	♔e7
48	♕f8+	♔f6
49	♕g7+	♔e7
50	♖a8!	

The threat of a check at a7 forces the black pieces to retreat.

50	...	♕d7
51	♕f8+	♔f6
52	♖a6+	♖e6
53	♕h8+	♔e7
54	♖a8	♖e1
55	♔g3	h5
56	♔f2	♖e6

(see diagram next page)

57 ♖c8!

Now Black can only move his rook, since his queen is tied to the defence of d5 and e8. In the event of 57...♕d6 White wins by 58 ♖e8+ and 59 ♖d8+, and pawn moves are impossible.

And since 57...♖c6 fails to 58 ♕f8+ ♔f6 59 ♖d8 ♕c7 60 ♕h8+ ♔e7 61 ♖e8+ ♔d7 62 ♖e5, when White carries out a favourable regrouping, Black's reply is forced.

57 ...   ♖d6
58 ♕f8+?

An imperceptible, but significant mistake, which in the heat of the moment went unnoticed by both players. It is not possible to occupy, or more precisely, to take control of all the squares around the black king with the queen and rook alone, and, as Chekhover later showed, White should have mobilised his pawns with 58 g4! Then 58...♖e6 loses to 59 g5 (taking away the f6 square) 59...♖c6 60 ♕f8+ ♔e6 61 ♖e8+ ♔f5 62 ♖e7 ♖c2+ 63 ♔g3 ♕d6+ 64 ♖e5+. The alternative is 58... hxg4 59 ♕f8+ ♔f6 60 fxg4. Now on 60...♖e6 there follows 61 ♖c3 ♖e4 62

♖f3+ ♔e6 63 g5, with an unavoidable invasion at f6, while if 60...♖c6 61 ♖e8 ♖c2+ 62 ♔f3 ♖c3+ 63 ♔f4 ♕c7+ 64 ♖e5!, with the decisive threat of g4-g5 mate.

After the move played Black breathed a certain sigh of relief.

58 ...   ♔f6
59 ♖e8

Here 59 g4 is no longer so effective on account of 59...♖e6, and White prefers to threaten mate in two moves.

59 ...   ♖e6
60 ♕h8+   ♔f5
61 ♕h6

Either capture of the rook again leads to mate, and White continues the attack on the dark squares, although it is no longer dangerous.

61 ...   ♔f6
62 ♕h8+

Winning a pawn by 62 ♖d8 ♕c6 63 ♕g5+ ♔g7 64 ♕xd5 (64 ♖xd5 f6) would have allowed Black to seize the initiative after 64...♕c2+ 65 ♔g3 ♕c7+ 66 ♔f2 ♕f4.

62 ...   ♔f5
63 ♖d8

White should now have admitted that he had missed the win, and agreed to a draw, but in the heat of the battle how difficult it can be to soberly assess a change in the chess climate!

63 ...   ♕c6!

Threatening for a start to check at c2 and c7.

64 ♖c8?

White should have concerned himself over his own king — 64 ♔g3, when he is still within the safety zone.

64 ...   ♕a6
65 ♔g3   ♕d6+
66 ♔h3

No better is 66 ♔f2 ♕b4, when it is the black pieces that "invite themselves" to a reception with the white king — with evil intentions. Had White left his rook at d8, this would not have been possible on account of the capture on d5, forcing mate.

66 ...   ♖e1
67 g3

Or 67 g4+ hxg4+ 68 fxg4+ ♔f4 69 ♕h6+ ♔e4! 70 ♖e8+ ♔f3, and the white king is mated.

67 ...   ♖g1
68 f4   ♖e1

Black has excluded the counter g3-g4+, which was possible in certain cases, and has taken complete command. He now threatens 69...♕e6 with a discovered check and a quick mate. The only way to defend against this was 69 ♖e8, but then after 69...♖xe8 70 ♕xe8 ♕e6 the d4 pawn is soon lost — and with it the game.

Rather than suffering without end, White prefers an end without suffering.

69 ♖c2   ♕e6
70 ♖f2   ♖h1+

71 ♔g2   ♕e4+
72 ♖f3   ♔g4
73 ♕c8+   f5

White resigns: after 74 ♕c3 Black has the simple, but elegant 74...♖f1, and in the pawn ending he can, if he wishes, have four extra pawns.

WHAT WOULD YOU HAVE PLAYED?

No.26

White is on the attack, and he would appear to have achieved a great deal. He has broken up the black king's pawn shelter, and after the fall of the f5 pawn he will begin a direct assault on h7 and f7.

True, it is Black to move, but his counterplay with 22...♗d4+ 23 ♔h1 ♘f2+ 24 ♖xf2 ♗xf2 does not work on account of 25 ♘xe8. What then should he do?

No.27

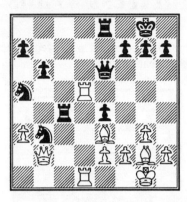

No.28

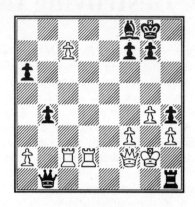

For the pawn White has gained more than sufficient compensation. He has seized the open file in the centre, the black knights have been lured to the edge of the board, and finally, there is the possibility of an attack on g7 (24 ♖g5). But from its ideal position the "central defender" — the black queen — is capable of withstanding the assault...

No.29

For a long time Black's position in No.28 was lost. But what is it now? The black pieces have, after all, entered the white king's residence...

It is true that the white rooks have occupied the 7th rank, on which, incidentally, there is not a single pawn. But what next?

9 Destroying the Fortress Walls

AN ENGLISHMAN'S HOME is his castle. This saying is also encountered in various versions among Russians, Germans, Spaniards, and, of course... chess kings. The pawn rank f7/g7/h7 (kingside castling does after all occur much more frequently than queenside, at least for the defending side) is that wall behind which the king seeks shelter. And for a time he finds it until — or if — an attack achieves its goal: the destruction of the fortress walls.

Moreover, the pawns are most solidly placed when they are on their initial squares. Firstly, in this case the attacker must spend much more time on the concentration of force (we will see how a rapid attack is possible from afar against a pawn that has advanced to h6), and secondly, the advance at the required moment of the required pawn is capable to cutting a trajectory of the attacking pieces. But as is known, a pawn is not able to reverse its move, and a step forward may irreparably reduce the further defensive resources, as occurred, for example, in the following game.

Black already has his sights set on the enemy king position, his rook is on course for h5, and the simplifying attempt 15 ♗xg4 ♘xg4 16 h3 is fraught with danger: 16...♘xf2! 17 ♔xf2 ♕h4+ with a powerful attack. White could still have maintained approximate equality by the calm 15 ♗e1, defending f2 and now planning the exchange of bishops. Instead, an incautious advance presented Black with a clear target.

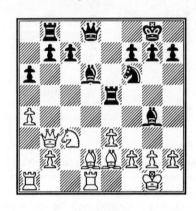

Gilfer-Böök
Stockholm Olympiad 1937

15 h3? ♗xh3! 16 gxh3 ♕d7 17 ♗f1

Now the king's escape is cut off to the centre, where it would be covered by the e- and f-pawns.

The only way of prolonging the resistance (although it would not have changed the outcome) was by 17 f4 ♕xh3 18 fxe5 ♗xe5 19 ♗f3 (otherwise mate) 19...♕xf3 20 ♗e1 ♘g4 21 ♖d2, when a possible finish would be 21...♘xe3 22 ♖f2 ♕g4+ 23 ♔h1 ♕h3+ 24 ♔g1 ♗h2+ 25 ♔h1 ♗g3+ 26 ♔g1 ♗xf2+ 27 ♔xf2 ♖e8, and wins.

17...♖g5+ 18 ♔h1 ♕c6+ 19 e4 ♘xe4 20 ♘xe4 ♕xe4+ 21 f3 ♕e5 22 f4 ♕e4+ 23 ♔h2 ♗xf4+ 24 ♗xf4 ♕xf4+ 25 ♔h1 ♕f2 White resigns.

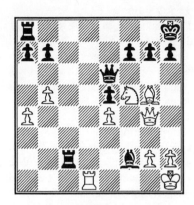

Castaldi-Euwe
Stockholm Olympiad 1937

In this game from the same Olympiad, for the exchange White has a powerful attacking grouping against a king, whose pawn shelter is not supported by pieces. Now 32 ☐d6 followed by ♗h6 is threatened, and attempts to avert this by the advance of any of the three black pawns merely make things worse.

E.g.: 31...h6? 32 ♗xh6, or 31...f6? 32 ♗h6 g6 33 ♗g7+ ♔g8 34 ♘h6+, or, finally, 31...g6 32 ♘h6 ♔g7 (32...♕xg4?? 33 ♗f6 mate) 33 ♕xe6 fxe6 34 ☐d7+ ♔f8 35 g3!, with the irresistible threat of ♘g4, mating. Only in this last variation does Black retain a draw after 32...☐f8 33 ♕xe6 fxe6 34 ☐d8 ♔g7 35 ☐d7+, although here too White has other possibilities, such as 33 ♕f3, with the idea on 33...f5, 33...f6 or 33...♔g7 of replying 34 ♘g4.

Black did not disturb his pawns prematurely, after **31...☐ac8 32 ♗h6 g6** (now is the right time!) **33 ♕g5 ♗d4 34 ♗g7+ ♔g8 35 ♗f6 ☐2c7 36**

h4 ♗c5 he retained hopes of a defence, and after mistakes by White he even won.

Therefore an assault on the royal fortress often begins with the discovery and creation in it of weak points, which then provide targets for a decisive blow. As, for example, in the following game.

Salov-Sax
World Cup, Skelleftea 1989

White's powerful piece outpost at d5 gives him an appreciable advantage, but even so it is hard to imagine that the walls of the royal fortress, which have no vulnerable points, will collapse within a few moves. After all, Black intends ...♗c5 and ...♘e7, eliminating the main enemy, after which his queen will reach the kingside via c6.

21 ♕f3!!

By the threat of 22 ♘xe7+ White gains time to transfer his knight to f5, and — most important — to force the opponent into a fatal weakening of one of the links in his pawn chain.

21...☐fe8

Forced, since 21...♖ae8 22 ♘f5 leaves Black either the exchange down — 22...♕c8 23 ♘dxe7+ ♘xe7 24 ♘d6, or simply in a bad position — 22...♕b8 23 ♘dxe7+ ♘xe7 24 ♘d6 ♖d8 25 ♖c3.

22 ♘f5 ♗f8

Apparently satisfactory, but the f7 pawn is no longer covered by the rook.

23 ♘h6+! gxh6 24 ♘f6+ ♔h8 25 ♖xd7

Now 25...♕c8 26 ♕f5 leads to mate, while the game continuation **25...♕xd7 26 ♘xd7 ♘d4 27 ♕d5 ♗g7 28 e3 ♘e6** merely allowed Black to prolong a hopeless struggle.

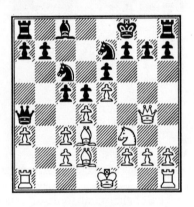

Murey-Poldauf
Podolsk 1991

By combining two opening schemes (...♔f8 and ...♕a5-a4) Black has not equalised fully, although he has created some counterplay. Thus, in particular, he threatens 11...c4 12 ♗e2 ♕xc2, when on the kingside the black queen becomes the central defender.

So White begins trying to break up the enemy king's pawn shelter.

11 ♕h5! h6

Forced, since in the event of 11... cxd4 12 ♘g5 ♘xe5 13 ♘xh7+ ♖xh7 14 ♕xh7 ♘5g6 the advance of White's h-pawn is decisive. And after 11...g6 he mounts a swift attack on the dark squares.

12 dxc5 ♕a5

Simplification by 12...♘g6 13 ♗xg6 fxg6 14 ♕xg6 ♕e4+ 15 ♕xe4 dxe4 16 ♘h4 ♔f7 17 f4! leaves White too many pawns ahead — even with opposite-colour bishops.

13 0-0 ♕xc5 14 ♖fb1 ♘a5 (15 ♖b5 was threatened) **15 ♘g5 g6 16 ♕h4**

White has forced another weakening advance. The g6 and h6 pawns have now become targets for attack, and there is an invasion point at f6. Is this sufficient?

16...♘c4 17 ♘xf7!

Quite sufficient! The shelter's last support is destroyed, after which there is no defence.

17...♔xf7

If 17...♘xd2, then 18 ♘xh8 ♘xb1 19 ♘xg6+ ♘xg6 20 ♕f6+ is more than adequate.

18 ♕f6+ ♔g8 19 ♗xg6 ♘xe5

No better is 19...♖h7 20 ♗xh7+ ♔xh7 21 ♕f7+ ♔h8 22 ♕f8+ ♔h7 23 ♗xh6, when the pinned knight is unable to defend g7.

20 ♗h5 ♘7c6

Otherwise (for example, after 20... ♕d6) the white rook joins the attack along the 4th rank.

21 ♗f4 ♕f8 22 ♗xe5 ♕xf6 23 ♗xf6, and White won easily and quickly: **23...♖h7 24 ♖e1 ♖c7 25 ♖e3 ♔h7 26 f4 ♗d7 27 f5! exf5 28 ♖ae1 f4 29 ♖e7+! ♘xe7 30 ♖xe7+ ♔g8 31**

罝g7+ 會f8 **32 罝h7**. The attack on the bare king continued even after the exchange of queens.

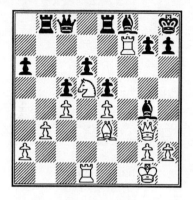

Tal-Rantanen
Tallinn 1979

White's advantage comprises several factors (powerful piece outpost in the centre, rook on the 7th rank, occupation of the open f-file, and, finally, superior pawn formation and great piece activity), but is this not all temporary? For example, 24 罝df1 兔h5 25 罝a7 罝b7, and the pressure of the rook along the 7th rank has already been neutralised; and besides, after each exchange of heavy pieces Black's position becomes increasingly safe.

But White finds another way: he creates weaknesses around the enemy king. For the moment g7 is securely defended, and there is no way of increasing the pressure on it, while not one of his pieces is aimed towards h7.

24 ᐃf6!! gxf6

This forced (24...兔xd1 25 罔h4 h5 26 罔g5 罝b7 27 罔g6, and mates) capture of the knight immediately

transforms h7 into a real weakness, and the attack proceeds against it.

25 罔h4 兔g7 26 兔h6 兔xd1

The only way to resist was by 26... 罝g8 27 罝xd6 罝b7 28 兔xg7+ 罝xg7 29 罝xb7 罔xb7 30 罝d8+ 罝g8 31 罝xg8+ 會xg8 32 罔xg4+, although with an extra pawn and more secure king, White must win the queen ending.

27 兔xg7+ 會g8

After the game it transpired that, strangely enough, both(!) players had aimed for this position. Alas...

28 兔h8! 會xf7 29 罔xf6+ 會g8 30 罔g7 mate

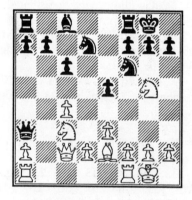

F.Olafsson-Donner
Lugano 1970

While Black has been engaged in exchanging White's fianchettoed dark-square bishop, White has "launched" his knight to g5 and now embarks on an attack against the king's fortress. His first task is to weaken the pawn screen, to prepare breaches in the fortress walls.

13 f4 exf4 14 罝xf4 h6

The threat of 15 兔g4 forces Black

to make this advance, but this is only the start.

15 ♘f3

There was little point in playing 15 ♘ge4: at the required moment the defender could have begun simplifying.

15...♕e7 16 ♖f1 ♖e8

Black vacates a square for his queen's knight. This weakens his defence of f6, but how else is he to complete his development? This problem is not solved by 16...c5 17 ♘h4! b6 18 ♘f5 ♕e6 19 ♗f3 ♖b8 20 ♘d5, when he can essentially resign: 21 ♗g4 followed by ♘xh6+ is threatened, and 20...♘xd5 allows the crushing 21 ♗xd5 ♕e8 22 ♘xh6+ gxh6 23 ♕g6+.

17 ♘d4 ♘f8 18 ♗d3 ♗e6 19 ♖xf6

After this the walls of the king's fortress lie in ruins.

19...gxf6 20 ♘e4 ♘d7 21 ♕d1 f5

Otherwise 22 ♕h5 and 23 ♖f3 with a quick mate.

22 ♘xf5 ♗xf5 23 ♖xf5

Now the attack continues with material practically equal.

23...♕e6 24 ♕f3 ♘e5 25 ♕g3+ ♔f8 (25...♔h8 26 ♖f6) **26 ♘f6! ♘xd3 27 ♘h7+ ♔e7 28 ♕c7+ ♕d7 29 ♖xf7+ ♔xf7 30 ♕xd7+ ♖e7 31 ♕f5+** and **Black resigned**, since after 31...♔g8 White wins most quickly by 32 ♕g6+.

After playing the opening badly (*see diagram next column*), Black is already obliged to parry the threat of 10 ♘g5 g6 11 h4.

9...♖e8 10 ♗d3 h6

Insufficient is 10...♘f8 11 ♘g5, when 11...h6 is bad in view of 12 ♗h7+. Black immediately has to grant the opponent a "chink" in his defences.

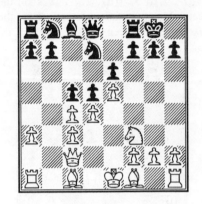

Salov-Taulbut
Moscow 1983

11 h4 ♘b6 12 ♖h3 dxc4 13 ♗e4 cxd4 14 ♖g3 ♔h8

No better is 14...d3 15 ♕d2 ♔f8, when a blow is landed on another section of the wall — 16 ♖xg7!

15 ♗xh6 g6 (15...gxh6 16 ♕d2) **16 ♗g5 ♕d7 17 ♗f6+ ♔g8 18 ♗xg6 Black resigns**.

Sacrifices on h7

Yes, Black's h7 pawn (or White's at h2) is always slightly weak, even with the ideal pawn formation, if, of course, it is defended only by the king. The attacking mechanism has been too well known for 150, if not 200 years, for us to give a detailed discussion here. A bishop sacrifice at h7 draws out the king, the knight advances to g5 with check, clearing the way for the queen (usually to h5) and a rook (usually along the 3rd rank). It is probable that thousands of such games throughout the world have been played – and won!

– so we have included here some that are complicated by certain additional motifs. After all, for a chess player, as for a musician, it is not enough to know only the rudiments, and to be able to perform only a single song...

In the table of the Taxco Interzonal Tournament, 1985, the result of the game **Speelman-Tal** was quite different. But it ended rather too quickly in a draw, and the players sat down... to play blitz!

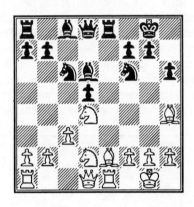

It is easy to see that the framework of the combination is in place (13... ♗xh2+ and 14...♘g4+), but will not the entire concept collapse? After all, it appears that White has a defence...

13...♗xh2+! 14 ♔xh2 ♘g4+ 15 ♔g3

The only way to avoid inevitable defeat was by 15 ♗xg4 ♕xh4+ 16 ♗h3 ♗xh3 17 gxh3 ♕xf2+ 18 ♔h1 ♘xd4 19 cxd4 ♕xd4...

M.T. ...but in this case I simply would not have shown this game. Speelman, fortunately, played differently, reckoning after the queen check at d6 to block with the f2 pawn.

15...♖e3+!

Diversion of the defender, obstruction — call it what you will: 16 fxe3 ♕d6+ 17 ♔f3 ♘ce5+ 18 ♔g3 ♘d3+ 19 ♔f3 ♘h2 mate.

M.T. Quite an attractive concept?

I.D. In-struc-tive!

This same mechanism can work even when the g5 invasion square is securely controlled.

Veresov-Dzentelovsky
Minsk 1956

Nominally Black has no weaknesses, and his position would be ideal, but - with his knight at f6 (defending h7) and his rook at f8 (defending f7). Without them White's thematic attack is perfectly correct.

16 ♗xh7+! ♔xh7 17 ♘e5!

The f7 pawn is attacked, and the queen's invasion at h7 will be supported by the rook, whose path along the 3rd rank has been cleared.

The further course of the game is of no interest, since Black made a blunder. But even the comparatively best 17...♔g8 18 ♕h5 ♖f8 19 ♖e3 f6 20

♘g6! (in the variation 20 ♘xd7 ♕xd7 21 ♕xa5 e5! Black has serious counterplay for the pawn, while for the reckless 20 ♖h3 fxe5 21 ♕h7+ ♔f7 22 ♖g3 ♗f6! 23 dxe5 ♗xe5! 24 ♕h5+ ♔g8 25 ♕xe5 ♕f6 there is no need) leaves White with a very strong attack, e.g.: 20...♘c4 21 ♖g3 ♗c6 22 ♗h6, or 20...♗e8 21 ♘xe7+ ♕xe7 22 ♕xa5 ♖f7 23 ♗a3 ♕c7 24 ♕h5, and he is simply a "healthy" pawn to the good.

Tal-N.N.
Simultaneous Display, Berlin 1974

With his last move 14 ♗g5 White has removed Black's control of g5, and if 14...♗xg5 the sacrifice 15 ♗xh7+ works, so to speak, in pure form (e.g. 15...♔xh7 16 ♘xg5+ ♔g6 17 ♘xf7!). However...

14...♘xe5

M.T. To be completely honest, I overlooked this capture. But in "justification", this was perhaps because I intuitively sensed that you can't play like this in the opening, and I had to find a reason why this move was bad. And I found one.

15 ♗xe7 ♘xf3 16 ♖xf3 ♕xe7 17 ♗xh7+ ♔xh7 18 ♖h3+ ♔g8

Now the routine 19 ♕h5 does not achieve anything after the equally routine 19...f6. But in this ancient idea it proves possible to include a relatively new motif.

19 ♘f5 ♕g5 20 ♕h5! Black resigns: he is mated after both 20...♕xh5 21 ♘e7+, and 20...f6 21 ♘e7+.

For the successful pursuit of a king it is by no means always essential to destroy its pawn shelter. It can be quite sufficient to break up the formation, by doubling the pawns on the f-file. This immediately gives rise to a whole complex of weak squares, on which the enemy pieces can approach the king, and, more important, the pawn at h7 (h2) is always practically indefensible.

Popov-Malevinsky
Sevastopol 1969

For a minimal payment Black has managed to "ruffle the hair" of the white king, which has prudently taken shelter in the corner. Without losing time, he continues the attack.

14...♘h5! 15 ♖g1

White has no time to take the bishop: 15 fxg4 ♕h4, and the h2 pawn is vulnerable (16 f4 ♘g3+).

15...♕h4 16 ♖g2 ♗h3 17 ♕d1

If 17 ♕f1 Black wins prettily by 17...♖xe3! 18 fxe3 ♘g3+! 19 hxg3 ♗xg2+ 20 ♔xg2 ♕xg3+ and 21... ♕h2 mate.

17...♗xg2+ 18 ♔xg2 ♕xh2+ 19 ♔f1 ♖xe3 20 fxe3 ♗g3 21 ♕d2 ♕h1+ 22 ♔e2 ♘f4+! White resigns.

I.D. For probably twenty years I have been pressing you to disclose that mechanism by which you seek — and, more important, find, your famous combinational attacks. But you always point to your nose and say that you readily sense something attractive, and not necessarily on the chess board...

M.T. I am also happy to repeat all this now! But to be serious, the following example is indeed very apt, and a book is a book.

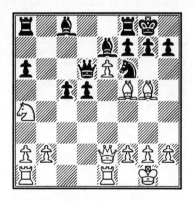

Nikhamkin-Gruzdev
Klaipeda 1984

That White has prepared an attack

— this is evident. The e-pawn has advanced a long way, his bishops are well employed, while Black's hanging pawns, although defended, are nevertheless hanging on open files, and in this position the advance of either of them is not a breakthrough, but a weakening. After the exchange of the knight at f6, the h7 pawn is supported by the king alone, and this may prove insufficient. So that of all the kingside pawns, only the one at g7 feels secure.

As soon as I saw this position, two quite old games immediately flashed through my mind.

Tal-Spassky
Candidates Final, Tbilisi 1965

Here White's light-square bishop is operating with an "X-ray" beam along the pawn-free a2-g8 diagonal, the d5 square is the key one in Black's defences, and it was in the hope of the "ricochet" **28 ♘xc6 ♖xc6 29 ♖a8!** that White made his 28th move.

Black, however, saw through White's threat, replied **28...♗xc6**, and managed to draw without difficulty.

Tal v. Brinck-Claussen
Havana Olympiad 1966

Here there is a similar pattern, and after **33 ♘xd5 ♗xd5 34 ♖a8! ♗xa2 35 ♖xd8+ ♔f7 36 ♕c6! ♘e7 37 ♕e8+ ♔e6 38 ♖c8** White successfully concluded his pursuit of the king: **38...♕d5 39 ♖c3 ♕d7 40 ♖e3+ ♔d6 41 ♕b8+ ♔c6 42 a4 ♘d5 43 ♖e1 ♕d6 44 ♖c1+ ♔d7 45 ♕c8+ Black resigns**.

I.D. Yet in our example the light-square bishop is not in the same place, and also...

M.T. After the capture on f7 the diagonal will be opened, the d5 pawn's defence can be removed, and in general one senses the "ricochet" theme.

I.D. Again intuition, sensing, and all these hunting associations!

M.T. Precisely! But with one nuance: the position is not difficult to calculate, knowing the idea of the attack, and if there is nothing concrete, then for the moment White still has strengthening moves — ♖ad1 and, perhaps, ♘c3.

A concrete and forcing variation was found, including the "h7 theme".
18 ♘b6!! ♕xb6
Otherwise simply 19 ♘xc8 and 20 exf7+, winning the exchange.
19 ♗xf6 ♗xf6 20 ♗xh7+!
The wall of another royal fortress collapses.
20...♔xh7 21 ♕h5+ ♔g8 22 exf7+ ♖xf7 23 ♖e8+ ♖f8 24 ♕xd5+
Black resigns. Even the best move, 24...♗e6 does not save him after 25 ♖xe6, e.g. 25...♖ad8 26 ♖d6+ ♖f7 27 ♕xf7+ ♔xf7 28 ♖xb6.

Sacrifices on h7 and g7

Of the attacks on these squares, after which the king proves completely "bare", pride of place goes to the double-bishop sacrifice, which was discovered on the chess board by the then World Champion in the following game. A rare instance, where the time that an important tactical device was conceived is known to the very day!

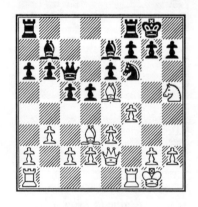

Lasker-Bauer
Amsterdam 1889

The white knight has just advanced from g3 to h5, and White's subsequent blows are as inevitable as the rising of the sun.

14...♘xh5

There is nothing else. 14...♘e8 is decisively met by 15 ♗xg7 ♘xg7 16 ♕g4, and 14...h6 by 15 ♗xf6 ♗xf6 16 ♘xf6+ gxf6 17 ♕g4+ ♔h8 18 ♕h4 ♔g7 19 ♖f3 ♖fd8 20 ♖g3+, winning the f6 and h6 pawns. If 14...d4 15 ♗xf6 ♗xf6 16 ♕g4 e5 Black runs into 17 ♗e4!, while 16...♔h8 17 ♖f3 ♖g8 allows 18 ♗xh7 ♖gd8 19 ♕h3.

15 ♗xh7+!

"The start of a very deep and elegant combination" (Steinitz).

15...♔xh7 16 ♕xh5+ ♔g8 17 ♗xg7!!

Lasker's contemporaries were very well familiar with the sacrifice on h7, but the second sacrifice on g7 was a revelation to them.

17...♔xg7

Or 17...f6, as Nimzowitsch subsequently played against Tarrasch (cf. the next example), but then 18 ♖f3 ♕e8 19 ♕h8+ ♔f7 20 ♕h7.

18 ♕g4+ ♔h7 19 ♖f3 e5 20 ♖h3+ ♔h6 21 ♖xh6+ ♔xh6 22 ♕d7

A finale, without which the combination would be incorrect: a double attack on the two bishops. Here the curtain could already have been lowered...

22...♗f6 23 ♕xb7 ♔g7 24 ♖f1 ♖ab8 25 ♕d7 ♖fd8 26 ♕g4+ ♔f8 27 fxe5 ♗g7 28 e6 ♖b7 29 ♕g6 f6 30 ♖xf6+ ♗xf6 31 ♕xf6+ ♔e8 32 ♕h8+ ♔e7 33 ♕g7+ Black resigns.

Since then more than a hundred years have passed, and although only a small number of such combinational routs have appeared in print, they have long become textbook examples. Moreover, the difference lies only in the preparation of the attack and the nuances in its implementation.

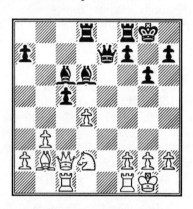

Nimzowitsch-Tarrasch
St Petersburg 1914

A brilliant tactician like Tarrasch could easily, had he wished, have found a way of shattering the peace of the white king — 19...♗xg2!, and after 20 ♔xg2 (20 dxc5 ♕g5, and wins) 20...♕g5+ 21 ♔f3 (21 ♔h1 ♕f4) 21...♖fe8! 22 ♖g1 ♕f4+ 23 ♔g2 ♖e2 White could have resigned with a clear conscience. But Tarrasch had no desire to conduct the attack in this way: he already knew of Lasker's combination! Hence:

19...♗xh2+ 20 ♔xh2 ♕h4+ 21 ♔g1 ♗xg2 22 f3

The bishop is immune on account of a similar double attack to that of 25 years earlier, made at the end of the combination: 22 ♔xg2 ♕g4+ 23 ♔h1 ♖d5 24 ♕xc5 ♖h5+! 25 ♕xh5 ♕xh5+ 26 ♔g2 ♕g5+ and 27...♕xd2.

22...♖fe8!

Preparing ...♕g3, which if played immediately would have been parried by 23 ♘e4.

23 ♘e4 ♕h1+ 24 ♔f2 ♗xf1 25 d5

Naturally, White cannot take the bishop on account of the loss of his queen, but he can try to give mate on the a1-h8 diagonal...

25...f5!

Here too Black should not be criticised! The choice was to win prosaically by 25...♕g2+ 26 ♔e3 (26 ♔e1 ♕xf3) 26...♕xc2 27 ♖xc2 f5 28 ♔f2 fxe4, or to go in for a forcing and pretty variation calculated to the end.

26 ♕c3 ♕g2+ 27 ♔e3 ♖xe4+! 28 fxe4 f4+

One imagines that Tarrasch deliberately avoided the "crude" mate in three moves: 28...♕g3+ 29 ♔d2 ♕f2+ 30 ♔d1 ♕e2 mate.

29 ♔xf4 ♖f8+ 30 ♔e5 ♕h2+ 31 ♔e6 ♖e8+ 32 ♔d7 ♗b5 mate

Also a pure mate, but here Black has no "superfluous" inactive pieces.

22 ♗xf6 ♗xa4 23 ♗xh7+ ♔xh7 24 ♕h5+ ♔g8 25 ♗xg7 ♗xh2+

So as somehow to include the queen in the defence. If immediately 25... ♔xg7 26 ♕g5+ ♔h7 27 ♘f5, and Black has no adequate defence, e.g. 27...♗e5 28 ♕h5+ ♔g8 29 ♘e7+ ♔g7 30 ♕xe5+ ♕f6 31 ♕g3+ ♔h8 (intending to answer 32 ♖e3 with 32... ♗c2!) 32 ♕h3+ ♔g7 33 ♕g4+ ♔h8 (33...♔h7 34 ♖e3) 34 ♕h5+ ♔g7 35 ♘f5+ ♔g8 36 ♕g4+! and 37 ♖e3, winning the queen.

26 ♔xh2 ♔xg7 27 ♘f5+ ♔f6 (or 27...♔g8 28 ♕g5+ ♕g6 29 ♘e7+) **28 ♕h6+ ♔xf5 29 ♕xb6 ♗b5 30 ♖e3 f6 31 ♕e6+ Black resigns**.

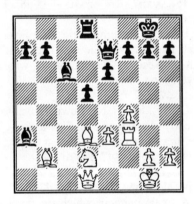

Alekhine-Drewitt
Portsmouth 1923

For the knight Black has three pawns, but... There was Amsterdam 1889, St Petersburg 1914, and...

20 ♗xh7+

"A similar sacrifice of two bishops had already occurred earlier. Here its interest lies solely in the way in which this combination was prepared," writes

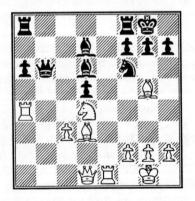

Gaudin-Oskam
Bromley 1920

Alekhine, and he goes on to assert that White's earlier pressure on the queen-side was merely a camouflage for the attack on the king.

20...♔xh7 21 ♖h3+ ♔g8 22 ♗xg7

If he takes the bishop, Black is mated in three moves, while on 22...f6 White does not need to win the queen for rook, bishop and pawn (23 ♕h5 ♕xg7 24 ♖g3), since he has 23 ♗h6! ♕h7 24 ♕h5! ♗f8 (or 24...♗e8 25 ♖g3+ ♔h8 26 ♗g7+ ♔g8 27 ♗xf6+) 25 ♕g4+ ♔h8(f7) 26 ♗xf8. It is not clear whether Drewitt saw all this, or if he took his opponent "at his word", but at any event **Black resigned**.

Kuzmin-Sveshnikov
41st USSR Ch., Moscow 1973

In the next diagram, for the pawn White has a lead in development and a huge spatial advantage, but if he attacks in the approved manner with 16 ♗xh7+ ♔xh7 17 ♕h5+ ♔g8 18 ♗xg7 ♔xg7 19 ♕g4+ ♔h7 20 ♖f3, Black's defences hold after 20...♘xf4 21 ♖xf4 f5. Therefore the combination begins with an overture!

16 ♘b6! ♘xb6, and now that given above. In the final position, although three pieces down, White gives mate from h3.

Sacrifices on g7

Here everything is more or less clear, if the attacking side succeeds in opening a file for his heavy artillery.

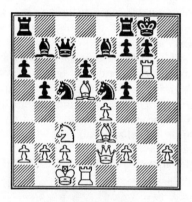

A.Sokolov-Salov
USSR 1983

At the cost of a piece White has opened the g-file and the a2-g8 diagonal for his attack, but the success of it depends on whether he can further break up the black king's pawn shelter: otherwise one of White's strikers, his light-square bishop, will be exchanged.

18 ♖xg7+! ♔xg7 **19 ♖g1+** ♘g6 (the only move) **20 exf5** (with the terrible threat of 21 ♕h5) **20...♖h8 21 ♗d4+ ♗f6 22 fxg6 fxg6**

The defence is not eased by 22...♗xd4 23 gxf7+ ♔f6 24 ♕g4 (threatening 25 ♕g5 mate) 24...♔e7 25 ♕xd4, and although a rook up, Black cannot save the game.

23 ♕g4 ♖h6 24 ♗xf6+ ♔h7 (24... ♔xf6 25 ♕d4+) **25 ♖e1 ♗xd5 26 ♘xd5 ♕c8 27 ♖e7+ ♔g8 28 ♖g7+ ♔f8 29 ♖g8+ ♔xg8 30 ♘e7+**, and **Black resigned**.

I.D. Misha, it would seem that we will be unable here to achieve an ideal arrangement of our topics. It should be said that the sacrifice on g7 is especially effective when the pawn rank has already been disturbed, but the vulnerability of the h6 pawn is our next theme.

M.T. Well, so what! Remember how they exhorted us in University: "Marxism is not a dogma, but a guide to action". Life has confirmed all this to be the exact opposite, but to chess this is indeed applicable.

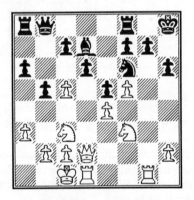

Hartston-Richardson
Westergate 1983

In this position position, where, incidentally, White won the brilliancy prize, the centre is blocked by pawns, and the absence of his bishops means that his only chances of an attack lie on the open g-file. But Black has made

preparations to parry it, by vacating g8 for his rook, and he could have faced the future with confidence, had not his h-pawn made a step forward in the opening. True, for the moment there is nothing to attack it with, but it can be weakened...

18 ♖xg7! ♔xg7 19 ♖g1+ ♔h7 20 ♘g5+! ♔h8

The acceptance of this second sacrifice would merely have hastened the end.

21 ♘e6

This does not come into the category of quiet moves, but such an idea is worth "memorising". (Besides, the "natural" 21 ♘xf7+?? simply loses, since it brings in the black rook to the defence of g7 and h7). Now Black could have resigned, but he steadfastly played on to the end.

21...♘h7 22 ♕xh6 ♖g8 23 ♖g7 ♖xg7 24 ♕xg7 mate

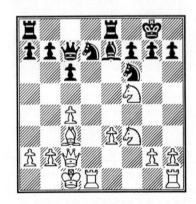

Kasparov-Nikolic
Manila Olympiad 1992

Nominally Black has achieved everything, or nearly everything. He is developed and he has an ideal pawn formation, but for an instant, before he plays his bishop to f8, his g7 pawn is protected only by the king. And it is this instant that White grasps!

17 ♘xg7! ♔xg7 18 ♕f5 ♘f8

Otherwise the threat of 19 ♖xd7 cannot be parried: 18...♖ad8 19 ♖df1 ♘f8 20 ♕g5+ ♘g6 21 ♘h4, and the pin on the long dark-square diagonal is decisive, while 18...♔f8 loses to 19 ♘g5 h6 20 ♖xd7 ♕xd7 21 ♘h7+.

19 h4!

White unhurriedly prepares to take the g6 square away from the black knight, and in doing so not only to re-gain his piece, but also open the h-file.

19...h6

The only move. Just how dangerous Black's position is can be judged from these variations:

(a) 19...♔g8 20 h5 h6 21 ♗xf6 ♗xf6 22 ♕xf6 ♖e6 23 ♕c3 ♖ae8 24 ♖d4, with the decisive threat of 25 ♖g4+;

(b) 19...♖ad8 20 ♖df1 ♔g8 21 ♕g5+ ♘g6 22 h5 ♘e4 23 hxg6 ♘xg5 (23...fxg6 24 ♕xg6+ hxg6 25 ♖h8+ ♔f7 26 ♘g5 mate) 24 ♘xg5 f6 (24...fxg6 25 ♖xh7) 25 gxh7+ ♔h8 (25...♔g7 26 ♘e6+) 26 ♖xf6 ♗xf6 27 ♗xf6+ ♕g7 28 ♘f7 mate. Very attractive!

20 g4

Probably even stronger was 20 ♕g4+ ♘g6 (20...♔h8 21 ♘g5 ♗d8 22 ♖xd8) 21 h5 ♕b6 22 hxg6 ♕xe3+ 23 ♔b1 fxg6 (23...♕xc3 24 ♕f4, mating or winning the queen) 24 ♕h4, with numerous irresistible threats (later Kasparov himself also thought so — **I.D.**).

20...♕c8! 21 ♕xc8

The attack could also have been continued with the queens on — 21 ♕c2 ♔g8 22 g5 ♘g4 23 gxh6 f5 24 ♖hg1 ♕e6 25 ♘d4 ♕xe3+ 26 ♔b1. But even after the exchange the black king has no peace: its residence has been destroyed.

21...♖axc8 22 g5 ♘8h7 23 e4! ♖cd8 24 ♖df1 ♔f8 25 gxf6 ♗xf6

Or 25...♘xf6 26 ♘e5!, when there is simply nothing that Black can move, and ♖f5 then ♖hf1 is threatened.

26 e5 ♗g7 27 ♖hg1

White also has an overwhelming position after 27 ♗b4+ ♔g8 28 ♖hg1 ♘f8 29 ♖g4 ♘e6 30 ♗d6.

27...c5 28 ♔c2 ♖e6 29 ♖g4 ♗h8 30 b4 (opening the b-file for a decisive attack from the flank) **30...b6 31 bxc5 bxc5 32 ♖b1 ♖a6 33 ♖b2 ♗g7 34 ♖b7! ♖xa2+ 35 ♔b3 ♖a6 36 e6 ♖xe6 37 ♖xg7 Black resigns**.

I.D. It is difficult to explain why, but for some reason sacrifices on g7 are very often of an intuitive nature. Perhaps the point is that there is no clear-cut attacking mechanism, such as ♗xh7+, ♘g5+ and ♕h5+ (♕g4), about which we have already talked...

M.T. Well, there are some attacking procedures on g7 — the sacrifice followed by an attack along the a1-h8 diagonal, for example, but in principle I agree with you. Here it makes sense to rely on your intuition and... to believe that boldness will win the day.

Especially since, in contrast to the patented sacrifice on h7, here a precise calculation is not usually possible — at the board, of course.

I will never forget, for example, my

game with grandmaster Yevgeny Vas-yukov from the 32nd USSR Championship in Kiev, 1964/5. It was given in Chapter 3. There we reached a very complicated position, in which I was intending to sacrifice a knight. It was a not altogether obvious sacrifice, leading to a mass of variations. I began trying to calculate them, and realised to my horror that nothing was coming of this. My thoughts piled up one on top of another. A subtle reply by the opponent, suitable in one case, was suddenly transferred by me to another situation, and there, of course, it proved quite unsuitable. In general, in my mind there arose a completely chaotic accumulation of all kinds of moves, sometimes not even linked to one another, and the notorious "tree of variations", from which trainers recommend cutting off one branch at a time, grew with incredible speed.

And suddenly, for some reason, I remembered the classic couplet by Koren Chukovsky:

Oh, what a task so harsh
To drag a hippo out of a marsh.

I don't know by what association this hippopotamus climbed onto the chess board, but although the spectators were convinced that I was continuing to study the position, in fact I was at that time trying to understand how indeed you would extract a hippopotamus from a marsh. I remember that in my thoughts there figured jacks, levers, helicopters and even a rope-ladder. After lengthy reflection I couldn't find a single way of dragging it out of the quagmire, and I maliciously thought: "Well, let it drown!" And suddenly the

hippopotamus disappeared. Just as it had come onto the chess board, so it went away. Of its own accord! And suddenly the position did not seem so complicated. Somehow I immediately realised that it was impossible to calculate all the variations, and that the knight sacrifice was purely intuitive. And since it promised an interesting game, of course, I did not restrain myself.

And the following day I read with great pleasure in a paper that Mikhail Tal, after careful thought, made an accurately calculated piece sacrifice...

The winner of the following game also admitted that his queen sacrifice was absolutely intuitive.

Suetin-Bagirov
Leningrad 1963

It appears that White's piece attack on the kingside will be exhausted with the exchange of dark-square bishops — 18 ♗xd6 ♖xd6, and 19 ♕xd6?? fails to 19...♗xg2+. The attempt 18 ♖xf6 ♗xe5 19 ♖xc6 is also clearly insufficient, since Black interposes

19...♕xb2! After weighing up these straightforward variations and trying in vain to work out an alternative, White took an intuitive risk.

18 ♕xg7+!? ♚xg7 19 ♗xf6+ ♚h6
Much later, in a "collective" — but by no means joint! — grandmaster analysis, doubts were cast on the correctness of the sacrifice by 19...♚g6, when the tempting 20 ♗d3 is parried by the almost paradoxical 20...♗e7! 21 ♗xe7 ♖xd3 22 ♖g5+ ♚h6 23 cxd3 ♖e8! 24 ♗f6 ♖e6!

M.T. I too analysed this position, and after 20 ♖af1 ♕e3 21 ♗d3 ♚h6! I suggested 22 ♘d1 ♕d2 23 ♖5f2, but then 23...♕xf2! 24 ♖xf2 ♖de8 25 ♗c3 f5! favours Black.

I.D. During the game White considered 22 ♗xd8 ♖xd8 23 ♖xf7 ♖d7 24 ♘d5, and only then established that his idea would be ruined by the counter 24...♗xd5 25 ♖xd7 ♗xg2+ 26 ♚xg2 ♕g5+ 27 ♚f3 ♕f4+.

M.T. But as they say, a game and analysis are very different things.

Indeed, after **20 ♖af1!** (threatening 21 ♖h5+ ♚g6 22 ♖h4, with a deadly bishop check at d3 or h5) **20... ♕e3 21 ♖h5+ ♚g6 22 ♖h4 ♗f4!** (the only defence) **23 ♖hxf4 h5** (there is no other defence against 24 ♖g4+ or 24 ♖h4) **24 ♗xd8 ♖xd8 25 ♗d3+ ♖xd3** (the strongest) **26 cxd3 ♕xd3 27 ♖f6+ ♚g5 28 ♖xf7 h4 29 ♚g1 ♕e3+ 30 ♖7f2** objectively the chances were already with White, and the time trouble mistake **30...♚h5?** (it was still possible to save the game by 30...h3! 31 gxh3 ♗f3) **31 ♘e2! ♚h6 32 ♘f4 a5 33 ♖d1 a4 34 h3 ♚h7 35 ♘d5** allowed him to secure his king completely

and to create a new phase of the attack. After **35...♕c5 36 ♘f6+ ♚g7 37 a3 ♚g6 38 ♘g4 ♚h7 39 ♖e1 ♕d6 40 ♘e3 ♚g6 41 ♘f5 ♕d8 42 ♖e6+ ♚f7 43 ♘d4+ ♚g7 44 ♖e4 ♗d7 45 ♘f3** White won the h4 pawn, and on the 84th move — the game.

Sacrifices on f7

The enticing of a king out of his fortress by a sacrifice at f7 has already been examined — and in considerable detail — in Chapter 1. Therefore here we will limit ourselves to a single, but highly instructive game.

Sveshnikov-A.Sokolov
Sochi 1983

In the evaluation of this position, three factors stand out: Black's minor pieces are bunched together on the queenside, his f7 has been weakened by the departure of the rook from f8, and his queen has clearly come out prematurely. All this suggested to White the idea of an unusual combinational attack.

15 ♗h5 ♕f6 16 ♗g5!!

Diverting the last defender (of course, apart from the king) of f7.

16...♕xg5 17 ♗xf7+ ♔xf7 (otherwise 18 ♘xe6, 19 ♘xd8 and mate on the 8th rank) **18 ♘xe6 ♕g6 19 ♕d5 ♘f6** (if 19...♔e8 the simplest is 20 ♘d6+ ♗xd6 21 ♕xd6) **20 ♘xd8+ ♔f8** (20...♔e8 21 ♖xe7+ and wins) **21 ♕e5 ♗c5** (Black must keep control of the dark squares in the centre; after 21...♗xd8? 22 ♕d6+ his king has nowhere to hide) **22 ♘d4** (22...♗xf2+ was threatened) **22...♔g8**.

Now the energetic **23 ♖e3! ♗d7 24 ♘xb7 ♖e8 25 ♕f4 ♖xe3 26 fxe3 ♗xd4 27 exd4 ♗c6 28 d5 ♗xb7 29 ♕d4** led to a position with an unusual balance of forces, but nevertheless won for White.

Until now we have been pointing out various ways of demolishing the initial, untouched wall in front of the castled position. But it only requires one of the pawns to make a step forward, for it immediately to become, if not a target for attack, then at least an object of attention by the other side.

Pawns at f7-g6-h7

This pawn formation, if it is "cemented" by the dark-square bishop at g7, is virtually the most secure wall around the king. But Black still has to reckon with the rapid advance of the white h-pawn, even in those cases when he has his "own play" (or counterplay).

M.T. Even so, it should once again be mentioned: there is no need to be afraid, but simply to reckon with this possibility.

I.D. Instructive here are both the following example, and the notes to it by the winner, taken from *Shakhmatnye Olympiady* (Moscow, 1974).

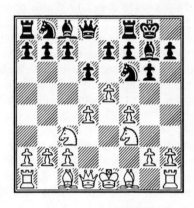

Bronstein-Palmiotti
Munich Olympiad 1958

From this advance (6 e5) there is much to be gained: (1) the knight at f6 is driven from its post; (2) the scope of the bishop at g7 is temporarily restricted; (3) the defence of the squares h5 and h7 is weakened.

White promptly exploits this last factor, by beginning a sharp attack on the kingside. However, he does not succeed in achieving any immediate gains, and, perhaps for this reason, in many games where this position was reached, White played 6 ♗e2 or 6 ♗c4, but hardly ever h2-h4. I say "hardly ever", since I am not sure that I am familiar with all the games. Indeed, Black's threat of breaking up the white centre by ...c5 looks very imposing, but I have never feared ghosts, and, after specifically weighing up the variations, I came (of course, at the board) to an unexpected conclusion: is White's centre really so necessary? Especially after the weight of the struggle has switched to the h-file!

Incidentally, in the given position it is not White's centre that crumbles, but his central pawns.

I should like to draw the readers' attention to a certain chance factor in White's success — the availability to the white queen of the favourable manoeuvre ♕d1-d4-f2-h4. But chance factors of this type are present in any position, and the skill of a player consists in finding and exploiting such features.

6...♘fd7 7 h4 c5 8 h5 cxd4

The plans of the two players are more than transparent: White is playing for a direct mate on the h-file, while Black is trustingly following the dogma "play in the centre is the best form of defence against a flank attack".

Precise calculation is now required. For example, can't White rush straight into the mass of variations with the tempting 9 hxg6!? Alas, for the moment such an attack is unjustified: 9... dxc3 10 gxf7+ ♖xf7 11 ♘g5 ♘f8 etc.

There is ample scope for analysis, but since a conclusion to the attack is not apparent (which means that no real gain is also apparent), without any great regret White "courageously" captured the d4 pawn with his queen, which is fully in accordance with his strategic plan and is not at all a loss of time. All the same the white queen has to make its way to the h-file, and it makes no difference by which route it goes!

9 ♕xd4 dxe5

Black has achieved the maximum — he has broken up the enemy centre and won a pawn. Nevertheless, after White's next move the position is, to say the least, double-edged.

10 ♕f2 exf4

As shown by later analyses, 10...e4! was correct.

11 hxg6 hxg6 12 ♗xf4 ♘f6 13 ♕h4 ♕a5

A clever defence: Black threatens ...♕h5! Here I understood the optimism of my opponent — 14 ♗g5 or 14 ♗e5 is pointless, while if 14 ♘g5 ♗g4, and how is White going to castle? Meanwhile threats against c3 are imminent. But even so...

14 ♘g5 ♗g4

The impression is that White's plans have been ruined — castling on the queenside is difficult, and there is no mate on the h-file. But in fact White had altogether no intention of giving an immediate mate. It was important for him to open the file, in order to have the opportunity of using this threat, and as for queenside castling, well, it is not obligatory: the king will even feel more secure in the right-hand corner, among its own pieces. But won't this weaken White's attack? After all, the rook will move off the open file. Of course not. On the h-file there is already one heavy piece, and, in view of the threatening position of the knight at g5, this is more than sufficient.

On the contrary, there was nothing for the rook to do at h1, whereas after kingside castling it opens fire on the f-file.

15 ♗d3 ♘bd7 16 0-0 ♗h5 17 ♖ae1 e5

This decisively weakens a number of important squares (d5, f7, f6), but with passive defence too White's attack can no longer be stopped.

It has to be admitted that, in deciding on his main strategic plan of action, White has been able to delve more deeply into the resulting complications.

18 ♗d2 ♕c5+ 19 ♗e3 ♕c6 20 ♗b5

The most accurate solution, but by no means the only one. The manoeuvre ♘e4-g3 would have achieved the same aim.

20...♕c7 21 ♗e2!

White attacks the opponent's most vulnerable point. If the bastion at h5 falls, Black's entire army will be demoralised. And the bastion falls!

21...♗xe2 22 ♖xe2 ♖fc8 23 ♘ce4

Bringing up the last reserves. The black king starts running.

23...♔f8 24 ♘xf6 ♘xf6 25 ♖xf6 ♗xf6 26 ♘h7+

The white forces have broken into the Promised Land.

26...♔e7 27 ♕xf6+ ♔e8 28 ♖d2

28 ♗d4 would possibly have led to Black's resignation, but the rook move, cutting off the king from the queenside, leads to mate.

28...a5

Indecision, or belief in a miracle.

29 ♕g7

Black resigns in view of inevitable mate.

In the following example Black certainly has sufficient compensation for the pawn, but what was it that made White create in his position another target for attack? After all, he

could have covered the d3 square, for which the black queen and knight are clearly aiming, by 18 ♕b5, preparing ♗d2, and at least completing his queenside development. In view of his pawn mass in the centre, there would still have been all to play for. But...

Sliwa-Stahlberg
Göteborg Interzonal 1955

18 g3? h5! 19 ♔g2 h4 20 ♘e2 f5

21...f4 is threatened, and after 21 f4 with what can White cover all the light squares around his king, and of what use is such a white bishop?

21 ♕c2 ♘f6 22 ♕c4 f4!

With fresh pawn sacrifices Black opens the attacking files.

23 ♘xf4 ♗xf4 24 exf4 b5!

Ensuring an invasion at c2 or e2.

25 ♕xb5 ♕c2+ 26 ♔h3 hxg3 27 ♕b3

If 27 hxg3 Black wins immediately by 27...♔f7!

27...♕f5+ 28 ♔xg3 ♖e2 29 ♗e3 ♕g6+ 30 ♔h4 ♕h6+ 31 ♔g3 ♘h5+

Two moves before mate, **White resigns**.

Pawns at f7-g6-h6

Here it is not only the g6 pawn that is vulnerable, but also the adjacent pawn at h6, and there is a whole range of "keys" to this fortification, as an examination of the following examples will reveal.

Yuferov-Nikitin
Moscow 1972

The piece-pawn formation around the black king is typical of many games in which Black employs the kingside fianchetto. Typical too are both White's attack on what is here the most real weakness of this set-up — the h6 pawn, and the defence chosen by Black, who by threatening an exchange is trying to drive back the white queen. But note should be taken of the typical and spectacular manoeuvre that allows White to continue his attack. By accepting the sacrifice — and there is nothing else! — Black opens the h-file for his opponent.

17 ♗g5! hxg5 18 ♘xg5 ♖e8 19 ♗d5!

In the given instance it all proceeds very smoothly. Black has no choice.

**19...♖e7 20 ♖ad1 ♘c7 21 ♗xf7+!
♖xf7 22 ♕h7+ ♔f8 23 ♕xg6 ♕xg5**

Forced, since if 23...♖e7 White's offensive resembles an avalanche: 24 f4 e4 25 f5, while after 23...♖f6 24 ♘h7+ ♔g8 25 ♘xf6+ ♕xf6 26 ♕xf6 ♗xf6 27 ♖xd7 further losses are inevitable.

**24 ♕xg5 ♘e6 25 ♕h5 ♘c4 26
♖xd7! ♖xd7 27 ♕g4**

A quiet move, attacking both black knights and — by X-ray — the rook at d7. White increased his material advantage still further, and realised it without any particular problems.

Tal-Petrosian
Moscow 1974

Black is so far behind in development that in his kingside assault White can even include quiet moves. It is the same idea: his pieces engage in a "hand-to-hand" fight with the controller of the dark squares.

19 ♘eg5+! hxg5

Even if he declines the sacrifice, Black cannot avoid a decisive attack on f7 — queen from c4, rook from e7 and, if necessary, knight from e5.

20 ♘xg5+ ♔g8 21 ♕f4

The threat against f7 is incidental, the main one being ♕h4-h7 mate.

21...♘d7 (heading for f6) **22 ♖xd7!** ♗xd7 (the other capture would have allowed mate at h7) **23 ♗xf7+** (now this too is possible) **Black resigns**.

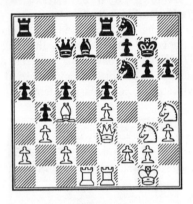

Turnhuber-Persig
correspondence 1991

In principle it is just the same in this position, except that the invasion square is the adjacent one. As soon as the white queen invades at h6, the black king will succumb. But for the moment the transit square f5 is covered, and so White begins by eliminating the defender.

22 ♖xd7 ♕xd7

Capturing with either knight is no better, e.g. 22...♘6xd7 23 ♘hf5+ gxf5 24 ♘xf5+ ♔f6 25 ♕xh6+ ♘g6 26 h4 ♖g8 27 ♕g5 mate.

23 ♘gf5+!, and as a way of capitulating Black chose **23...♔g8 24 ♘xg6 ♘xg6 25 ♕xh6**, which differs little

from 23...gxf5 24 ♘xf5+ ♔g8 25 ♕g3+.

M.T. In general it is rather optimistic to regard the h6 pawn as a reliable guard of the g5 square...

I.D. ... with which the immediate approaches to the king's fortress can be considered to begin, and an invasion on which is nearly always either the overture to an attack, or its beginning. However, the following practical examples are already from another act...

M.T. ... of the same opera!

Pawns at f7-g7-h6

If variations with the fianchetto of the king's bishop in the opening are disregarded, it is the h-pawn, more often than its colleagues, that makes a step forward, sometimes even in the opening, and, as a rule, in order to drive back or at least determine the intentions of a white bishop at g5.

Tal-Byrne
Biel Interzonal 1976

Black has just invited the white

bishop to "declare its intentions", and in the event of 15 ♗h4 he is threatening the typical counter 15... ♘xe4, since at h4 the bishop is unprotected. But here too White is prepared, at the cost of a piece, to effect the opening of the rook's file.

15 h4! hxg5 (15...♖fd8 was nevertheless better, freeing in good time a flight path for the king) **16 hxg5 ♘xe4** (on this counter Black was pinning all his hopes; after 17 ♘xe4 ♕xd2 his position is quite acceptable) **17 ♕d3!**, and it transpires that Black loses after either 17...♘xc3+ 18 bxc3 g6 19 ♕h3+! ♔g7 20 ♕h6+ ♔g8 21 ♖h1, or 17...♘xg5 18 ♖h1+ ♔g8 19 fxg5 f6 20 g6, or 17...f5 18 ♕h3+ ♔g8 19 ♘xe4 ♗xe4 20 g6 ♗h4 21 ♕xh4 ♖fe8 22 ♘xf5!

He chose **17...♗xg5 18 ♘xe4 ♗xe4 19 ♖xe4 ♗h6 20 g4 f5 21 ♖xe6 ♗xf4 22 ♘xf5**, and in view of the threats of 23 ♘xg7, 23 ♘e7, 23 ♖h1+ and 23 ♖e7, after thinking for 40 minutes he **resigned**.

In the game **Shabalov-Smirin** (*Manila Olympiad 1992*) in the well known variation **1 e4 c5 2 ♘f3 d6 3 d4 cxd4 4 ♘xd4 ♘f6 5 ♘c3 ♘c6 6 ♗g5 e6 7 ♕d2 ♗e7 8 0-0-0 0-0 9 f4 h6 10 h4** White showed that he has his opinion regarding the position after 10...♘xd4 11 ♕xd4 hxg5 12 hxg5 ♘g4 13 ♗e2 e5 14 ♕g1 exf4 15 ♗xg4 ♗xg5 16 ♕h2 ♗h6 17 ♗f3 ♕f6, which theory evaluates in favour of Black.

M.T. Yes, we analysed it in our school (the Latvian School for Young Chess Players under the direction of Mikhail Tal - **I.D.**), and Shabalov was

there. But now the theme is different...

10...♘xd4 11 ♕xd4 a6 12 ♗e2 ♕a5 13 ♗f3 ♖d8 14 g4 ♗d7

Thus the h6 pawn has not forced the white bishop to abandon its aggressive post, and it now becomes that brick, a blow at which can break up the entire defensive wall.

15 ♗xh6! gxh6 16 g5 ♘e8

Alas, the simplifying attempt 16... ♕c5 leaves Black both a pawn down, and under pressure by the white pieces — 17 ♕xc5 dxc5 18 gxf6 ♗xf6 19 e5 ♗e7 20 ♗xb7 ♖a7 21 ♗f3.

17 ♖dg1!

The threat (18 gxh6+ ♔h7 19 ♖g7+ ♔xh6 20 ♖xf7) is stronger than its immediate execution (17 gxh6 ♗f6).

17...h5 18 ♗xh5 ♗f8 19 f5 ♕e5 20 ♕d2 exf5 21 g6! fxg6

This opens files for the opponent's attack, but after 21...f6 22 g7 ♘xg7 23 ♗g6 (or 23 ♕h6 ♗e8 24 ♘d5) 23...f4 24 ♘d5 it is hard to find any defence for Black.

22 ♖xg6+ ♔h7 23 ♖hg1 fxe4 24 ♖h6+!! ♗xh6 25 ♗g6+ ♔g7 26 ♗xe8+ ♔h7 27 ♗g6+ ♔g7 28

♗xe4+ ♔f7 29 ♕xh6 ♖h8 30 ♗d5+
♔e8 31 ♕d2 ♔d8 (32 ♖e1 was
threatened) 32 ♖e1 ♕h5 33 ♘e4 ♕h6
(otherwise 34 ♕a5+) 34 ♘g5 ♔c7 35
♖e7 ♖ae8 36 ♕a5+ b6 (36...♔c8 37
♗xb7+), and although White missed
the quickest win by 37 ♕xa6, and if
37...♖xe7 38 ♕b7+ ♔d8 39 ♕xb6+
♔c8 40 ♗b7+, mating, he nevertheless concluded the pursuit of the king:
37 ♕c3+ ♔d8 38 ♖xd7+! ♔xd7 39
♕c6+ ♔e7 40 ♕c7+ ♔f6 41 ♕xd6+
♔f5 42 ♕d7+ ♔e5 43 ♗f7 etc., that
began with the sacrifice on h6.

(This game and another extract from
a game played in Manila, were analysed for this book by the authors in a
Moscow hospital, four days before the
death of Mikhail Tal, the eighth World
Champion in the history of chess —
I.D.).

The illusory defence of g5 was even
more energetically emphasised in the
next game, in which White decisively
weakened the defence of one of two
vulnerable points — h6 or f7.

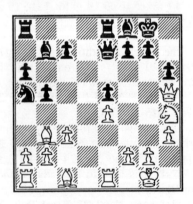

Geller-Portisch
Moscow 1967

18 ♗g5!! ♕d7

It transpires that there is nothing
else: on 18...♕xg5 White mates by 19
♕xf7+, while if 18...hxg5 19 ♘g6!

19 ♖ad1 ♗d6 20 ♗xh6

Now, when the over-protection (as
Nimzowitsch expressed it) has been
eliminated, the wall can be attacked.

20...gxh6

No better is 20...♘xb3 21 ♗xg7!
♔xg7 22 ♘f5+, when on 22...♔g8
there follows 23 ♕g5+, while if 22...
♔f6 23 ♕h6+.

21 ♕g6+ ♔f8 22 ♕f6 (threatening
23 ♘g6+ and 24 ♕h8 mate) **22...♔g8
23 ♖e3 Black resigns**.

Sometimes a less mobile piece can
succeed in breaking through onto the
seemingly well-defended "penalty
spot", opposite the king.

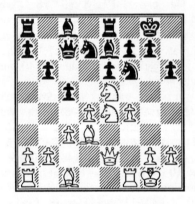

Bronstein-Zamikhovsky
Leningrad 1970

14 ♘g5! ♖f8

If 14...hxg5 15 fxg5 ♘d5 16 ♗h7+,
with mate in a few moves.

15 ♘g6! ♖e8

Alas, on this knight too there is a

taboo: 15...fxg6 16 ♕xe6+ ♔h8 17 ♕xe7 hxg5 18 fxg5 ♘h7 19 ♖xf8+ ♘hxf8 20 ♗e4 ♗b7 21 ♗f4 ♕xf4 22 ♗xb7 ♖b8 23 ♖f1, and it is difficult for Black to coordinate his pieces.

16 ♘xe6! ♕d6 17 f5! fxg6 (if 17...fxe6 White would have continued as in the game, but with even greater effect) **18 ♗f4 ♕c6 19 ♗b5 ♕e4 20 ♕xe4 ♘xe4 21 fxg6**, and although he was a piece up, Black was unable to free himself.

The game concluded **21...♘df6 22 ♘c7 ♗d7 23 ♗xd7 ♘xd7 24 ♖ae1 ♘df6 25 ♘xa8 ♖xa8 26 ♖xe4! ♘xe4 27 ♖e1 ♗d6 28 ♖xe4 ♗xf4 29 ♖xf4**, and White easily realised his material advantage.

Since from time to time the defender's control over g5 proves simply to be illusory, the move ...h6 should be regarded with particular caution and scepticism. Of course, in chess, as in life, there are no absolute truths: what is bad in one situation may prove good in another, and the advance of the h-pawn may avoid, for example, a mate on the back rank. But much more often it proves ruinous, by presenting a target for a pawn or piece attack.

In the following position White's pieces are unusually well coordinated: they are all aimed at the black king, the undoing of which is the h-pawn. Indeed, if it were at h7 with the knight at f8, Black's defensive resources would not yet be exhausted. As it is, the advance of a white pawn completely breaks up the king's fortress.

22 g4! ♕d6

In the hope of 23 g5 ♕d5, since 22...♘df8 is clearly insufficient.

Alekhine-Weenink
Prague 1931

23 ♗g6 ♖f8 24 g5 ♗xd4 25 gxh6 ♘df6 26 hxg7+ ♔xg7 27 ♕h6+ ♔h8 28 ♘xd4 ♕xd4 29 ♗b2

Black resigned, since if 29...♕d7 30 ♖d3!

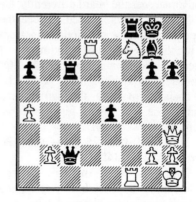

The weakness of White's back rank apparently does not allow him to continue his attack in the "natural" way — 30 ♘xh6+ ♗xh6 31 ♖xf8+ ♔xf8 32 ♕xh6+ ♔e8, and it is Black who wins. But the assault ratio reaches its maximum after 30 ♕xh6!! The queen is immune on account of mate in two moves, 30...♖xf7 loses to 31 ♖d8+ and 30...♖f6 to 31 ♕h8+!! ♗xh8 32 ♘h6 mate, and the only defence 30...g5 leaves Black both two pawns down (31 ♕xg5), and under attack.

To the delight of one of the authors, the game **Schneider-Tal** *(Lucerne 1982)* took a quite different course...

I.D. Before this next example it should be said over and over again: to conduct an attack, relying on one single "pure" stratagem, even a standard one, is practically impossible.

M.T. At one time, in my youth, David Bronstein's maxim about the great benefit of knowledge seemed something of an affectation. Now it is simply banal for us to talk about this: a player who is scientifically "equipped", not only in the opening, but also in the endgame, sees the board differently.

Gradually this procedure became typical in similar positions, and from being the possession of grandmasters it became "common property". Of course, although the sacrificial mechanism may be the same, each game has its own features *(see diagram next column)*.

24 ♗xh6! gxh6 25 ♘f6+ ♔h8 26 ♕d2 ♗f4 27 ♕d4!

Within two moves we will see why White lured the black bishop to f4, and did not play 26 ♕c3 immediately.

27...c5 28 dxc6 ♗xc6 29 ♘h5+ f6 30 ♘xf4

This is the whole point. White regains his piece, he is a pawn up, and, most important, his attack on the broken king's position continues.

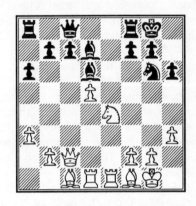

Ivanchuk-Rakhmanov
Junior Tournament, Klaipeda 1985

30...♕f5 31 ♘e6 ♖g8 (31...♖f7 32 ♘d8) **32 ♗d3! Black resigns.**

Since if 32...♕h5 33 ♕xf6+ ♔h7 34 ♘f8+! ♖gxf8 (34...♖axf8) 35 ♖e7+.

Even when it appears that nothing can threaten the h6 pawn, it sometimes proves possible to exploit this very important nuance of the position.

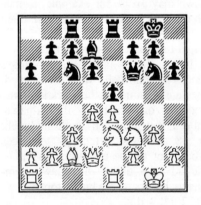

Tal-Keres
Tallinn 1973

16 ♘d5!

White was ready to content himself with a positional advantage after 16...♕d8, but Black decided to accept the challenge.

16...♕xf3 17 ♗d1 ♘h4 18 gxh4 ♕h3 19 ♘f6+!

This Black did not expect, and he gave up the exchange by **19...♔h8 20 ♘xe8 ♖xe8 21 h5**, after which he gradually lost.

Of course, essential was 19...gxf6 20 ♕xh6 exd4 21 ♔h1 ♘e5 22 ♖g1+ ♘g4 (22...♘g6 is insufficient — 23 ♖xg6+ fxg6 24 ♕xg6+ ♔h8 25 ♕h6+ ♔g8 26 ♗h5) with a sharp game, but White's entire manoeuvre became possible precisely because of the advance of the h-pawn from its initial post.

It is worth studying the possibility of an explosive attack on h6, even when the opponent has obvious counterplay.

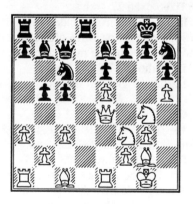

Varanin-Moskvin
USSR 1989

For example, here Black is ready by ...♘d4 to set White serious problems, and at the least to exchange part of the attacking forces, while maintaining control of the open file. And yet White still risked the sacrifice: after all, the advanced pawn at h6 is as though created for this.

31 ♗xh6!

After 31 ♘xh6+ gxh6 32 ♗xh6 ♗f8 White has no good continuation.

31...♘d4 32 ♕f4 ♘c2

Preferable was 32...♗xf3 33 ♗xf3 ♘xf3+ 34 ♕xf3 ♘g5 35 ♗xg5 ♗xg5, with some compensation for the pawn.

33 ♗xg7! ♔xg7 (33...♘xe1 34 ♘h6+ ♔xg7 35 ♕xf7+ ♔h8 36 ♘h4!, and Black loses too much) **34 ♘f6!!**

The culmination of the attack. Exploiting the fact that his knight is immune, White again creates a threat against f7.

Again Black has no time for 34...♘xe1 on account of 35 ♘g5! ♗xg2 36 ♘e8+! ♔h8 37 ♘xf7+ ♔g8 38 ♕g4+ ♔xf7 39 ♕g6+ ♔f8 40 ♘xc7 ♘g5 41 h6.

34...♖h8 35 ♖ed1! (forcing the opponent's reply) **35...♘xa1 36 ♘g5!**

All White's pieces are now in the attack, whereas after 36 ♖d7 ♕xd7 37 ♘xd7 ♗xf3 38 ♗xf3 ♘g5 there would have remained insufficient force.

36...♖ad8

Black loses amusingly in the forcing variation 36...♘xg5 37 ♕xg5+ ♔f8 38 ♖d7 ♕xd7 (38...♗xf6 39 exf6 ♕xd7 40 ♕g7+ leads to mate) 39 ♘xd7+ ♔e8 40 ♘f6+ ♗xf6 41 ♕xf6 ♖xh5 42 ♗xb7 ♖b8 43 ♗f3 ♖h7 44 ♗e4 ♖h5 45 g4 ♖h3 46 ♔g2.

37 ♘e8+!

And in view of mate in three moves (37...♔h6 38 ♘xf7+ ♔xh5 39 ♕h6+

♔g4 40 ♕h3) **Black resigned**.

In addition, the appearance of a pawn at h6 immediately provokes (or should provoke) in the player with White the seditious thought: is it not possible to carry out an "attack from afar": sacrifice the dark-square bishop from its initial position, and then with a quiet move bring the queen onto the c1-h6 diagonal.

I.D. I came across this manoeuvre in some games from the 1920s...

M.T. ... but even so it received full recognition only after the following game.

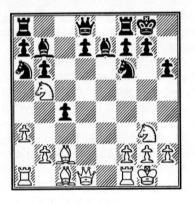

Bronstein-Keres
Göteborg Interzonal 1955

For the moment White has sacrificed two pawns, obtaining in return the f5 square for one of his knights, d6 for the other, and the real possibility of regaining one of the pawns almost by force: 14 ♘f5 ♖e8, and apart from the possible sacrifice on h6 he also has 15 ♘bd6 (which, however, does not lead to the win of the exchange: 15... ♗xd6 16 ♘xd6 ♖e6! and if 17 ♘xb7 ♕c7).

But he made use of a different attacking mechanism.

14 ♗xh6!? gxh6 15 ♕d2 ♘h7

Later analyses showed that by immediately bringing up his reserves — 15...♘c5!, with the aim of blocking the b1-h7 diagonal, Black would have had better chances of defending his king, e.g. 16 ♖ae1 ♘d3 17 ♗xd3 cxd3, and if 18 ♘f5 ♗e4 19 ♘bd4 ♖e8 20 ♘xh6+ ♔f8 21 ♕g5 ♗g6 22 ♖xe7 ♖xe7 23 ♕xf6 ♗e4! 24 ♕h8+ ♔e7 25 ♘hf5+ ♗xf5 26 ♘xf5+ ♔e6 27 ♕h3 ♕h8, when nothing forcing is apparent, and he remains the exchange up.

But the attack can also be continued by 18 ♕xh6!, when 18... ♘h7 19 ♘f5 ♗f6 20 ♖e3 ♖e8 21 ♖g3+ ♔h8 22 ♖g7 is bad for Black, and 18...♖e8 can be met by 19 ♘f5 ♗f8 20 ♕g5+ ♔h7 21 ♘bd6 ♖e6 22 ♖e3 ♘g8 23 ♕h5+ ♘h6 24 ♘xh6 ♗xh6 25 ♕xf7+ ♔h8 26 ♖xe6 dxe6 27 ♕xb7.

In the game Black decided simply to extinguish the first wave of the attack, keeping a favourable material balance.

16 ♕xh6 f5 17 ♘xf5 ♖xf5

He has to give up the exchange; if 17...♖f7 18 ♕g6+ ♔f8 19 ♘bd6 ♗xd6 20 ♕xd6+ ♔g8 21 ♘h6+.

18 ♗xf5 ♘f8 19 ♖ad1 ♗g5 20 ♕h5 ♕f6 21 ♘d6 ♗c6 22 ♕g4 ♔h8

Parrying two threats, 23 ♕xc4+ and 23 h4. But the king's fortress has been completely destroyed, and with his very next move White succeeds in creating a further three(!) threats, which cannot all be parried simultaneously.

23 ♗e4!

On the agenda is 24 ♕xg5 followed by 25 ♘f7+, and 24 ♗xc4 followed by 25 ♘e4, and — the game continuation.

23...♗h6 24 ♗xc6 dxc6 25 ♕xc4 ♘c5 26 b4 ♘ce6 27 ♕xc6

White now has a material advantage, and the pursuit of the king is merely postponed for the moment.

27...♖b8 28 ♘e4 ♕g6 29 ♖d6 ♗g7 30 f4 ♕g4 31 h3 ♕e2 32 ♘g3 ♕e3+ 33 ♔h2 ♘d4

Or 33...♘xf4 34 ♖h6+ ♘h7 (if 34... ♔g8 35 ♕c4+ ♘4e6 36 ♖xf8+) 35 ♕d6! ♗xh6 36 ♕xb8+ ♘f8 37 ♕d6, and the ending after the exchange of queens should be won for White.

34 ♕d5 ♖e8 35 ♘h5 ♘e2 36 ♘xg7 ♕g3+ 37 ♔h1 ♘xf4 38 ♕f3 ♘e2 39 ♖h6+ Black resigns.

If the king's position is even more weakened, it can be very straightforward to mount an attack of this type, as in the following example.

Voitsekh-Morozov
USSR Correspondence Ch. 1973-5

The pawn formation around the black king suggests only one solution. An experienced player would not even bother calculating variations in advance, since this can be done later: the weakness of the b1-h7 diagonal is just too gaping, the f- and h-pawns, which have incautiously stepped forward, are just too vulnerable.

22 ♘xh6+! gxh6 23 ♕g4+ ♔h8 24 ♗xh6!

I.D. Misha, how much time would you have spent considering this second sacrifice?

M.T. One second at most. Firstly, White's rook at e1 was undefended, and the exchange at e8 would bring up the black queen to the defence. Secondly, it is a pseudo-sacrifice: after 24...♗xh6 25 ♕g6 White, at the least, regains the piece. And thirdly, if you and I are writing a book about attacking procedures, it means that they are familiar to us...

I.D. In my opinion, from this example one can best of all not so much understand, as sense what is meant by the weakness of a single square or a complex of squares. Once David Bronstein gave a classic formulation of this: by moving to a weak square, a piece is able to attack the neighbouring squares and the forces standing on them. An ideal illustration is the variation 24... ♗xh6 25 ♕g6. Such an invasion would not be possible, for example, with a black pawn at f7, i.e. without the "holes" in Black's position.

24...♖e7 25 ♗xf8 ♕xf8 26 ♕h5+ ♔g8 27 ♖xe7 ♕xe7

In principle, simplification favours the defending side, if he also has a material advantage. But here exchanges have eliminated defenders that are difficult to replace, whereas all White's reserves can easily join the attack.

28 ♘f5 ♕d7 29 ♕g6+ ♔f8

(29...♔h8 30 ♕xf6+ ♔g8 31 ♘h6 mate) **30 ♕xf6+ ♕f7 31 ♕h6+ ♔e8** (31...♔g8 32 ♖e1 ♘bd5 33 ♖e6) **32 ♖e1+ ♔d7 33 ♖e7+ ♕xe7 34 ♘xe7 ♔xe7 35 ♕g7+**

And in view of the forced variation 35...♔d6 36 ♕e5+ ♔d7 37 ♗f5+ ♔d8 38 ♕f6+ ♔e8 39 ♗e6, with a quick mate or major loss of material, **Black resigned**.

Tal-Gurgenidze
36th USSR Ch., Alma-Ata 1969
Caro-Kann Defence

1	e4	c6
2	d4	d5
3	♘c3	b5
4	a3	dxe4
5	♘xe4	♗f5

The game has immediately taken an unusual course, but even so Black decides against finally leaving the safety zone, by taking the pawn, either now (6...♕xd4 7 ♘f3 ♕d5 8 ♕e2), or two moves later.

7	♗xe4	♘f6
8	♗d3	e6
9	♘f3	♗e7
10	♕e2	♘bd7
11	0-0	0-0
12	♖e1	♖e8
13	♘e5	♘xe5
14	dxe5	♘d5
15	♕g4	

Not objecting to a few exchanges, White has removed from d4 a target for counterplay — the pawn, driven away a defender — the knight at f6, and created all the preconditions for an attack on the king. Therefore prophylaxis by 15...g6 was indicated for

Black, when nothing now is achieved by the hasty 16 h4 ♗xh4 17 g3 ♗e7 18 ♔g2 on account of the simple 18...h5. White would have had to prepare it with 16 g3. But Black did not yet sense the danger.

15	**...**	**a5**
16	**h4!**	

Threatening a direct win after 17 h5 and 18 ♗h6 ♗f8 19 ♗xg7 ♗xg7 20 h6. So the pawn sacrifice, which, however, serves merely as an overture to a planned rook sacrifice, has to be accepted.

16	**...**	**♗xh4**
17	**g3**	**♗e7**
18	**♔g2**	**g6**

Black no longer has time for counterplay such as 18...b4, since White is threatening 19 ♗xh7+ ♔xh7 20 ♕h5+ ♔g8 21 ♖h1, and barricades such as 18... ♗f8 19 ♖h1 f5 cannot be maintained: 20 ♕h5 h6 21 ♕g6 ♔h8 22 ♗xh6 gxh6 23 ♖xh6+ ♗xh6 24 ♖h1 ♘e3+ 25 fxe3 ♕d5+ 26 e4.

19	**♖h1**	**♗f8**
20	**♗g5!**	

An important interposition, not allowing the opponent to complicate the game to his advantage in the event of the immediate 20 ♖xh7 ♔xh7 21 ♗g5 ♘e3+! 22 fxe3 (or 22 ♗xe3 ♗g7 23 ♖h1+ ♔g8 24 ♕h3 ♕c7 or 24...♕d5+ and 25...♕xe5) 22...♕d5+ 23 ♗e4 ♕xe5 24 ♕h4+ ♔g8 25 ♗f6 ♕h5.

20	**...**	**♕c7**

The black queen has to give up the idea at some point of checking at d5, because of variations such as 20...♗e7 21 ♖xh7 ♗xg5 (or 21...♔xh7 22 ♕h5+ ♔g8 23 ♗xg6) 22 ♖ah1 ♔f8 23 ♗xg6, or 20...♘e7 21 ♗xg6 fxg6

(21...hxg6 22 ♗f6 ♗g7 23 ♕h4 also concludes matters) 22 ♕xe6+, and of the many mates, this one is rather elegant: 22...♔h8 23 ♖xh7+ ♔xh7 24 ♖h1+ ♗h6 25 ♖xh6+ ♔g7 26 ♗f6+ ♔xh6 27 ♕h3 mate.

21   ♖xh7!   ♕xe5

If 21...♔xh7 22 ♖h1+ ♔g8 23 ♗f6 ♘xf6 24 exf6 ♕e5 25 ♗xg6 ♕xf6 26 ♗h7+ ♔h8 27 ♕g8 mate.

22   ♖xf7!

Persisting with his desire to offer this rook.

22   ...   ♔xf7
23   ♗xg6+   ♔g8

Or 23...♔xg6 24 ♗f4+.

24   ♗xe8   ♗g7

After 24...♖xe8 the black queen would have been attacked from the other side — 25 ♗f6+. As it is, White continues his offensive, now with a material advantage.

25   ♗d7   ♘c7
26   ♗xc6   ♖f8
27   ♖d1   ♕c5
28   ♗f3   ♕xc2
29   ♖d7   ♖f7
30   ♖d8+   ♖f8

31   ♗f6   ♕h7
32   ♗e4   ♕h6
33   ♗g5   ♕h8
34   ♖d7

Black resigns: if 34...♖f7 35 ♖xc7.

Spassky-Tal
Montreal 1979
Queen's Indian Defence

1   d4   ♘f6
2   c4   e6
3   ♘f3   b6
4   e3

The Queen's Indian Defence is an opening that until recently had a very quiet reputation. Sometimes in newspaper reports one would even read comments such as: "The players used the Queen's Indian Defence for peaceable aims." However, a certain reassessment of values is currently taking place, and in particular, this opening is often and very successfully employed by Karpov.

There is no denying that White, if he wishes, can play with a high degree of solidity (the move that best meets this aim is 4 g3). But peaceableness on the part of my opponent was the last thing I expected in this game.

4   ...   ♗b7
5   ♗d3   d5
6   b3

This is no better and no worse than 6 0-0. Perhaps the only slight nuance is that White does not allow his opponent the opportunity for relieving manoeuvres such as 6...dxc4 and 7...c5.

6   ...   ♗d6
7   0-0   0-0
8   ♗b2   ♘bd7

9 ᐁbd2   ♕e7
10 ᔕc1   ᔕad8

Up to now the moves have been more or less obligatory. Both sides are deploying their forces as well as possible in anticipation of the coming battle. The alternative here was 10... ᐁe4, but the position after 11 ♕c2 f5 12 ᐁe5 did not particularly appeal to me. With his last, consolidating move, Black invites his opponent to determine the position of his queen. In reply to 11 ♕e2 I was now intending 11... ᐁe4, while after the continuation chosen by Spassky, I thought that the advance of the c-pawn would gain in strength.

11 ♕c2   c5
12 cxd5

The other, roughly equivalent possibility was 12 ᔕfd1, against which I had prepared 12...cxd4 13 exd4 ᔕc8. In such situations the loss of a tempo is not so significant.

12 ...   exd5
13 dxc5

But this exchange is, I think, bad. The weakness of the hanging pawns in not apparent at all, and Black's pieces operate together most harmoniously. In my opinion, 13 ♗b5 or 13 ♗f5 was stronger.

13 ...   bxc5
14 ♕c3

And this is simply a challenge... When after the game I asked Spassky why he made this move, he spread his hands: "A beggar isn't afraid of being robbed".

The idea of a pawn breakthrough now becomes very possible. I spent some time examining the immediate

14...d4, and came to the conclusion that for the moment it did not promise anything real, and so, guided by general considerations, I brought into play my last, "sleeping" piece.

14 ...   ᔕfe8
15 ᔕfd1

That day it would seem that Boris was betrayed by his sense of danger. I expected 15 ᔕfe1, in reply to which I was intending seriously to consider 15...c4 (16 bxc4 ♗b4 17 ♕c2 dxc4). But now White himself provokes the breakthrough in the centre, and Black's pieces are so ideally placed that there is no sense in delaying it.

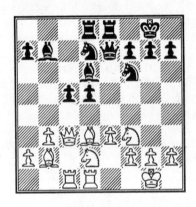

15 ...   d4
16 exd4   cxd4
17 ♕a5

Good or bad, White should have accepted the pawn sacrifice. It is true that 17 ♕xd4 loses material after 17...ᐁc5, but after 17 ᐁxd4 I could see no forcing way of developing the attack. For the sake of my conscience, so to speak, I had prepared a reserve variation: 17...♕e5 18 ᐁ4f3 ♕h5, with full compensation for the pawn, but even so I would probably have been unable to resist the temptation — it is not often that opportunity occurs for sacrificing a bishop at h2 in games at grandmaster level. But here things are not completely clear. After 17... ♗xh2+ 18 ♔xh2 ♘g4+ 19 ♔g3 (bad is 19 ♔g1 ♕h4 20 ♘4f3 ♕xf2+ 21 ♔h1 ♖e5! 22 ♗f5 ♘e3) 19...♕e5+ 20 f4 (after 20 ♔xg4 ♘f6+ White is mated) 20...♕e3+ 21 ♘4f3 ♘df6 Black's attack is very dangerous, but White is by no means doomed (there is the possibility of 22 ♗xh7+, for instance).

At any event, the continuation chosen by Spassky is bad. Firstly, because the "condemned" pawn is still alive, and in addition the position of the queen on the 5th rank shortly gives Black the opportunity, with gain of tempo, for the decisive inclusion of his rook in the attack.

17 ...   ♘e5
18 ♘xe5

18 ♖e1 was perhaps slightly more tenacious, although Black has a very attractive choice between 18...♗xf3 and 18...♘xd3!?

18 ...   ♗xe5
19 ♘c4

Black's attack develops slightly more slowly, but probably just as effectively, after 19 ♘f1 ♘d5 20 ♘g3 ♘f4 21 ♗f1 h5.

19 ...   ♖d5

Here it is, the decisive tempo. For the bishop sacrifice all is ready.

20 ♕d2

I was expecting 20 ♗a3 (with the idea of driving the queen off the d8-h4 diagonal), which is decisively met by 20...♕e6 21 ♕d2 ♗xh2+! 22 ♔xh2

♖h5+ 23 ♔g1 ♖h1+!, with mate in two moves.

20 ...   ♗xh2+

A familiar theme in a slightly new setting.

21 ♔xh2   ♖h5+!

White was evidently counting only on 21...♘g4+ 22 ♔g3, but now the way forward for the king is blocked. After 22 ♔g3 Black has the immediately decisive 22...♘e4+ (however, 22...♖g5+ is also good) 23 ♗xe4 ♕h4+.

22 ♔g1   ♘g4
White resigns

Against the two threats, the prosaic 23...♕h4 and the elegant 23... ♖h1+ (in reply, say, to 23 ♖e1) there is no defence.

Tal-Stean
Alekhine Memorial, Moscow 1975
Tarrasch Defence

1	♘f3	♘f6
2	c4	c5
3	♘c3	e6
4	g3	d5

5	cxd5	exd5
6	d4	♘c6
7	♗g2	♗e7
8	0-0	0-0
9	♗g5	cxd4
10	♘xd4	h6
11	♗e3	♖e8
12	♕b3	

From the fact that after this my opponent thought for a long time, I concluded that I had succeeded in devising something new.

| 12 | ... | ♘a5 |
| 13 | ♕c2 | |

At a5 the knight stands no better than at c6, but for the moment Black plays logically.

| 13 | ... | ♗g4 |
| 14 | h3 | ♗d7 |

But this is inconsistent. 14...♗h5 was clearly stronger, keeping the e2 pawn under attack. The continuation could have been 15 ♖ad1 ♖c8 16 ♘f5 ♗b4, with an unclear game.

15   ♖ad1

It transpires that at d7 the bishop is only in the way of its own pieces.

15   ...   ♖c8

16   ♘f5

Not so much play against the isolated pawn (White has in reserve the strategic manoeuvre ♗d4 and ♘e3), as the start of an attack on the king. It was for this reason that on the previous move the d1 square was occupied by the *queen's* rook. The point is that in reply to 16...♘c4 White has a combination: 17 ♘xd5 ♘xd5 (17...♘xe3 18 ♘fxe7+ ♖xe7 19 ♕xc8!) 18 ♗xd5 ♘xe3 19 ♘xh6+! ♔f8 20 fxe3!, and the rook at f1 has its say.

Comparatively best was 16...♗e6,

but this would have meant admitting that all the preceding manoeuvres with this bishop were pointless.

16   ...   ♗f8

17   ♗xd5   ♖e5

Possibly Stean was hoping to gain positional compensation for the pawn after 17...♘xd5 18 ♖xd5 ♕c7, but then noticed that 19 ♗f4 leads to further loss of material. Otherwise Black would hardly have willingly allowed the following piece sacrifice.

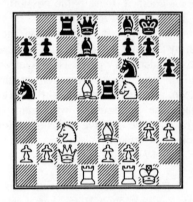

18	♘xh6+	gxh6
19	♕g6+	♔h8
20	♗xf7	♖c6

The only move. The game would have concluded instantly after 20...♗g7 21 ♗xh6 ♗xh6 (21...♕f8 22 ♕xf6) 22 ♖xd7!

21   ♖d5

My old illness — trying for too much. Far simpler was 21 ♗xh6 ♗xh6 22 ♕xh6+ ♘h7 23 ♕f4, when all Black's pieces are "hanging".

But now he should have played 21...♖xd5 22 ♘xd5 ♗g7, when it appears that White has nothing better than 23 ♗xh6, which, however, is quite sufficient for a win.

21 ...   ♛e7

It was this very move that White was reckoning on, since the resulting position very much appealed to him.

22   ♗d4   ♞c4
23   f4

It transpires that if 23...♗f5, as planned, White wins simply with 24 ♖xe5 ♞xe5 25 ♛xf5 ♞xf7 26 ♞d5.

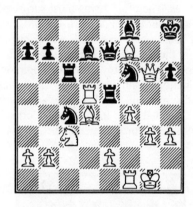

23   ...   ♗g7
24   ♗xe5   ♞xe5

White would have been set greater problems by 24...♞e3, but of course this too could not have saved the game. For example, 25 ♖f3 ♞exd5 26 ♞xd5, or 25...♗f5 26 ♗xf6 ♖xf6 27 ♖e5, and several pieces disappear from the board, but they are mainly Black's.

25   ♖xe5   ♛f8

White has such a large material reserve that it is by no means essential to hang on to the exchange.

26   ♗b3   ♞g4
27   ♛d3   ♞xe5

In reply to 27...♗xe5 White wins most simply by 28 ♛xd7.

28   fxe5   ♛c5+

29   ♔h2   ♗e8
30   e6

White's extra material does not prevent him from continuing his attack.

30   ...   ♖d6
31   ♛e4   Black resigns

Tal-Portisch
Candidates Quarter Final, Bled 1965
French Defence

1	e4	e6
2	d4	d5
3	♞c3	♞f6
4	♗g5	dxe4
5	♞xe4	♞bd7

Until 1962 this variation was not especially popular, and was employed only rarely — and on those occasions when Black very much needed a draw. At the Candidates Tournament in Curacao, this variation was chosen against me by Petrosian in round eight, and by Benko two rounds later. In the game with Petrosian I played 6 ♞xf6+ ♞xf6 7 ♞f3 c5, and after an hour's thought I chose the absolutely unique plan of 8 ♛d3 ♗e7 9 ♗xf6 ♗xf6 10 ♛b5+. Naturally, White lost very quickly. The game with Benko developed more normally, but during the encounter with Portisch I could not recall the precise move order (until now I have endeavoured fairly successfully to forget all the games that I played in Curacao).

6   ♞xf6+

Perhaps the most accurate. After 6 ♞f3 ♗e7 Black succeeds in simplifying the position, since 7 ♞xf6+ can be answered by 7...♗xf6.

6	...	♞xf6
7	♞f3	c5

8   ♗c4

I think that it is in this way, without trying to refute Black's opening, that White attains the most promising position. Attempts to force matters by 8 ♘e5 or 8 ♗b5+ do not achieve anything real against accurate defence.

8   ...   cxd4
9   0-0   ♗e7
10   ♕e2   h6

Black's desire to get rid of the bishop at g5 is understandable. But in the future the pawn at h6 will draw the attention of the white pieces aimed at the kingside. The h6 square is a very convenient one on which to sacrifice.

Perhaps more in the spirit of the position was 10...0-0 11 ♖ad1 ♘d5 12 ♗xe7 ♘xe7, when Black's knight can begin shadowing its white opponent: in the event of ♘e5 Black replies ...♘g6, while with the white knight at d4 Black will prepare ...♘c6. In positions of this type the exchange of knights is to the advantage of the defender.

11   ♗f4   0-0
12   ♖ad1   ♗d7
13   ♖xd4

White thought for about half an hour over this move. It was difficult to decide which was stronger — the openly aggressive move in the game, or the more reserved 13 ♘xd4, after which White could have manoeuvred his rook along the third rank without loss of time. In nearly all variations White's attack would have developed completely unhindered.

But what did not much appeal to me was that Black could reply 13...♘d5 14 ♗e5 ♗f6 15 ♗xd5 exd5 16 ♗xf6 ♕xf6, and although White has an un-

disputed positional advantage, it may prove insufficient for a win. White can easily obtain three quarters of a point, but after a defeat one wants more...

13   ...   ♕b6
14   ♕d2!

It was with this continuation in mind that on his previous move White decided to capture the pawn with his rook. I did not consider any other moves. Therefore I was most surprised when after the game Portisch informed me that only here had we diverged from the Tal-Benko game, where I had chosen the, in my (present) opinion, ridiculous continuation 14 ♖d3. It was not surprising that here, having come up against an innovation, Portisch thought for some forty minutes.

14   ...   ♗c6

Black could also have defended his bishop, and simultaneously prepared to meet the coming bishop sacrifice, by 14...♖fc8. After this I was intending once more to check the sharp variation 15 ♗xh6 gxh6 16 ♕xh6 ♕xd4! 17 ♘xd4 ♖xc4 18 ♖d1 with dangerous threats, and if this proved insufficient I had in reserve the unpretentious retreat 15 ♗b3, maintaining an attractive position. Now White's reply is practically forced, since otherwise 14 ♕d2 is simply a waste of time.

15 ♗xh6 ♘e4

The only move. In the event of 15... gxh6 White would have continued the attack by 16 ♕xh6, when if 16...♗xf3 he has the decisive 17 ♕g5+ ♔h8 18 ♖h4+ ♘h7 (or 18...♗h5 19 ♗d3, with the irresistible threat of 20 ♖xh5+) 19 ♕xe7, when 19...♖g8 fails to 20 ♕f6+, while 16...♘e4 is very strongly met by 17 ♗d3. If Black changes the move order by playing 15...♗xf3, if he wishes White can transpose into variations already considered by 16 ♗xg7. Besides this, the simple 16 gxf3 gxh6 17 ♔h1 is also good.

16 ♕f4 gxh6
17 ♖xe4

This gives the game a rather different direction. In return for the sacrificed exchange, White counts on maintaining a persistent initiative. The attempt to force matters by 17 ♕xh6 succeeds after 17...♗c5 18 ♘g5!, 17... ♖fd8 18 ♗xe6!, or 17...♕c5 18 ♗d3, but after the only good move 17... ♖ad8!, keeping f7 defended, White probably has nothing better than to force a draw by perpetual check: 18 ♗xe6 ♖xd4 19 ♗f5 ♘f6.

17 ... ♗xe4
18 ♕xe4

Here Portisch again thought for a considerable length of time. He has a minimal advantage in force — the exchange for a pawn. But the exposed position of his king and the presence of opposite-colour bishops call on him to be extra-careful. Thus 18...♕xb2 loses almost immediately to 19 ♘e5!, when it is impossible to defend against the various sacrifices on e6 and f7 (19... ♗f6 20 ♗d3). I thought that the best defensive resource was 18...♗f6 19 ♗d3 ♖fd8 20 ♕h7+ ♔f8 21 ♕xh6+ ♔e7 (21...♗g7 is weaker: 22 ♕f4 or 22 ♕h5) 22 b3, but here White now has two pawns for the exchange, and his initiative shows no signs of diminishing. Portisch aims to include his rook in the defence.

18 ... ♖ad8!
19 b3

The prospect of reestablishing material equality after 19 ♗d3 ♖xd3 and 20...♕xb2 appeared insufficient.

19 ... ♗c5

Now the idea of Black's defence is revealed. First of all, for the moment he is restricting the white rook by the attack on f2, and he plans for the bishop to take part in the defence from d4. The following manoeuvre by White is aimed at further weakening Black's kingside. It involves the calculation of a lengthy variation, a calculation which, unfortunately, is inaccurate. Meanwhile, by continuing simply 20 c3, White would have retained all the advantages of his position, and the defence would have involved enormous difficulties. However, White's oversight is a rather amusing one.

20 ♕f4 ♔g7
21 ♕e5+

This forces the advance of the pawn, since it is hopeless to allow the queen in at f6.

21 ... f6
22 ♕g3+

Naturally, White did not even consider capturing on e6.

22 ...   ♔h7
23 ♖e1

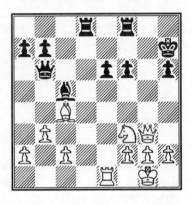

Here Black had a very interesting defensive possibility: 23...♗b4. I had taken this into account, and had prepared what I imagined to be a winning variation: 24 ♗xe6 ♗xe1 25 ♗f5+ ♔h8 26 ♕g6 ♗xf2+ 27 ♔f1 ♖d1+ 28 ♔e2 ♕e3+ 29 ♔xd1. But while Portisch was considering his move, I noticed to my horror that, by playing 28...♖e1+, Black would give mate first. White would probably have had to move his rook, or else force a draw by 24 c3 ♗xc3 25 ♘h4 ♗xe1 26 ♕g6+. After the mistake committed by Black, White's attack gains in strength with every move.

23 ...   ♖g8
24 ♕h4   ♖d6
25 ♔f1

I do not feel inclined to attach a question mark to this move. It looks perfectly logical. White frees his queen from having to defend the f2 pawn, since nothing is gained by capturing it

without check.

But here he had a very fine opportunity of instantly gaining a decisive advantage, by playing 25 c3 a5 26 a3!! (this possibility was pointed out, immediately after the game, by my trainer, Koblenz). Now, in view of the threat of 27 b4, Black is forced to move either his queen or his rook, but then White captures one of the pawns, e6 or f6, with decisive effect. E.g., 26...♖c6 27 ♕xf6 ♗xf2+ 28 ♔f1 ♖xc4 29 ♖xe6, or 26...f5 27 b4 axb4 28 axb4 ♖g4 29 ♕e7+ ♖g7 30 bxc5 ♕xc5 31 ♕f8! ♖g8 32 ♕f7+ ♖g7 33 ♘g5+! hxg5 34 ♕h5+ ♔g8 35 ♖xe6. Fortunately, White's omission does not alter the general evaluation of the position. It is extremely difficult for Black to defend against the numerous threats, especially when in severe time trouble.

25 ...   f5
26 h3

Preparing for the g-pawn to come into play as a "battering-ram".

26 ...   ♖g6

26...♕c6, preventing White's next move, was perhaps more tenacious.

27 g4!

This destroys, once and for all, the black king's shelter. Black achieves nothing by 27...fxg4 28 hxg4 ♕c6 on account of the simple 29 ♘e5, when he does not have a single check. Here too the best defence was probably 27... ♕c6 28 gxf5 ♕xf3 29 fxg6+ ♔xg6, but then White is material up with an active position. The move played by Portisch loses very quickly.

27 ...   ♖d7
28 ♖xe6!

It was still possible to fall into a trap

— 28 ♗xe6? ♗xf2!, and Black succeeds in simplifying the position. But now it is all over.

28	...	♖d1+
29	♔g2	♖xe6
30	♗xe6	fxg4
31	♕xg4	♖d8
32	♘e5	**Black resigns**

WHAT WOULD YOU HAVE PLAYED?

No.30

The white outpost at e5 creates the preconditions for an attack, but it is inadequately supported and sooner or later will inevitably become a target for Black's counterattack. Nevertheless White has some initiative, and...

At first sight position No.31 seems fairly simple, but in fact it is extremely difficult for Black. 13 ♗g5 is threatened, and the simplifying attempt 12... ♘xd5 loses quickly to 13 ♗xd5+ ♔h8 14 ♗g5 ♕e8 15 ♕h5!

No.31

Black could have defended with 12...♘e7 13 ♘xf6+ ♖xf6 14 ♖xf6 gxf6, although here too White has a great advantage. In fact he chose **12... h6** (preventing the pin) **13 ♕d3 ♗e6**. Now 14 ♘xf6+ ♖xf6 15 d5 does not work in view of 15...♘e5, but...

No.32

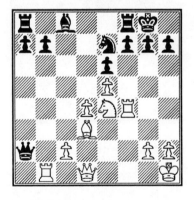

Combinations of this type should occur to a player "spontaneously"...

No.33

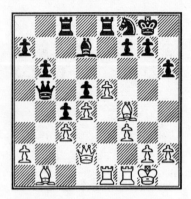

This applies even more so here...

No.35

Although nominally White has a material advantage, can his king feel safe? After all, the leading bastion of his fortress, the g3 pawn, seems securely defended..

No.34

But in this position a minute or two's thought is in order...

No.36

Here the cement from the fortress walls has already been washed away...

Answers to:
What would you have played?

No.1 (p.30)
Tal-Simagin
23rd USSR Ch., Leningrad 1956

We do not know, because the knight did not even think of retreating. It offered itself as a sacrifice, depriving the black king of the right to castle.

12 ♘xf7! ♔xf7 13 f5

Naturally, lines have to be opened for the attack on the king.

13...dxe5 14 fxe6+ ♔xe6 15 ♖b1!!

Unexpectedly White's attacking potential is increased, for example, in the variation 15...♕a5 16 ♖xb7, when his threats become irresistible. The rook also comes in useful on the b-file in the event of 15...♕a6 16 ♕g4+ ♔d6 17 dxe5+ ♔c7 18 ♗f4, and therefore Black accepts the challenge.

15...♕xb1 16 ♕c4+ ♔d6 17 ♗a3+ ♔c7 18 ♖xb1 ♗xa3 19 ♕b3!

For the queen Black has sufficient material compensation, but White's lead in development makes his attack irresistible.

19...♗e7 20 ♕xb7+ ♔d6

The king is forced to go back.

21 dxe5+ ♘xe5 22 ♖d1+ ♔e6 23 ♕b3+ ♔f5 24 ♖f1+ ♔e4 25 ♖e1+ ♔f5 26 g4+ ♔f6 27 ♖f1+ ♔g6 28 ♕e6+ ♔h7 (28...♗f6 29 ♕f5+ and 30 ♕xe5) **29 ♕xe5**, and apart from the initiative White now has also a material advantage.

No.2 (p.30)
Tal-Tukmakov
Sochi 1970

Yet, strangely enough, it practically has no choice. If, with such strong "X-ray" pressure along the a2-g8 diagonal you do not begin an attack on the black king, then when do you ever attack? Unless perhaps White's extra pawn could have raised its voice after the retreat of the knight and the slow realisation of his extra pawn. But what player listens to the opinion of a pawn?!

22 ♘xf7! ♔xf7 23 dxe5 ♗xc5

Black decides not to be obstinate, and promptly returns the piece. After 23...♘h7 24 ♕f3+ ♔g8 25 ♖d1 he would nevertheless have had to do this, but in even more unfavourable circumstances.

24 exf6 ♖xe1+ 25 ♕xe1 ♕xf6 26 ♘e4 ♕e7 27 ♕e2 ♖d8 28 ♕xb5 ♕xe4 29 ♕xb7+ ♔f8 30 ♗e3

Returning part of the material won, White opens the f-file for the concluding attack on the king. Therefore **Black resigns**.

No.3 (p.31)
Tal-Zaid
Moscow 1972

Nothing of the sort! Chess is not

draughts (checkers), capturing, as we know, is not obligatory, and important intermediate moves are sometimes available.

19 ♗xf7+!

In this way the black king is kept in the centre, there being no question of White's attack being calculated as far as mate. It is based on the sincere belief (and knowledge!) that a king in such a situation is bound sooner or later to succumb.

19...♔xf7 20 ♕d5+ ♔g6

If 20...♔f8 21 ♖xe4, and 21...♕d6 fails to 22 ♖f1+.

21 ♕xe4+ ♔f7 22 ♖f1+ ♗f6

Now, after interposing 23 ♕d5+, White could have brought to the centre his last reserve his knight. But:

23 ♘c5

M.T. I did not anticipate the brilliant defence of my young opponent; the game was played in a clock simultaneous, and Zaid was then only a candidate master.

23...♖e8!! 24 ♕d5+

If 24 ♖xf6+ Black would not have replied 24...gxf6 25 ♕h7+, with mate in a few moves, but 24...♔xf6!, while on 24 ♖xe8 ♕xc5+ 25 ♔h1 he had prepared 25...♕c6 (the showy 25...♗f5 does not work, since White again interposes 26 ♖xf5 ♖xe8 27 ♕xe8+), and after the forced exchange of queens the black bishops are ready to show their strength.

24...♔f8 25 ♕d6+ ♔f7 26 ♘xb7 ♕a4?!

Time scramble; 26...♗xb7 27 ♕xa3 ♖xe5 was better.

27 ♕d5+ ♔f8 28 ♘d6 ♗e6 29 ♖xe6 ♖xe6 30 ♕xe6 ♕d4+ 31 ♔h1

♕a7 **32 ♘f5 ♕f7 33 ♕d6+ ♗e7 34 ♕c6 ♖d8 35 ♕xa6 Black resigns**.

No.4 (p.31)
Tal v. Gomez-Baillo
Termas de Rio Hondo 1987

But the f7 square is already "ripe", and White immediately exploits this.

13 ♘d6! cxd4

Or 13...♕e7 14 ♗f4 ♘h5 15 ♖fe1 ♕f6 16 ♗e5 ♘xe5 17 dxe5 with a great advantage, since the pressure on f7 continues.

14 ♘xf7 ♘c5

White also wins the exchange after 14...♖xf7 15 ♗c4 ♘c5 16 ♗xf7+ ♔h8 (16...♔f8 17 ♗b4) 17 ♕a3.

15 ♘xd8+ ♘xb3 16 ♗c4+ ♔h8 17 ♗xb3 ♖xd8 18 ♘g5 (the unfortunate f7 square!) **18...♖d5 (18...♖f8 19 ♗b4) 19 ♖fe1**

And **Black resigned** in view of the variation 19...♗b7 20 ♘f7+ ♔g8 21 ♘d6.

No.5 (p.31)
Barcza-Tal
Tallinn 1971

And Black found a way of keeping the white king in the centre!

9...♗h3! 10 ♘fxd4

After 10 0-0 ♘xf3+ White loses the exchange, while 10 ♘exd4 ♗xg2 11 ♖g1 exd4 12 ♘xd4, in the hope of 12...♗h3 13 g4 followed by ♖g3, is countered by 12...c5! 13 ♘b3 ♗f3 14 g4 f5!

10...♗xg2 11 ♖g1 exd4 12 ♘xd4 c5 13 ♘b5 ♗f3 14 g4

For the piece White has only a

pawn, but the black bishop may be trapped at any moment, and after 14... f5 15 gxf5 gxf5 16 ♖xg7+! ♔xg7 17 ♗h6+ ♔g8 18 ♗xf8 ♕xf8 19 ♘xd6 fxe4 20 ♕g5+ ♘g6 21 ♕d5+ the situation becomes complicated. And so Black strikes from the other side.

14...d5! 15 ♗xc5 ♖c8 16 ♗a3 dxe4 17 dxe4

Now both 17...♕xd2+ 18 ♔xd2 ♖fe8 19 ♔e3 and 17...♗xe4 18 ♕xd8 ♖fxd8 19 ♗xe7 are bad for Black. But on the other hand, the continuation in the game is good.

17...♕b6! 18 ♗xe7 ♕xb5 19 ♗xf8 ♕xb2 20 ♗xg7 ♔xg7

In this position, where he has a quite appreciable material advantage, **White resigned**.

He has no defence. 21 ♖d1 is met by 21...♖xc2, mating after 22 ♕f4 ♖e2+ or winning a rook in the variation 22 ♕d4+ ♕xd4 23 ♖xd4 ♖c1+. And after 21 ♖c1 ♖d8 22 ♕e3 the game is concluded in highly spectacular fashion by 22...♕xc2!

No.6 (p.31)
Kapengut-Kupreichik
Minsk 1969

Not altogether. White found a way of keeping the black king in the centre, even at the cost of weakening his pawn formation.

15 ♘d6+! exd6 16 ♖e1+ ♔f8 17 gxf3 f6

17...♖g8 18 ♗e3 and 19 cxd6 is even worse for Black.

18 ♖e6 dxc5 19 ♗xc5+

After 19 ♖xf6+ ♔g7 20 ♖d6+ ♘xd4 the attack on the king comes to

an end, and for the queen Black obtains quite sufficient compensation.

19...♔g7 20 ♖d6 ♕e8 21 ♖d7+ ♔h6 22 ♕d6 (22 ♖b1 came into consideration) **22...♕e5 23 ♗e3+ ♔h5?**

23...g5 offers more chances, although after 24 ♕d2 Black has to reckon with the threat of 25 f4.

24 ♕d1! ♕e6 25 ♖d6 ♕e7 26 f4+ ♔h6 27 f5+ g5 28 h4 ♖ad8 29 hxg5+ ♔g7 30 gxf6+ ♕xf6 31 ♕g4+ Black resigns.

No.7 (p.41)
Veresov-Osnos
Grozny 1969

By breaking through in the centre. This is the only way for White to bring his reserves into play, since otherwise he has no way of intensifying the pressure on the kingside.

17 e5! dxe5 18 ♘e4

Not so much attacking the f6 square (the exchange of queens will reduce Black's problems), as threatening the dagger-blow 19 d6!

18...♕d7

Now on 19 d6 Black has a retreat square for his bishop at d8, and he is not especially afraid of 19 ♘xf6+. But...

19 ♕xf6!

The defensive lines are breached in a different way. Simplification for Black is unacceptable: after 19...♗xf6 20 ♘xf6+ ♔h8 21 ♘xd7 ♘xd7 the invasion 22 ♖f7 leads to the loss of a piece.

19...♗d8 20 ♖f2 ♕e7 21 ♕f3 ♘d7

Other moves too would not have avoided loss of material. For example,

21...♖c8 22 ♗g5 ♕c7 (22...♕d7 23 ♗xd8 and 24 ♘f6+) 23 d6, and 23...♕c6 is completely bad on account of mate in three moves.

22 ♗g5 ♕xg5 23 ♘xg5 ♗xg5 24 d6 e4 25 ♕f7+ ♔h8 26 ♕xd7, and White won easily.

No.8 (p.41)
Capablanca-Alekhine
New York 1924

He has to open files, otherwise Black will create counterplay. But 18 cxb6 axb6 immediately makes apparent White's pawn weaknesses on the queenside, and so he prepared a different manoeuvre.

18 ♖fd1! bxc5

Castling is dangerous (19 a4), and it is not possible to find anything else.

19 d5! ♕d6

The only move, since Black loses quickly after 19...exd5 20 ♘xd5 ♕d6 21 ♖ab1 with the threat of 22 ♘b6.

20 dxe6 ♕xe6 21 ♕xc5 ♕b6 22 ♕f2!, and the five black pawn islands were a more than sufficient basis for a win. White easily won a pawn and... failed to realise his advantage, through his own fault. But this bears no relation to our theme.

No.9 (p.41)
Gipslis-Borer
Berlin 1991

First of all White opened a path for his queen to the kingside.

22 d5! ♗d7

It is clear that the pawn cannot be captured (22...exd5?? 23 ♖e8+), while

22...f6 fails to a sacrifice that is thematic in such positions: 23 ♖xh5!! gxh5 24 ♕xf6, with numerous threats.

23 ♖xh5!! gxh5 24 ♕f6 ♕xd5

Forced in view of 24...♗e8 25 ♖e5 exd5 (26 ♖xh5 was threatened) 26 ♖xe8+, and hoping for 25 ♖e5 ♗e8 26 ♖xd5 ♖xd5, when there is still some play in the position. Even here White should win — 27 ♘e5 followed by ♕g5xh5, but he wants more.

25 ♘e5 ♗e8 26 ♖e3 ♕d1+ 27 ♔h2 ♖d4 28 ♖g3+ ♔g4 29 ♘xg4 hxg4 30 h5!!

Another reserve joins the attack, and there are hardly any defenders.

30...♕d8 31 ♖xg4+ ♔f8 32 ♕g7+ ♔e7 33 ♖f4 ♕a5?

A tougher defence was offered by 33...♗c6 34 ♖xf7+ ♔d6 35 ♕d4+ ♗d5 36 ♕b4+ ♔c6 37 ♕xb7+ ♔d6, when although White continues attacking with material now equal, there is no forced win. Now, however, the game concludes quickly.

34 ♕f6+ ♔f8 (34...♔d6 35 ♖d4+) 35 h6 ♖d8 36 h7 Black resigns.

No.10 (p.50)
Troinov-Popov
USSR 1962

It gives him not only the right, but also the obligation — to attack. White rightly "launches" his queen into the vicinity of the black king.

13 ♕h5 ♖e8

Black intends to parry the attack on h7 (♖f3-h3) by transferring his knight to f8. But the move played creates other weaknesses, and White now strikes from the other side.

14 ᐯxd5!! exd5 15 ♕xf7+! ♔xf7
The Greek gift has to be accepted
(15...♔h8 16 ᐯe6).
16 ♗xd5+ ♔g6
Evidently Black considered the
variation 16...♔f8 17 ᐯe6+ ♔g8 18
ᐯxd8+ ♔h8 19 ᐯxc6 bxc6 20 ♗xc6
♖b8 21 e6 ᐯf6 22 ♗xe8 ᐯxe8 23 f5
to be too cheerless (23...♖xb2 24
♖ab1), and he sends his king out into
the storm.
**17 f5+ ♔h5 18 ♗f3+ ♔h4 19 g3+
♔h3 20 ♗g2+ ♔g4 21 ♖f4+**
And, two moves before mate, **Black
resigned**.

No.11 (p.50)
Geller-Polugayevsky
28th USSR Ch., Moscow 1961

Alas, there does not appear to be
any combination breaking up the king's
shelter: after all, Black has drawn up
nearly all his forces for the defence,
and his queen, although temporarily
"lagging behind", is ready to come into
play by taking on d5, although he then
has to reckon with ᐯxg7.
But White has a possibility of further increasing his attacking potential.
27 ᐯe3! ♖d2 28 ᐯg4
With gain of tempo White has kept
the black queen passive, and, more
important, he has increased the offensive power of his rook at f1 and
found a new target for his knight to
attack: not only the h6 pawn, but also
f6. Now all his pieces are operating at
full power.
28...♕d7 29 h4!
There is no point in hurrying with
29 ♕xh6+, since now this threat is

intensified: 30 ♕xh6+ gxh6 31 ᐯf6+
♔h8 32 ᐯxd7+ ♗g7 33 ♗xg7+
♔xg7 34 h5, winning a piece.
**29...♕e7 30 ♖e3 ♕d7 31 ♕xh6+
♔g8**
Or 31...gxh6 32 ᐯf6+ ♔h8 33
ᐯxd7+ ᐯe5 34 ♗c3 ♖c2 35 d4.
32 ♖xe8
Mate at g7 and the rook at d2 are
both "hanging". **Black resigns**.

No.12 (p.72)
Rubinstein-Teichmann
Vienna 1908

No, because the opening of lines for
attack could have been carried out
more quickly, and perhaps more effi-
ciently: 18 g6 (nevertheless!) 18...fxg6
19 hxg6 h6 20 ᐯxe4 dxe4 21 ᐯg5,
and the game is over: both 22 ♗e6+
and 22 ♕xc4+ are threatened, and
21...♗d5 is met by the decisive 22
♗xe4.

No.13 (p.73)
Adorjan-Ribli
Riga Interzonal 1979

By interposing **18 ♗h6!** And since
counterplay with 18...♖xc3 is now
clearly too late — 19 gxf7+ ♔xf7 20
♖xg7+ ♔e8 21 bxc3 ♕xc3 22 ♕xc3
♖xc3 23 ♖xh7, and since the bishop is
immune — 18...gxh6 19 ♕xh6,
mating, Black has to defend his g7.
**18...♗f6 19 gxh7+ ♔xh7 20
♗xg7! ♗xg7 21 h6 ♗f6 22 ♕g2**
Black resigns, since against the invasion 23 ♕g7+ (23...♗xg7 24 hxg7+
♔g8 25 ♖h8 mate) there is no defence.

No.14 (p.73)
Kochiev-F.Wade
Moscow 1983

White used his occupation of the light squares to invade the opponent's position.

29 ♕f3 ♘f7 30 ♘fe3 ♗e7 31 ♕f5+ ♔g7 32 ♕e6 ♖xd1 33 ♖xd1 ♖d8 34 ♖xd8 ♕xd8 35 ♔h2

Contrary to the usual state of affairs, the exchanges have not eased Black's position. White's queen is tying its black opponent to the defence of the bishop, and on the light squares the reserves will soon be brought up.

35...♔f8 36 ♘f5 ♕c7 37 ♘ce3 h5 38 ♘xe7 ♕xe7 39 ♕c8+ ♘d8 40 ♘f5 ♕e8 41 ♕c7

Mate can be avoided only at the cost of the queenside pawns. **Black resigns**.

No.15 (p.73)
Levenfish-Eliskases
Moscow 1936

In fact Black nevertheless played **20...h5!**, since if 21 gxh5 he has 21...g5! (there is no need to resort to the sharp 21...♖h8) followed by 22...♖h8 and 23...♖xh5, with a very strong attack down the open h-file. The situation is similar after 21 h3 hxg4 22 hxg4 ♖h8, and so White's reply is practically forced.

21 ♗h3 ♖h8 22 ♔g2 ♗h4 23 ♘b5 ♗xe1 24 ♖fxe1 ♘a6 25 g5

Necessary, alas, otherwise after 25... hxg4 26 ♗xg4 ♗xg4 27 ♕xg4 ♖h4 White loses slowly, but surely.

25...♗xh3 26 ♕xh3 ♕xg5+ 27

♔h1 ♕e7 28 ♖g1 ♔h6 29 c5!?

A desperate attempt to break the unhappy course of events. Otherwise ...g5, ...♖af8, the advance of the king, and ...g4.

29...♘xc5!

Black is not afraid of ghosts! Especially since the only alternative was the passive 29...♖ae8, since 29...g5 or 29...♖ag8 would have handed White the initiative — 30 cxd6 cxd6 31 ♕e6!

30 ♘xc7 ♕xc7 31 ♖xg6+ ♔xg6 32 ♕f5+ ♔h6 33 ♕f6+ ♔h7 34 ♕f5+ ♔g8!

In giving up his queen, Black reminds his opponent that one piece on its own cannot do much.

35 ♖g1+ ♕g7 36 ♕f6 ♖h7 37 ♕xd6 ♘d3! 38 ♕e6+ ♔h8 39 ♖xg7 ♖xg7 40 ♕h6+ ♔g8 41 h4 ♘e1!

Avoiding the last pitfall: 41...♖a6, intending mate after 42 ♕xh5 ♖ag6, is refuted by 42 d6!

42 ♕e6+ ♔h7 43 ♕h3

It turns out that 43 ♕xe5 is not possible on account of 43...♖g1+!

43...♖ag8 White resigns.

No.16 (p.88)
Stolberg-Zak
USSR 1938

By the most ordinary interference! After **28 ♖d7!** Black could, of course, have prolonged his resistance in a hopeless position — 28...g6 29 ♖xc7 gxh5 30 ♘xf7, but he "preferred" to allow a smothered mate in the main variation **28...♗xd7 29 ♕xf7+ ♔h8 30 ♗c4 ♘g6 31 ♕g8+ ♖xg8 32 ♘f7 mate**.

No.17 (p.88)
Tal-Platonov
Dubna 1973

It fact Black's resignation was very timely! At the last moment he noticed that in reply to his planned 23...♖xg3 there would follow 24 ♗g6!!, when the rook's retreat is cut off, and mate is inevitable.

No.18 (p.88)
Polugayevsky-Osnos
36th USSR Ch., Alma-Ata 1969

The last straw for Black was 21 e5! This unusual interference move severs Black's connections on the b8-h2 diagonal, and his position collapses.
21...♕d2 22 a3 ♖f8 23 ♗xe6! g5
If 23...fxe6 24 ♕xe6+ ♔h8 25 g3, and White's material advantage is enough for a win.
24 g3 fxe6
No better is 24...♕e2 25 ♖xf4! gxf4 26 ♕g5+ ♔h8 27 ♕h6! ♖g8 (27... ♔g8 28 ♗f5) 28 ♕f6+ ♖g7 29 ♗xf7 ♕d1+ 30 ♔a2, when the e-pawn cannot be stopped.
25 ♕xe6+ ♔g7 26 gxf4 ♕g2
Equally hopeless is 26...♖xf4 27 ♖xf4 ♕xf4 28 ♕d7+ ♔g6 29 ♕xb5 ♕xh2 30 ♕d3+ ♔g7 31 ♕e4.
27 ♖d1 gxf4 28 ♕d7+ ♖f7 29 e6 Black resigns.

No.19 (p.88)
Fridman-Tørnblom
Stockholm 1974

A move away from victory, this would have been a strange decision!

By **1...♖e3!** Black blocked the e2 pawn. If 2 fxe3, then 2...♘h3 is now decisive, and at the same time 2...♖xf3 is threatened. **White resigned**.

No.20 (p.104)
Tal-Andersson
Match, Stockholm 1976

Yes, and relying on this outpost (the f6 square is under control) White began a direct attack on the king.
19 ♖g3 ♕xc2 20 ♕e3 (with the threat of 21 ♕h6) **20...♕c4 21 b3 ♕d5 22 ♘f6+ ♗xf6 23 exf6**
The white outpost has moved to the 6th rank, and although it is insufficiently defended, the attack has been strengthened.
23...g6 24 ♖g4 ♔h8 25 ♗b6! ♖c8
Taking the unprotected bishop — 25...♘xb6 — diverts Black's attention from the kingside, and he is mated or loses his queen: 26 ♕h6 ♖g8 27 ♖h4.
26 ♕h6 ♖g8 27 ♖d4
Here 27 ♖h4 is parried by 27...♘f8, when Black himself launches a counterattack.
27...♘xb6
If 27...♕b7 White achieves his aim — 28 ♕xh7+, mating.
28 ♖xd5 ♘xd5 29 ♖f3 ♖c3 30 ♖xc3 ♘xc3 31 ♕e3 b4 32 ♕a7 ♖f8 33 ♕c5 ♖b8 34 ♕d6, and in view of the unavoidable loss of his queenside pawns, **Black resigned**.

No.21 (p.104)
Kask-Kamenetsky
USSR Corr. Team Ch., 1974-5

Firstly, White's main forces are

concentrated on the queenside, and the black outpost at e4 greatly restricts their possible rapid regrouping. Secondly, there is a classic target for attack — the advanced pawn at h3. And thirdly, also classic is the deployment of Black's queen and bishops, which are aimed at the kingside. In short, there are more than sufficient grounds for the decision.

23...♗xh3! 24 gxh3 ♕xh3 25 ♘e5 ♖d6 (renewing the threat of mate in a few moves) **26 ♗g4 ♖g6 27 ♘xg6 ♕xg4+ 28 ♔f1 fxg6 29 ♕c4+ ♔h7 30 ♖a2**

The threat of 30...♖xf2+ 31 ♔xf2 ♗g3+ with a quick mate has been parried, but the pursuit of the king continues — incidentally, with level material.

30...h5 31 ♔e1 h4 32 ♕f1 h3 33 ♔d2 ♗g3 34 ♔c3 ♖f3 35 ♕g1 ♕e6 36 ♖d2

Compared with the initial diagram, the queen has "castled very long", but has not gained any peace. By destroying the pawn chain around the king, Black drives it back. To its doom.

36...♗xf2! 37 ♖xf2 ♖xe3+ 38 ♔d2

Even in a non-correspondence game it would not be difficult to calculate the forcing variation 38 ♔b2 ♖b3+ 39 ♔c2 (or 39 ♔a1 ♖xa3+ 40 ♔b1 ♕b3+ 41 ♖b2 ♕a4, mating) 39...♕c4+ 40 ♔d1 ♕xd4+ 41 ♔e1 ♕e3+ 42 ♔d1 ♖d3+ 43 ♔c2 ♖c3+ 44 ♔b1 ♖xc1+, leading to a queen ending where Black is five(!!) pawns up.

38...♕b3 39 ♕f1 ♖d3+ 40 ♔e1 ♕xa3 41 ♖cc2 ♕a1+ 42 ♔e2 ♕xd4 43 ♕c1 ♖g3 44 ♖d2 ♕e3+ 45 ♔f1 ♕g5

There are too many threats, and **White resigned**.

No.22 (p.104)
Menchik-Thomas
London 1932

At any event, the first Women's World Champion concluded matters by force.

20 f6+ ♔h8

After 20...♔xf6 White gains the tempi required for the creation of a mating net: 21 ♕g5+ ♔g7 22 h6+ ♔g8 23 ♕f6.

21 ♕h6 ♖g8 22 hxg6 fxg6 23 ♕xh7+!

And **Black resigned**, since he is mated by the opponent's minimal forces: rook and f6 pawn.

No.23 (p.115)
Botvinnik-Chekhover
Moscow 1935

This position was reached after a prolonged sacrificial attack. White concluded by eliminating the main defender: **32 ♖xf6! ♗xf6 33 ♕h7+ ♔f8 34 ♖e1! ♗e5** (what else?) **35 ♕h8+ ♔e7 36 ♕xg7+ ♔d6 37 ♕xe5+ ♔d7**, and White, still a rook down, announced mate in six moves: **38 ♕f5+ ♔c6 39 d5+ ♔c5 40 ♗a3+ ♔xc4 41 ♕e4+ ♔c3 42 ♗b4+ ♔b2 43 ♕b1 mate**.

No.24 (p.115)
Tal-Najdorf
Leipzig Olympiad 1960

White has assembled a striking

force of pieces on the kingside. But everything turns on the position of Black's knight: it is not attacking, but is primarily defending the approaches to his king, in particular f6. Therefore:

21 ♖xe4! dxe4 22 ♗f6! ♕b6

The "slightest movement" of the g7 pawn would have allowed mate in one or two moves.

23 ♗xg7 ♖fe8 24 ♗e5 ♕g6 25 ♘h6+ ♔f8 26 f5!

Black resigns: 26...♕g5 is met by 27 ♘xf7!, while if 26...♕c6 White wins by either 27 ♕h5 ♕d7 28 ♗d6+!, or 27 ♕g3 ♕xh6 28 ♗d6+ ♖e7 29 ♗xe7+ ♔xe7 30 ♕e5+.

No.25 (p.115)
Spassky-Geller
Candidates ¼-Final, Sukhumi 1968

Alas, the defenders of the black king can be eliminated, and Spassky, who was on his way to the chess throne, did this on nearly every move!

23 ♖xf6!! exf6 24 ♕h7+ ♔f8 25 ♘xf7!

The f7 pawn was also playing a defensive role, and now 25...♔xf7 26 ♗h6 ♖g8 27 ♘f4 is a very convincing variation. The attackers that have perished on the decisive part of the battlefield are replaced by fresh troops, whereas the defenders (of the g6 pawn, at least) cannot be replaced. Therefore:

25...♖xc2 26 ♗h6 ♖c1+

It is too late for 26...♕xd3 27 ♕xg7+ ♔e8 28 ♖xc2 ♘xc2 29 ♘f4, when White wins.

27 ♘xc1 ♔xf7

Or 27...♗xh6 28 ♘xh6 ♔e8 29 ♘g8!, and the pursuit of the black king

continues.

28 ♕xg7+ ♔e8, and now White could have quickly decided matters by 29 e5 ♗xg2 30 e6, mating. But the game continuation **29 g5 f5 30 ♕xg6+ ♔d7 31 ♕f7+ ♔c6 32 exf5+** also led to a win.

No.26 (p.126)
Brink-Claussen v. J.Littlewood
Varna Olympiad 1962

He should divert the white queen from the defence of f2 and exploit the weakness of the back rank.

22...♕xd6! 23 ♕xd6 ♗d4+ 24 ♔h1 ♘f2+

White resigns: he is either mated, or is left a piece down: 25 ♔g1 ♘e4+.

To be fair, it should be mentioned that the less spectacular 22...♗e5 would also have won.

No.27 (p.127)
Makogonov-Smyslov
12th USSR Ch., Moscow 1940

This means that the queen must be driven away, exploiting the barely perceptible weakness of the back rank.

24 ♖e5!! ♕c8 (the rook is clearly immune) **25 ♗h3!**

One blow after another. If now 25...♕b8, then 26 ♖g5 g6 27 ♖b5, and there is no defence against the threat of ♗h6 (27...♘c5 28 ♗h6 ♕e5 29 ♕xe5, and again the back rank is Black's downfall). At the same time the immediate 25 ♖g5 would not have achieved its aim on account of 25...♖c3.

So Black decides on a sacrifice.

25...♖d8 26 ♗xc8 ♖xd1+ 27 ♔g2 ♖xc8

Alas, the attack continues.

28 ♖g5 g6 29 ♖b5 (the way for the bishop to h6 is opened) 29...♖d6 30 ♖xb3 ♘xb3 31 ♕xb3 **Black resigns**.

No.28 (p.127)
Bouaziz-Miles
Riga Interzonal 1979

The position is now drawn, and after **45...♖xh3!** White should have reconciled himself to this, by playing 46 ♕f1! ♖g3+ 47 ♔f2 ♖xf3+ 48 ♔xf3 ♕xf1+, with perpetual check after 49 ♔e4.

But through inertia he chose **46 ♔xh3??**, overlooking the fearful blow **46...♕h1+ 47 ♕h2 ♕xf3+ 48 ♔xh4 ♗e7+ 49 g5 ♗xg5+!**

Only here did White realise that he would be prettily mated: 50 ♔xg5 f6+ 51 ♔h4 g5 mate, or 51 ♔g6 ♕g4 mate.

No.29 (p.127)
Stein-Sokolsky
Odessa 1960

Even without his queen White was able to create decisive threats against the king.

27 ♖g7+! ♗xg7 28 ♖xg7+ ♔h8 29 ♖c7!

White's material advantage becomes decisive. He threatens 30 ♗g7+ ♔g8 31 ♘f6+, and the black knight is attacked.

A few moves later **Black resigned** (if 29...♕e5 30 ♗f4 ♕f5 31 ♖xc6 etc.).

No.30 (p.165)
Mikhalchishin-Yudasin
Nikolayev 1983

Everything depends on whether White can break up the pawn screen around the black king.

20 ♗h6! ♖xd1+ **21 ♔xd1** (otherwise the e5 outpost falls) **21...♕f8 22 c3 ♘d7**

The attempt to exchange bishops by 22...♗d5 does not succeed: 23 ♗c2, and 23...♗xa2 is not possible on account of 24 ♕e4. Therefore Black aims by pressure on the e5 pawn to tie down the opponent's forces.

23 ♔c1 a5 24 ♗c2 a4 25 ♖e3! ♔h8 (26 ♖g3 was threatened) **26 ♗g5** (maintaining in certain variations the possibility of ♗f6) **26...♖a5 27 ♖h3 h6 28 ♕f4 ♘xe5?**

This leaves f6 undefended and loses by force. White has more problems after 28...♖xe5 29 ♗xh6 gxh6 30 ♖xh6+ ♔g8, when Black's defensive resources are by no means exhausted.

29 ♗xh6! gxh6 30 ♖xh6+ ♔g8 31 ♗h7+ ♔h8, and without waiting for White's reply, **Black resigned**: 32 ♕f6+ ♔g7 33 ♕d8+ leads to mate.

No.31 (p.165)
Tal-Plaskett
Sochi 1984

But White can exploit the target created to begin an attack.

14 ♗xh6 ♗xd5 15 cxd5 ♘b4 16 ♕g6 ♕e7

Has the first wave been repulsed, and can Black now pick up the d5 pawn?

17 a3!

White even urges him to! After 17... ♘bxd5 18 ♗xg7 ♕xg7 19 ♗xd5+ ♘xd5 20 ♕e6+ White is a pawn up and the black king is "bare" .

17...♘c2 18 ♗xg7 ♕xg7 19 ♕xc2, and Black could have spared himself the following five moves.

No.32 (p.165)
Tal-Gedevanishvili
Georgian Championship 1970

Of course, White's concentration of force against the black king is not the maximum, but it is evidently quite sufficient. Queen, rook, bishop and knight — part of them can be sacrificed to break up Black's defensive lines.

18 ♘f6+! gxf6 19 ♗xh7+ ♔h8

No better is 19...♔xh7 20 exf6 ♘g6 21 ♕h5+ ♔g8 22 ♖bf1(g1) or 22 ♖ff1, and against the mate at g7 there is no defence.

20 ♖h4 ♔g7 21 ♕c1 ♘g8 22 ♗xg8 Black resigns.

No.33 (p.166)
Tal-Taimanov
Blitz Tournament, Leningrad 1977

Were the black pawn still at h7, there would be a long and hard struggle in prospect, although White has every chance (pawn majority with an outpost at e5) of an attack on the kingside. But the pawn has "stuck out", and this leads to the rapid collapse of Black's position.

29 ♗xh6! gxh6 30 ♕xh6 ♕c6 31 ♕g5+ ♘g6

Or 31...♔h8 32 f4, and the way for the rooks to h3 is open.

32 f4 ♕e6 33 f5 ♕e7 34 f6 ♕f8 35 ♗xg6 fxg6 36 ♕xg6+ ♔h8 37 ♖f4 Black resigns.

No.34 (p.166)
Tal-Miles
Porz 1981/2

But hardly any more, since the insufficiently defended f7 pawn may also be attacked through a blow at another link of the pawn chain, a device that is as typical as it is simple.

15 ♗xh7+! ♘xh7

After 15...♔xh7 the defender of the h5 square is diverted by 16 ♖xd7, and if 16...♘xd7 17 ♕h5+ ♔g8 18 ♕xf7+ ♔h7 19 ♘h5 with a quick mate.

Therefore Black prefers immediately to remain a pawn down, which, however, is equivalent to capitulation.

16 ♖xd7 g6

If 16...f6 17 ♘g6 ♕c6 White wins by 18 ♖xb7!, while after 16...♘f6 he does not content himself with an extra pawn, but continues his decisive attack: 17 ♘h5! ♘xd7 18 ♕g4 g5 (18... ♗f8 19 ♘xd7 and 20 ♘xf8, or 18...g6 19 ♘xg6) 19 ♘xd7 ♕d8 20 ♖d1!

17 b4

White could have simply set about realising his material advantage, but instead he makes use of a chance possibility: 17...♕xb4 diverts the queen from the defence of e6 and allows 18 ♘xg6, while 17...cxb4 clears the way for the white c-pawn.

17...♗c8 18 bxc5 ♕xc5 19 ♘e4 ♕b6 20 ♕f3

I.D. 20 ♖d3 with the idea of 21 ♖g3

is more natural, but the move in the game is prettier: on 20...♗xd7 White had prepared 21 ♗e3!, while if 20...f5 21 ♕g3.

20...♕b2 21 ♘xf7

None of White's pieces can be taken.

21...♕g7 22 ♘h6+ ♔h8 23 ♖c7

Winning the queen in the variation 23 ♗e5 ♗xd7 24 ♗xg7+ ♔xg7 does not satisfy White.

23...♖f8 24 ♖xe7

Black resigned in view of the dismal choice between 24...♕xe7 25 ♗e5+, and 24...♖xf4 25 ♖xg7 ♖xf3 26 ♖g8+.

No.35 (p.166)
Drike-Krantz
Correspondence 1989-91

Only at first sight. In fact White's defences collapsed instantly after **17...♘xh2!**, and in view of the unat-tractive choice between 18 ♔xh2 ♗xg3+ 19 fxg3 ♕xg3+ 20 ♔h1 ♖h8+, and 18 ♕h6 ♕xh6 19 ♗xh6 ♘hg4 20 ♗d2 ♘xf2!, **White resigned**.

No.36 (p.166)
Tal-Chepukaitis
Blitz Tournament, Leningrad 1977

There are obvious possibilities of sacrifices on h7 and g6.

23 ♘xh7! ♗xf6 24 ♘xf6+ ♔f8 25 ♕xg6 ♕f7 26 ♕g5

With the intention of winning the queen after 27 ♘h7+ ♔e8 28 ♗g6.

26...♕g7 27 ♘h7+ ♔f7 28 ♕d8

Threatening "only" 29 ♘g5+.

28...♕h6 29 ♘g5+ ♔g7 30 ♕e7+ ♔g8 31 ♗h7+

Black resigns, since White has an unusually pleasant choice between winning the queen and mating in a few moves.

Postscript

THIS BOOK did not turn out quite as we had planned. Unfortunately, there is no chapter about the offensive on the queenside: Mikhail Tal had some interesting thoughts about this, and regarded activity on this part of the board both as an independent operation, valuable in its own right, and as a diverting, as it were secondary operation, undertaken in order at a convenient moment to nevertheless assail the place where the enemy king was sheltered.

Of this planned chapter there remained only fragments, and two or three of the other sections could perhaps have been a little fuller. But we did not have time. One of the greatest of chess magicians, the former World Champion Mikhail Tal, has passed away. Right to his last day he maintained his interest in chess, and, of course, not only chess: from a Moscow hospital he travelled to a tournament in Spain, he went out for a day to play in a blitz-tournament, and he analysed and made recordings of the material for this book. To profound regret, all this was to be his last.

This is why the title planned earlier *Everything about Attack* has been changed. Tal was a wonderful master of attack, and in his career of more than a third of a century in top-level chess, what pleased him most was not a point in the tournament table, and not a victory, but a successful attack.

And I should like once again to repeat the words of Mikhail Tal, that appear in the introduction to this book: may the readers win their games, by attacking. Attacking brilliantly.

It was this that always made Tal happy.

Iakov Damsky

Index of Players

Illustrative Games